The Lords of Tikal

NEW ASPECTS OF ANTIQUITY

General Editor: COLIN RENFREW

Consulting Editor for the Americas: JEREMY A. SABLOFF

© T.W. RUTLEDGE 10/97

PETER D. HARRISON

The Lords of Tikal

Rulers of an Ancient Maya City

with 140 illustrations, 13 in colour

THAMES AND HUDSON

For Alexandra Carroll Madeira Harrison

Frontispiece: Reconstruction from Altar 5 showing Hasaw Chan K'awil and a lord from Calakmul at the exhumation of Hasaw's wife's remains (see ill. 81).

© 1999 Thames and Hudson Ltd, London

British Library Cataloguing-in-Publication Data
A catalogue record for this book is available from the British Library

ISBN 0-500-05094-5

Printed and bound in Singapore by C.S. Graphics

CONTENTS

FOREWORD FROM THE EDITORS

Ancient Maya civilization is renowned for the sophistication of its intellectual and aesthetic achievements. Stone temples on tall pyramidal bases rising above the jungle canopy and elaborately carved stone monuments covered with hieroglyphs are just two of the images of the ancient Maya that are etched in the public's imagination. There is also a popular impression of mystery surrounding the Maya, and photographs of tropical vegetation engulfing ruined temples and palaces are often used to characterize this seemingly enigmatic culture.

In recent years, however, modern scholarship has succeeded in cutting back some of the metaphorical foliage that has impeded understanding of the ancient Maya and has provided significant new insights into archaeological knowledge about the rise and growth of this complex culture. Breakthroughs in the decipherment of the Maya hieroglyphic writing system and new archaeological methods have both contributed heavily to these dramatic new understandings of the Maya.

Among the new scholarly understandings of Maya civilization are the appreciation that the ancient Maya had an urban civilization with numerous large cities and were not a "civilization without cities" as previously supposed; that the Maya had a mixed resource base and did not totally rely on maize; that the Maya also utilized varied agricultural techniques, such as intensive swamp reclamation, and did not just practice the slash-and-burn cultivation method that is often employed by the modern Maya; that Maya civilization arose many centuries before the beginning of the Classic period around AD 800; that Maya civilization was not isolated in its tropical rainforest heartland from its neighbors in ancient Mexico to the north or Central America to the south but was economically, politically, and ideologically embedded in the wider culture area that scholars call "Mesoamerica"; that the Maya were not a peaceful people but had a long history of intercity conflict; and last, but certainly not least, that the subjects of hieroglyphic texts found on monuments, buildings, and ceramic vessels were not limited to esoteric matters such as astronomy and calendrics but had a strong historical and political content that related to topics such as dynastic histories and the political and ideological glorification of individual rulers.

With the advantage of historical hindsight, it is now clear that one of the most significant and influential archaeological projects in this revolutionary change in scholarly thinking was the University of Pennsylvania Museum of Archaeology and Anthropology's research, in conjunction with the government of Guatemala, at the great Maya site of Tikal. The Tikal Project was in operation for more than a decade from the late 1950s through the close of the 1960s. This major project was initiated under the field directorship of Edwin Shook and subsequently led for most of its history by William R. Coe. From the close of the large Tikal Project around 1970 through the 1990s, Guatemalan archaeologists have continued important fieldwork at the site. In this engrossing volume, Dr. Peter Harrison, who participated for many years in the Tikal Project, discusses the many contributions of the Project and subsequent research that have led to a radically new appreciation of the cultural achievements of the ancient Maya. Dr. Harrison clearly places Tikal in its ecological context and takes the reader through the site's development over a 1,700-year period, from its rise around 800 BC to its demise in the ninth century AD. He brings the latest scholarship to bear on his interpretations of Tikal's architectural and political growth, the ups and downs of its rulers and their dynasties, and Tikal's competitive position vis-á-vis other major urban centers such as Calakmul. Throughout this interpretive narrative, the reader will continually see the stimulating role that the archaeological research at Tikal played in reshaping Maya scholarship. The pioneering study of Tikal's urban settlement, the new insights into the agricultural techniques and produce that supported the large population concentrations that were uncovered at Tikal, and the evidence for early cultural complexity prior to the onset of the Classic period at the site are just several of the areas in which Peter Harrison illustrates the key contributions that the Tikal Project made not only to the illumination of the site's history but the understanding of Maya civilization in general.

For those readers who are engrossed by the ancient Maya and the immensity of their cultural accomplishments, for those interested in the rise of preindustrial civilization throughout the ancient world, and for those who are fascinated by stories of scientific archaeological discoveries, this volume will certainly prove to be a delightful reading experience. We invite you to share Dr. Harrison's enchantment with the remarkable site of Tikal.

Jeremy A. Sabloff

Colin Renfrew

CHAPTER ONE

THE MAYA AND THEIR CIVILIZATION

Great cities, like great works of art, are the product of a great deal of time and expense, reflecting the full range of emotions of the people that made them happen. In the case of Tikal, its splendid setting, partially hidden in the rain-forest of Guatemala, and the hedonistic delights offered by the city's textures, colors, and shapes – and the mysteries that lie beneath its surface – invite interpretation.

This architectural splendor developed within the framework of a world-class civilization – the ancient Maya. The city of Tikal thrived and expanded from 800 BC until AD 900, spanning most of the known periods of archaeological classification imposed by scientific research upon the Maya civilization. To place the city in context we must first examine how it compares with the rise of civilizations in general, and how it fits within its own civilization.

By the time of its collapse in the 10th century, Tikal covered roughly 65 sq. km, with over 3,000 known surface structures. As many as 10,000 ruined buildings and platforms may lie below the surface. The population reached a figure of somewhere between 100,000 and 200,000, although arguments are entertained for even greater numbers. The peak of achievement, both politically and in terms of monumental architecture, fell during the reign of three successive kings in the 9th century when astonishing feats of construction were performed. These monuments still rise above the tropical forest, although the jungle has obscured most of the city, blessing the ruins with the added dimension of romanticism and mystery. Decades of archaeological research have lifted the veil of mystery only slightly.

Great civilizations began to emerge in the Old World out of an agricultural base around 4000 BC. The same process of emergence from a hunting and gathering stage into farmers and thence into complex societies took place in the New World at somewhat later dates, as far as is now known. Differences, however, attended the origins of the Maya. For example, in contrast to the dryness of the deserts of Egypt and its dependence upon the life-giving River Nile, the lowland setting of the Maya civilization was lush and varied, dependent upon a rain cycle that was not always reliable. The romanticism and mystery associated with the public image of the Maya civilization are very real at Tikal – features which continue to promote its popularity both as a film subject and a focus of serious research.

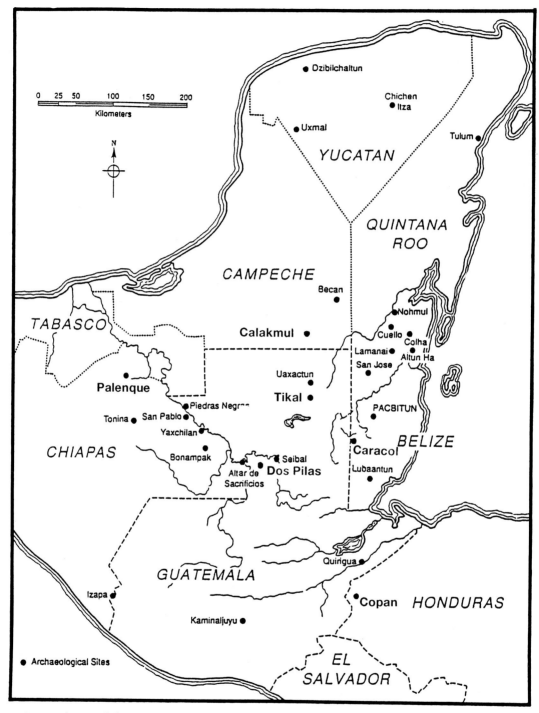

1 Regional map of the Maya area with selected cities. Tikal, and cities of major interaction are shown in larger print.

The Maya area

The land mass occupied by the Maya covers a significant part of modern Mexico, comprising the eastern portions of the states of Tabasco and Chiapas, and all of the states of Campeche, Yucatan, and Quintana Roo. In addition the Maya civilization extended into all of modern Guatemala and Belize and the northwestern parts of El Salvador and Honduras (*ill. 1*). This area is described in two geographic zones: the relatively flat Yucatan Peninsula and a series of mountain ranges which lie at the base of this peninsula. These ranges are divided between the northern and southern highlands. There is a slope forming a distinctive region that leads from the mountains down to the Pacific Ocean. The contrast between the hot, wet lowlands and the cooler, drier highlands has led to a misconception of uniformity within each of these two zones. In actuality, the lowlands are extraordinarily varied, exhibiting a variety of vegetational regimes, complex drainage systems and topographic relief. All this variety in land form must have been a welcome challenge for the ancient Maya who became adept at exploiting and adapting to micro-niches in their varied environment.

The evolution of Maya civilization

The Maya still live in this area today, numbering over 7½ million speakers of the 28 Mayan languages. Economically subsisting on agricultural practices that date back 3500 years, these people carry a rich and substantial remainder of the Classic civilization of their ancestors – beliefs and practices that manifest themselves in self-sustaining ways, reacting to the modern life that surrounds them (*ill. 2*). Although many of the 28 modern Mayan languages predated the Classic civilization it is now believed that only two of these languages, Chol and Yucatec, were used in ancient times as a basis for the hieroglyphic script that is a major feature of the ancient civilization. Many of the other separate Mayan languages have developed away from ancient base tongues in the intervening time.

Despite a century and a half of study, which has seen a recent acceleration in the rate of scholarly breakthroughs, improved archaeological techniques, and a more enlightened approach to non-Western cultures, much of the ancient Maya achievement remains poorly understood and hotly disputed. Adding to the problem of incomplete knowledge, there is a great deal of ethnocentrism and preoccupation with cherished models of how non-Western societies are thought to have operated. Some such models were forged in the 1960s under the influence of now-outdated Marxist thinking about the pre-eminence of "hydraulic societies" – societies with economic bases in irrigation techniques. Traditionally the Maya were put in the "second division" of civilizations because their agriculture supposedly relied exclusively on shifting, slash-and-burn cultivation methods. But now more current studies have proven that the

2 *Modern Maya Indians in the market center of Santiago Atitlan, at the highland lake of Atitlan. Ancient figurines show that costumes like these were present in ancient times and helped to identify the home village of the wearer.*

Maya utilized a large variety of irrigation, drainage, and intensive forms of agriculture as early as AD 1 preceding the appearance of hydraulic agriculture in the Mexican highlands.[1]

Civilizations have been defined in different ways in various parts of the world and in a variety of schools of academic thought. With reference to Middle Eastern high civilization, Gordon Childe required the presence of monumental architecture, a writing system, and at least rudimentary science. The Maya fulfilled all these requirements. They built in stone, raising public monuments that rival those of ancient Egypt in energy expenditure, as well as design and quality of fine art. Some of their ceramics were so finely crafted it is astonishing to realize that they were made without benefit of the wheel, and their painting at its best has been compared to that of Michelangelo. Knowledge of astronomy, time, and geometry equaled that produced by many high civilizations in the Old World. Perhaps, most important, the Maya possessed a written script by which they recorded their own history, albeit subject to the kinds of editing that characterize all historical accounts. In that sense, the Maya now may be admitted into the company of literate peoples. Still disputed is the degree of centralized authority that was established and maintained by them. "City state" – of which Tikal was one – seems the best term at present to describe the political dominance of certain centers over demarcated territories, although it borrows imperfectly from the Classical Mediterranean model. Recent studies of Maya warfare demonstrate its strong importance to the overarching Maya culture as well as the major role it played in the ultimate collapse.[2] The importance of internal warfare suggests that neither an overall cooperative nor totally despotic organization was ever achieved. The Maya were unique, with a distinctive history of development and a remarkable set of accomplishments as well as their own particular weaknesses.

Interaction with other contemporary cultures in the Mesoamerican realm and beyond functioned as an important source not only of shared ideas, but also of shared resources by trade. In Mesoamerica there existed an underlying common value system that goes back so far in time that its source is lost and remains a subject of future study. Examples of this inter-cultural sharing include the cults of the plumed serpent and jaguar, and the concept of a multi-class society dominated by an upper level of social elites.

Apart from academic arguments about whether the states of the Maya qualified as a civilization, the date of origin of the Maya as a distinct culture remains in dispute. There were people occupying the Maya lowlands with a stone-tool-using, non-agricultural economy before the appearance of distinctive Maya ceramics and agriculture. Santa Marta cave in the Chiapas river basin yielded evidence of Archaic (pre-Maya) groups who camped in the cave in a seasonal cycle. These semi-nomadic foragers are dated between 7000 and 3500 BC.[3] The true identifier of a culture would be its language, but the language spoken cannot be determined from the artifacts of those earliest sites. A small number of such sites are scattered throughout Mexico and Belize. These sites indicate a stone or lithic technology which pre-dates the appearance of ceramics, and with ceramics, agriculture. Therefore, ceramics have had to serve as a lame indicator of the earliest dates for the appearance of the Maya culture. Roughly, this appears to be around 1200 BC, although the ceramic forms and decoration by this time are already sophisticated enough to imply that even earlier versions probably existed. Regional differences in ceramics identify different groups of Maya.

At the site of Cuello in Belize the earliest evidence of sedentism in the Maya lowlands is an established agricultural community with ceramics and the remains of early village life at 1200 BC.[4] Several sites in northern Belize have produced both pottery and carbon-14 dates that corroborate the existence of well-established communities by this date.[5] While early Maya sites are known to the far west, Tikal is believed to have been settled from the east, from the direction of the earliest Belizean villages.[6]

The drainage divide of the Central Peten

It is the topography that helps to determine the reasons for the establishment of the site of Tikal in its particular locale and at a particular time. Chris Jones of the University of Pennsylvania first observed the role of this locale.[7]

The site where Tikal was established sits upon the equivalent of a continental divide. To the east are drainages and rivers leading towards the Caribbean coast. To the west are drainages and rivers leading towards the great Usumacinta River which flows directly to the coast of the Gulf of Mexico. This river also receives drainage from the uplands to the west. In other words, most of the Maya lowlands are divided by drainage at this strategic point, a place that would have to be crossed when trade routes extended from the west to the east side of the Yucatan Peninsula.[8] Tikal likely developed as a "toll" site receiving benefits from the overland flow of trade between major bodies of water . Further, the site is flanked by two large wetlands, the larger lying to the east and forming the headwaters of a water route leading directly to the Caribbean. A number of investigators have observed from the air signs of channelization below, leftover indicators of once intensive agriculture.[9] These channels have been observed in both the eastern and western flanking wetlands, but ground investigation has yet to provide confirmation. Such geographic and economic factors tell us why this great city was established where it is and also explain why its initial date of permanent habitation is somewhat later than in other areas. The earliest phase of Maya development as found elsewhere in the Maya lowlands, which has been dated at c. 1200–800 BC, has not been found at the site of Tikal. For such a large site, one of obvious eventual importance, it seems unusual that Tikal was not inhabited from the earliest known dates. Quite possibly no one dared to establish permanent residence on such a strategic point on an inland trade route during the earliest years of Maya development. The people of Tikal finally did just that, and despite centuries of conflict, the resulting city became a landmark.

The lowland forests of the Peten in Guatemala consist of the three-stage variety of rainforest. The three tiers of this tallest form of rainforest are known by botanists to each include separate micro-environments and ecosystems, each nourishing their own catalog of plant and animal life. The three levels are the relatively open, protected, shady forest floor; the lower branches of the taller trees, and mid-height bushes; and the upper canopy which provides the shade (*ills. 3 and 4*). The terrain varies in elevation, with many hills and ridges, broken by vast wetlands which today are characterized as seasonal swamps. The monsoon rains come in two intervals: one in the summer months and another, with heavier precipitation, in the autumn. Accurate prediction of the timing of this seasonal rainfall is essential to successful agriculture, which is why an agriculturally dependent society quickly develops an acute sense of time and a certain expertise with calendars. Evidence from recent studies of the Maya wetlands in places outside the Peten have shown that the Maya utilized such environments for a type of agriculture that was less dependent upon the rain cycle and more dependent upon the water levels in these swamplands. Such agriculture is called "intensive" and can yield more food than the usual farmer is capable of producing.[10]

Investigations at Tikal have shown that the site possessed no special or rare

3 (above) Looking out from Temple IV over the city of Tikal now covered by the re-grown rainforest which smothers most of the buildings of the city. The canopy of the forest averages 30 m in height.

4 (right) The rainforest canopy as seen from the ground level. The hardwood tree supports a parasitic fig which could eventually kill the host.

natural commodity to suggest settlement based on the presence of a tradable source material. There is locally available a source of chert of only middling quality. It was heavily exploited for manufacture of implements at the site, but there is no evidence that this locally produced stone was ever traded outside the confines of the site itself.

On the other hand, Tikal's swampside location readily suggests an excellent reason for its settlement in addition to trade considerations. In Central America, swamps are considered to be places just like towns, and accordingly are given names. The "Bajo de Santa Fe" lies immediately to the east side of Tikal, forming its eastern border. On the border of this swamp are a series of the earliest known settlements within what we now recognize as the confines of the city at its largest extent. In all likelihood, these earliest settlers reached the Tikal location by water routes and settled there because of ease of access, fertility of the uplands surrounding the flanks of the swamp, and the prominence of the ridges that characterize the center of the site. A ridgetop in any culture is a desirable location for ease of view of the surrounding territory and its defensible advantages. The settler has early warning of the approach of possible enemies and can communicate by heliograph (reflective mirror signals) with friendly nearby settlements. Whether or not the Maya employed this sun-based, efficient means of communication remains speculation, but its probability is supported by the presence of mirrors as part of the elite Classic paraphernalia.

15

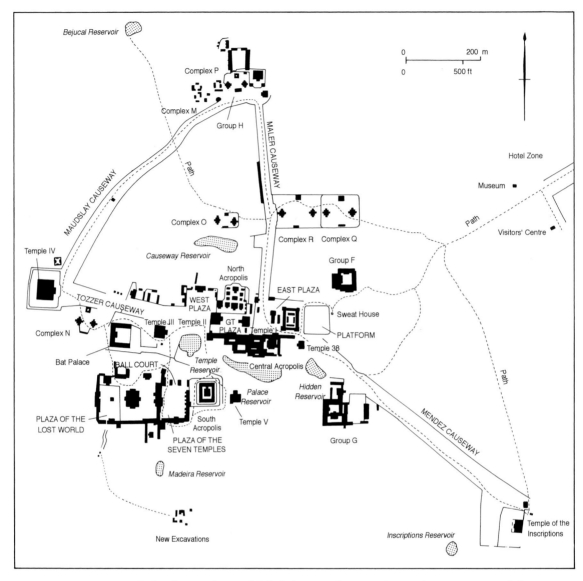

5 Stylized map of central Tikal showing the core of 16 sq. km. It is expected that thousands more structures lie beneath the surface.

At its peak of population, around AD 700, the site covered more than 65 sq. km of settled zone, containing many thousands of structures. The central core of the most densely populated zone was 16 sq. km and is easily identified as a major city, one of perhaps three that achieved such size, each with very different political histories (*ill. 5*). The other two are Coba in northern Quintana Roo and El Mirador to the northwest of Tikal. Settlement at Tikal began around 800 BC while the site fell into disuse sometime in the 10th

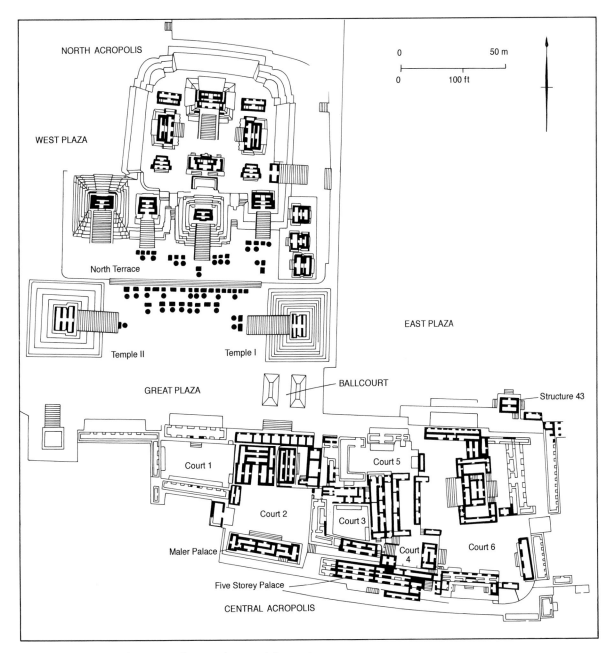

NORTH ACROPOLIS

WEST PLAZA

0   50 m

0   100 ft

North Terrace

Temple II   Temple I

EAST PLAZA

GREAT PLAZA   BALLCOURT

Structure 43

Court 1   Court 5

Court 2   Court 3

Maler Palace   Court 6

Court 4

Five Storey Palace

CENTRAL ACROPOLIS

6 The North Acropolis, Great Plaza, and Central Acropolis.

century AD. It appears that Tikal was a receiver of goods, and its occupation of a strategic position may well have led to its being surrounded by a ring of enemies, including Calakmul to the north, Caracol to the southeast, and Dos Pilas to the west (*see ill. 1*). This situation led to a stormy political history.

The forest environment

The rainforest is at the same time a source of usable plants and animals, and a challenge to survival. The soil is shallow which means that the trees extend their roots broadly, soaking up most of the minimally available nutrients in that frugal soil. The Maya learned very early in their development that they had to clear the forest before planting any domesticated crop and then to nurture that cleared land until its nutrients were mostly used up before moving on to another part of the forest. The cleared plot of land is called a *milpa* in Mesoamerica, the Spanish name for "field" (*ill. 7*).

The tall trees include some tropical hardwoods such as mahogany, *ciricote* and *pimienta*, as well as the tropical cedar, all still used today. The Maya recognized that the *sapodilla* tree, known today for its sap, chicle, the source of chewing gum, provided a wood very resistant to the voracious jungle termite, and so they used sapodilla timbers at Tikal, where they remain in place today. The *amapolla*, said to have been used by the Maya to make an intoxicating drink, grows all over Tikal; in the spring its flaming red foliage brings color to the city. Archaeologists at Tikal noticed an unusually high number of *ramon* trees whose fruit and nuts were heavily exploited by the Maya. These are perhaps wild remnants of orchards once nurtured near habitation. One of the first outstanding trees encountered by visitors on the path to the ruins is an ancient giant *ceiba*, sacred tree of the Maya, known as the "tree of life." The ceiba figured prominently in the ancient art, iconography, and mythology of the culture. Even today a ceiba is never cut in the process of clearing a milpa. Throughout the Maya area one often sees these tall trees standing majestically alone in a corn field. Those trees which were particularly useful or sacred to the Maya were nurtured within the confines of a settlement, be it village or city. This ancient nurturing resulted in the preservation of a number of species, not just of trees, but also of smaller useful plants such as those which produced condiments for cooking (cilantro, pimienta) and medicinal plants as well. There is also evidence that the ancient Maya appreciated plants for decoration, as found in illustrations on ceramic vessels showing flowers in headdresses and on the thrones of prominent figures. These elements of natural beauty in the forest environment today give us a glimpse of the palette of color and forms that inspired the ancient art – items that were adopted by certain rulers as personal emblems and livery. Depictions of flowers, plants, and animals used in this way are clearly shown on painted vessels.

The types of game prevalent in the forest included white tail deer, a smaller member of the deer family called *brocket*, the tapir and collared peccary, several rodentia, especially the *agouti*, the *tepesquintli*, and rabbit, all edible game. Non-edible but nonetheless valued animals of the forest included the fox, the feline members – jaguar, ocelot, and jaguarundi – as well as others (*pl. VII*). Animal hides were utilized and their characteristics were admired and appreciated. Notably, the jaguar reigned as the New World King of the

7 *A milpa, or corn field, in the burning process which takes place in the spring. The milpa fires must be set with precise timing, such that the ash will be driven in the soil by the first rains. If rains do not appear, fires often burn out of control.*

Beasts, and it was the spirit of this animal that served as the archetypal kindred spirit or *nahual* for the highest level of Maya leadership.

Amphibians include the herbivorous alligator and caiman, the meat-eating American crocodile (*ill. 8*), a variety of turtles, and a wide variety of frogs (*pl. V*). Most notable of the latter is a rare tropical species called in Maya *uo*, an animal whose strange life-cycle consists of a type of hibernation in the soil for most of the year, then emergence to the surface during the height of the monsoons for mating and breeding in the ground waters that collect at this time. Its mournful call sounds exactly like its name (pronounced "woe"), and this exotic creature appears as one of the Maya month names in the calendar.

The avian life of the forest included several different species of parrot, toucan, and the *guacamaya*, a host of migratory birds including humming-birds, hawks, doves, and two species of eagle. The bird life of Tikal is so wide-ranging even today that guide books have been published devoted to the site alone. Also important as edible species were the *pavo real* (*ill. 9*) or American turkey and the *curacao*. Prized for its long and springy feathers, the reclusive *quetzal* lives in cloud forest, the isolated ecological niche at about 4000 ft (1200 m), where rainforest and highlands collide, a region every Maya trader must have crossed on his way to highland markets (*pl. VI*). The quetzal feathers constituted a universally utilized feature of the headdress of every Maya leader throughout the lowlands and highlands, so much so that the bird has come very close to extinction. Colored feathers were clearly a valuable trade commodity at Tikal. Birds also appear in the iconography of costumes, often as head-

8 *This juvenile American crocodile represents a species that may have been second in importance at Tikal only to the jaguar.*

9 *The* pavo real *or royal turkey is the native American species and served as one food source for the ancient people. Nurtured by the Tikal Park, these birds have returned in large numbers and can be seen throughout the ruins.*

dresses and perhaps as nahual spirits, the "animal spirits" attributed to human beings.

This was the setting wherein a group of Maya took up residence around 800 BC and began the process that would lead to the realization of one of the grandest and most influential cities of this ancient and complex culture.

Chronologies: our view

The rough chronology which archaeologists have imposed upon the Maya culture recognizes and acknowledges changes through time in the form of clusters of cultural features. The word "classic" is borrowed inaccurately from Mediterranean civilization and applied to the Maya to distinguish the peak of achievement from its development and decline. The changes in clusters of cultural "packages" are expressed as major periods. They include: Preclassic (1500 BC–AD 250), Classic (AD 250–1100) and Postclassic (AD 1100 to the Spanish Conquest or roughly the mid-16th century). This kind of chronology at least allows a working framework, but it should be recognized as an expedient and not as a complete description of cultural variation.

The major periods are broken into finer divisions based largely on the changes in ceramics – one of the more plastic of arts and thus subject to fine differences that we can detect both by eye and by scientific analysis of chemical compositions. For the Preclassic period there are Early, Middle, and Late phases (*see Table 1*). The names selected by archaeologists to identify the ceramic phases at Tikal are distinctive to the site, as is customary in the analysis of individual sites in the Maya area. The names selected by Tikal's ceramicist, T. Patrick Culbert, are taken from the names of days in the month of the Maya calendar.[11] The Early phase dates from 1200–800 BC and has not been found at Tikal. The Middle phase has two ceramic complexes named Eb and Tzec and their dates are 800–600 BC and 600–350 BC respectively.

The Late Preclassic phase (350 BC–AD 250) is more complex than its predecessors and thus is divided into three distinct ceramic complexes. These are named Chuen (350 BC–AD 1), Cauac (AD 1–150), and Cimi (AD 150–250). These complexes are not arbitrary but represent real, observed differences in the development of the pottery that was being produced. They are the archaeologist's way of bringing order to the analysis of time and change, and are the handles which we use when discussing the development of the city.

The next major period, the Classic, has Early, Late, and Terminal phases at Tikal, represented by four ceramic complexes, two of which divide the Late Classic. These are: Manik (AD 250–550), Ik (AD 550–700), Imix (AD 700–850), and Eznab (AD 850–950). Finally, a Postclassic phase, represented by a single ceramic complex, is called Caban (AD 950–1200?). Excavations by Laporte in the so-called Lost World complex allowed him to further distinguish divisions in the Manik (Early Classic) phase which he labeled Manik 1, 2 and 3.[12] One ultimate goal of the archaeology performed by the Pennsylvania group is to determine and define elements of change in the culture other than ceramics which will then permit a more objective and refined method of describing the time/change continuum. For example, there are similar changes in architecture as in ceramics, both in style and in the mechanics of engineering, as well as changes in burial practice, settlement pattern and a number of other cultural features. Only when all of these have been thoroughly analyzed and amalgamated, will it be possible to re-define the cultural phases of Tikal.

Table 1	Tikal Ceramic Complexes	
Period	*Ceramic Complex*	*Approximate Date*
Postclassic	Caban	AD 950–1200 (?)
Terminal Classic	Eznab	AD 850–950
Late Classic	Imix	AD 700–850
Late Classic	Ik	AD 550–700
Early Preclassic	Manik	AD 250–550
Late Preclassic	Cimi	AD 150–250
Late Preclassic	Cauac	AD 1–150
Late Preclassic	Chuen	350 BC–AD 1
Middle Preclassic	Tzec	600–350 BC
Middle Preclassic	Eb	800–600 BC

Chronologies: their view

The Maya view of their own chronology was different from ours and was based upon their calendar. The Maya concept and manipulation of time has been studied and published extensively. It utilized a vigesimal system based upon units of 20, rather than the familiar European decimal system based on units of ten. Time was a sacred and magical concept. Its divisions and units – days, months, years – were viewed as deities carrying a bundle, the burden of time. The need for an accurate record of the passage of time arose out of the needs of agriculture. In the lowlands, the seasons are governed by a cycle of wet and dry months which determine the proper times for planting, growth, and harvest. Success in food supply was essential first to survival and then to development and population growth. The basic unit – the day – is based upon the movements of the sun, perceived as a primary male deity named Kinich Ahau. Those individuals who mastered the timing of the movements of the sun, the moon, and the stars came to be revered and honored – the priests and kings, the bearers of knowledge that resulted in a bountiful harvest. A consequence of association of the days with different deities was their association also with benevolent or malevolent natures. They were, after all, modeled upon human nature. Thus there were good and bad days – days beneficial or not – for giving birth, initiating war, planting, reaping, and so forth. Developed as a necessity to survival, the calendar became an instrument of astrology. It is now believed that every Maya of every social class had some understanding of this process of interaction between themselves and the gods of time. This was not an arcane knowledge held only by kings and priests, but one that was shared on some fundamental level with every member of the society. However, keeping a written record of time required literacy and mastery of a codified system of notation. This skill was restricted to the elite levels of the society.

There is no way to make explanation of the Maya calendar count system simple and this volume does not intend to explore the subject exhaustively. For the reader who wishes to understand the calendar in depth I recommend consultation of any one of a number of general volumes on Maya culture.[13] There follows a brief sketch of the complex Maya calendrical system.

It is from the hieroglyphic or written record of inscriptions that we know just how sophisticated the Maya calendar was. Two different calendars were maintained. The *Tzolkin* or sacred calendar was based upon a 260-day count, consisting of 13 numbers and 20 names which cycled together until the starting combination appeared again, after 260 days – 13 times 20. This "sacred year" was very important to the Maya and each of the 260 days was associated with a different deity.

The second cyclical count contained 365 days, the "Vague Year," the closest day count the Maya had to the true solar year of 365.25 days. We compensate with a leap year of 366 days every four years, but fractions were beyond the capabilities of Maya mathematics. The Vague Year was composed of

18 months of 20 days each, with an added short month of five days to approximate the true solar year. This counting cycle also consisted of a series of combined names and numbers, so that any given real day had a number and name from each of the two counting systems, for example a number and day name from the Tzolkin and a number and month name from the Vague Year such as 1 Ik 1 Pop. With the two counts intermeshed, the same four-part combination could not recur for 52 cycles of the Vague Year, or 52 times 365 days. Because it could re-cycle, the Maya needed yet another form of count that would distinguish similar dates that were 52 years or more apart. This system is called the "Long Count."

The Long Count days have a unique designation that can never recur again and for this type of count a fixed starting date is required, just as we use the assumed date of the birth of Christ as the start of the current era calendar. The Maya used a mythical starting date set on 11 August 3114 BC in our calendar. The Long Count was used to record dates on monuments that are associated with specific events. It is a notational system that was recorded in paired columns, reading from left to right (*ill. 10*). The count had to accommodate long periods of time and it does this through escalating positions similar to the way we record numbers in escalating positions. For example, the number 1625 indicates to us five units of 1, two units of 10, six units of 100, and one unit of 1000. The Maya used five positions in which the first represents the unit of a

10 *Stela 5 on the North Terrace displays an excellent example of a hieroglyphic text, including a number of dates in the Maya calendar. Texts read from left to right, and top to bottom.*

single day and was called a *kin*. The second position contained 20 kins to make up one Maya month, called a *uinal*. In the third position the Maya deviated from their vigesimal system to include only 18 instead of 20 uinals to make up a Maya year, called a *tun*. Each tun contained 360 days, the closest count possible with multiples of 20 (20 times 18). The next position reverts to vigesimal with 20 tuns (or 20 "years"), a period called a *katun*. At Tikal, the katun was a very important period marked for many cycles with the erection of a dated monument celebrating its end. The last position contain 20 katuns, a period of 400 "years" or tuns and is called a *baktun*. This position could accommodate enough time to count from the mythical beginning until the Maya present. At Tikal, recovered written dates begin during the 8th baktun and continue into the 10th baktun. The span of Tikal's written history is discussed in a later chapter.

On a written date of the Long Count, the recorded passage of days is followed by the full name of the day reached. We record such dates in the following manner: 9.14.0.0.0 6 Ahau 13 Muan . This reads that 9 baktuns, 14 katuns, no tuns, no uinals and no kins are counted from the starting date and brings us to the 6th day named Ahau in the Tzolkin, and the 13th day in the month named Muan. This happens to be the end day of the 14th katun which is why there are no tuns, uinals or kins. This is the dedicatory date on Stela 16 at Tikal and correlates with 1 December, in the year AD 711. While the Maya system is complex it is in many ways similar to our way of recording passed time from a fixed date.

Throughout this volume the Maya Long Count dates are provided in the notes in the short-hand notation shown above, although the correlated dates in our calendar are used as standard historical anchors in the text.

I *(right) Airview of the Great Plaza, with Temple I in the foreground, Temple II in the center and Temple IV in the far distance.*

Overleaf

II *One of the unique pieces from Burial 10 is a ceramic composite vessel referred to as the "Old Man Deity," probably depicting the sun god in his night guise.*

III *Some vessels of the Cauac period were spectacular in their size and shape. This red polished type of hourglass vessel is referred to as the "fire-hydrant" vessel in the Tikal typology.*

IV *This extraordinary ceramic lidded vessel depicts a cormorant resting on the surface of water with a turtle below. It was recovered in Tomb 1 of Structure 5D-88 in the Lost World group, dating to the late Early Classic period.*

III

IV

V

VI

VII

CHAPTER TWO

TIKAL DISCOVERED

In 1525 Hernan Cortes passed through the area that was to become the Peten Department of Guatemala, traveling from Mexico and headed for Honduras. His route brought him across Lake Peten Itza to a Maya city still occupied and thriving, by the name of Tayasal. His passage was friendly, and a horse was left behind with the king of Tayasal, an event which worked its way into the legends of Guatemalan history. Tayasal lies near the western end of the long Lake Peten Itza, a mere 60 km from the ruins of Tikal. It seems remarkable that such a large ancient city was missed by this intrepid explorer, but we must to remember that he was not interested in ruins *per se* but rather in people and their riches.

The centuries of Spanish exploration of this New World were a time of exploitation. The goals were to claim lands in the name of the King of Spain, to wrest away whatever "treasures" were perceived as valuable, and to convert souls to Christianity. For over a century after the arrival of Cortes, the Spanish explorers focused on the city of Tayasal which offered remarkable resistance to Spanish domination. In all that time the presence of one of the largest of Maya cities went undetected.

It is known from archaeological remains that during the 19th century there was a settlement at Tikal, probably of Yucatec speakers, like those who had settled on the northern shore of Lake Peten Itza in what are now the modern settlements of San Jose and San Andres. The exact years of this occupation are not known but the inhabitants are credited with one explanation of how the site got its name.

The name of Tikal

One reading of the word "Tikal" in Yucatec Maya divides the word into "ti'" meaning "place of" and "k'al" meaning "spirits." This renders such romantic translations as "place of spirits" or "place of spirit voices," and for one scholar as "where voices cry in the night."[1] Legend has it that on one occasion the

---

V *This colorful tree frog is one of many species of frog whose natural habitat was Tikal. Frogs were important in the art and iconography of the Maya calendar and as a symbol of the watery habitats that surround the city.*

VI *The quetzal's long tailfeathers were prized and traded for use in headdresses. The bird was likely never native to Tikal, but feathers were traded from the highlands.*

VII *The jaguar was lord of the forests, and its spirit or* nahual *was often claimed by kings as their personal name and protector. Images of jaguars appear frequently in the iconography of Tikal.*

people of the 19th century settlement were driven out of their humble houses in the ruins by a combination of fear of the "spirit voices" and a plague of bats. Bats, especially the small fruit bat, have always favored the standing, empty chambers of the palaces and temples as a suitable and desirable habitat. It is possible that an outbreak of rabies may account for the virtual abandonment of the site by the Maya re-occupants in the mid-19th century.

Quite apart from the origin of the name as we know it and its Maya meaning, there is the emblem glyph which the ancient Maya themselves used to identify the site (*ill. 11*). This raises two questions. Is the name "Tikal" possibly the original name preserved through time by oral tradition? Can this name be read from the emblem glyph? There are two schools of thought. Clemency Coggins and Christopher Jones both believe that the name is original and that there are several ways to translate it.[2] The primary translation is related to the reverence for the 20-year time period called the katun which is so strongly evidenced in the presence of many twin-pyramid groups at Tikal, built to mark the end of the katun time period. As Coggins has elucidated, in Yucatec Maya the word for the count of twenty is *k'al,* while *ti'* is "place of," providing a reading of "Place of the Count of the K'atun," or *Ti'k'al.*

Furthermore, time was regarded and depicted by the Maya as a burden or bundle carried by the gods. The glyph is read as a tied bundle, the burden of time, represented by the katun. This is a compelling interpretation.

11 This emblem glyph states "divine lord of Tikal." The tied bundle is the glyph designating the name of this city.

A more recent interpretation represents the other school of thought and is based upon a sculpture found at the site of Copan in Honduras. On this sculpture of an adult male, the hair arrangement, viewed from the rear, is formed exactly like the Tikal emblem glyph: a tied bundle. In this case, the tied bundle is the man's hairdo in the form of a topknot. David Stuart reads this configuration with the Maya word *mutul* which also means "flower."[3] The importance of a man's topknot in the iconography of Tikal had already been cited by Coggins as a means of emulating the emblem glyph of the site in art.

Whether the name of Tikal is original and refers to reverence for time, or whether the name was "Mutul" and refers to a flower with a visual pun expressed in a hairstyle remains a matter for academic debate. For the visitor and for the Guatemalan Tourist Board, the name remains Tikal.

The history of discovery

By the time that the 19th-century occupants had departed, the Peten had become a political entity with a population distributed mainly around the shores of the lake some 60 km away – clearly, the presence of the ruins of Tikal was commonly known to these people. However, it was not until 1848 that an official expedition to examine the ruins took place headed by two government officials: Modesto Mendez, the commissioner of El Peten, and Ambrosio Tut, governor of the Department. With them came an artist, Eusebio Lara, who was the first to make a record of some examples of the sculptured monuments at the site. An account of this journey, together with Lara's illustrations, was published by the Berlin Academy of Science in the year following the investigation. Mendez revisited the site in 1852, but no record survives of the later visit.

It was during this period of exploration that the famous American, John Lloyd Stephens, and his British companion and illustrator, Frederick Catherwood, traveled through the Maya area, recording sites and making them known to the Western world. By chance, they did not hear about the ruins of Tikal, and so this most important site does not appear in their record.

The next known visitor to the site was Dr. Gustav Bernoulli, a native of Berne, Switzerland, who had settled in Guatemala for his health on the recommendation of the great explorer Alexander von Humboldt. In 1877, while exploring Maya ruins, Bernoulli met with Teobert Maler at the site of Palenque, and traveled from there to Tikal shortly after, presumably on Maler's advice. Following this initial visit he ordered the removal of three of the carved lintels, two from Temple IV and part of Lintel 3 from Temple I. These lie today in the Museum fur Volkerkunde in Basel, where they remain the best preserved of all Tikal wooden lintels. Dr. Bernoulli acted according to the ethics of the day and obtained full official permission from the government to remove the carvings. These actions reflect the 19th-century view of the function of archaeology: to collect curiosities for exhibition and education.

Alfred Percival Maudslay was the next explorer to visit Tikal. An Englishman, he did for Tikal what Stephens and Catherwood did for so many other Maya cities elsewhere: made the site known to the Western world.[4] Maudslay's simple map was the first made and it reveals the initial hesitancy to explore thoroughly or to recognize more than the most prominent structures. Maudslay's contribution was a two-edged sword, however. His photographs of the major temples of Tikal, taken in 1881 and 1882, are spectacular, giving us a glimpse of what these massive structures actually looked like when first cleared of the foliage which had covered them after their abandonment (*ills. 12, 13*). Unfortunately, once the buildings had been exposed in this way to the elements, without any efforts at conservation, many details were lost due to erosion. In fact, the great temples of Tikal were exposed to erosion damage twice in this fashion before any effort was made to preserve them.

12, 13 *Taken by Alfred Maudslay in the late 19th century, these remarkable views of cleared Temples II, III, and IV are not accessible today.*

The next visitor to Tikal was Teobert Maler, who had directed Maudslay as well as Bernoulli to the site. A German by birth and Austrian by choice, Maler was employed by the Peabody Museum of Harvard University to visit the site after years of travel and exploration in the Maya region. His mandate was to attempt a definitive exploration and record of the city's ruins. He spent from 25 May till 5 June in 1895 making plans of the five so-called "Great Temples" and parts of what was to become known as the Central Acropolis.[5] This included the Palace of the Two Stories, which has been known as "Maler's Palace" ever since. Maler used this structure as his encampment headquarters and it must be remembered that the whole of the architectural group was heavily overgrown by tall trees (*ill. 14*). The first story of the palace, however, stood largely intact, and Maler's descriptions of having to build a large fire outside the central doorway to keep roaring jaguars at bay are romantic and intriguing, to say the least. The probability is that what he heard was the roar of the howler monkey, which closely resembles the call of the jaguar. This blood-curdling sound is still heard by visitors to the site today, and the howler monkeys do roar all night.

Maler returned to Tikal to complete his work in 1904 and remained this time from the beginning of August until the middle of November, some three-and-a-half months. Once again, he stayed in the front central room of the place that bears his name. His florid inscription, typical of European handwriting of the

14 Structure 5D-65, known as "Maler's Palace" was where Teobert Maler lived in 1895 and 1904. Chronology suggests that this great palace was built in the late 8th century by the 29th Lord of Tikal.

time, is incised into the east jamb of the central doorway. The dates under his name, 1895/1904, record the years during which he lived in this room, even if briefly. Although Maler handed over his written description and many plans of buildings to the Peabody Museum, he became a little paranoid in his later years about the uses that the Museum might be making of his work. Imagining that the Museum was realizing vast profits from his efforts at his expense seems humorous today, but it led Maler to withhold his detailed map of the site, a document which resurfaced much later.

In order to complete a publication, the Peabody Museum was forced to send a new expedition to Tikal in 1910. Thus, the next explorers were Alfred Tozzer, who was to become the first occupant of the prestigious Bowditch Chair at Harvard, assisted by a young Raymond E. Merwin, who would go on to become well known as a Maya scholar in his own right.[6] While previous explorers had entered the site from the west, approaching from the island town of Flores and Lake Peten Itza, the Tozzer/Merwin expedition was the first to enter from the east by way of British Honduras, now Belize, traveling from El Cayo to Lake Yaxha and overland northwards to Tikal. Tozzer deemed this the easiest route at the time and recommended it for future explorers. After a month at the site Tozzer and Merwin completed a map showing considerably more detail than Maudslay's but still tending to overlook the thousands of smaller structures in the center of the site and failing to realize the full scope of the city's extent. This map, together with more detailed data, was combined with Maler's report and published in 1911. The result is an exciting work which even today manages to convey the flavor of the site. It was this volume that came into my hands, while serving as a student at the Royal Ontario Museum in Toronto, an inspiration that eventually led me to become yet another explorer of Tikal.

Following this pioneer work by the Peabody Museum, the focus shifted from interest in Tikal's architecture to concern for recording the hieroglyphic inscriptions which were a feature at most major Maya sites. With the support of the Carnegie Institution of Washington, Sylvanus P. Morley undertook the major task of attempting to record all the inscriptions to be found in the province of the Peten.[7] Knowing what we do today of the enormous scope of both settlement and inscribed records of the ancient Maya, it is certain that this ambitious undertaking has still not been completed. However, Morley's effort remains a landmark of scholarship, and it brought him to Tikal for recording sessions in 1914, 1921, 1922, and 1928. Overlapping with this monumental effort was Morley's other major contribution to Maya studies, the excavations at the site of Uaxactun, about 18 km to the north. This project established an academic base for understanding the stratigraphy of a Maya site and its chronology. Among the archaeologists working with Morley at Uaxactun was Edwin M. Shook, a young student of engineering who came to be one of the most knowledgeable Mayanists of the 20th century, destined to become the first Director of the Tikal Project out of the University of Pennsylvania.

During his work at Uaxactun, Shook made side trips south to the much larger site of Tikal. It was a five-hour walk along a chiclero's trail, and there were no living inhabitants at the site then. Work continued in relative proximity to Tikal from 1926 until 1937, a period during which the essential principles of archaeological excavation were forged, suitable to the problems peculiar both to the setting and the culture.

The Tikal Project: University of Pennsylvania

It was only a decade later, in 1947, that Percy Madeira proposed to Froelich Rainey, Director of the University Museum of Pennsylvania, that major work be undertaken at one of the largest, oldest, and most important of Maya sites: Tikal in Guatemala.

Madeira, an old-family native Philadelphian, was President of the Board of Directors at the Museum, while Rainey was to serve as that institution's Director for 29 years. Although positively received, the proposal had to be put on hold for a number of years until after the collapse of the Arbenz regime when a pro-American government in Guatemala welcomed the University of Pennsylvania. This long-standing dream to mount an expedition to Tikal was finally realized in 1955, having its genesis in the drawing-rooms of prominent families in Philadelphia and Pittsburgh. The result was collaboration among several scholars and benefactors, mostly those connected directly with the University Museum. These were Percy Madeira, Froelich Rainey, John Dimick and his friend from earlier work in Guatemala, Ed Shook, formerly of the Carnegie Institution.

A small airstrip had been built in the 1940s on the east edge of the site by the Guatemalan military for use in case of conflict with British Honduras. This happy circumstance made air travel directly to the site possible and eased the logistics of working in the heart of the Peten. Thus it was that the threat of strife between Guatemala and the country now known as Belize made it feasible for work to begin at Tikal.

A camp had to be built to house the archaeological team as well as a village to serve the workmen, who were mostly Maya from the Cakchiquel-speaking area of the highlands of Guatemala. Aubrey Trik, an architect schooled in the *beaux arts* tradition with additional experience at the site of Zaculeu in highland Guatemala, joined the team in its early stages. He was able to apply his architectural training at first in the design of the village and later to the much more important work of restoring ancient structures of monumental size. As the first Project Director, Ed Shook oversaw the excavation from 1955 until 1961 and oversaw the mapping of the site. He initiated the trenching operations which led to the discovery of the necropolis that lay beneath the North Acropolis. This impressive collection of temples and platforms which form the north side of Tikal's Great Plaza served for centuries as the burial place of kings.

The University Museum had a long tradition of mounting large-scale expeditions, especially in the Near East where the custom was to engage enormous numbers of workmen who could move huge quantities of soil quickly in order to reveal monumental architecture in a reasonable length of time. Tikal was a site on this scale, and it was the conscious effort to introduce the Near Eastern excavation style that led to the appointment of Robert S. Dyson as the project's next director. For the year of 1962 Dyson took leave of his work at Hasanlu in Iran to oversee the operations at Tikal. The number of workmen rose to above 100, probably an unprecedented number for a Maya excavation, at least at the time. At this point, work in the Central Acropolis was initiated under the present author's supervision. Dyson had to return to his own research in Iran in 1963, and his succeeding director was William R. Coe II who had been with the Project from the start and by this time was serving as Curator of the American Section of the Museum.

The original program of consolidation and restoration was in the charge of Aubrey Trik who had earlier worked at the highland site of Zaculeu.[8] As the project grew in scope and budget, the allocation of responsibility similarly became diversified. As a roving architect/archaeologist for the University Museum, Trik was assigned to other museum projects elsewhere. Swiss archaeologist George Guillemin took over as field director and supervisor of the restoration operations. For three years I was in charge of budgetary matters and administration of the Project in the field, in addition to my excavation duties in the Central Acropolis. Coe held his position as overall project director until the formal end of the Project in 1969. His detailed and lengthy report, Tikal Report 14, describes the excavations in the North Acropolis and Great Plaza. It was published in 1992 and has been hailed by one reviewer as the masterpiece of the most accomplished living Maya archaeologist.

Funding for this massive project had to shift of necessity from privately raised sources to more official ones. The government of Guatemala recognized the benefits of this extensive project in the remote forests of the Peten, and agreed to fund several more years of investigation and restoration. This source of national support for a foreign-based project was unprecedented in the history of Maya archaeology. Such guaranteed funding allowed an expansion of the restoration and preservation effort, always more costly than the more modest costs of excavation. The concept of preserving what had been excavated, standard practice today, was pioneered in those days.

The project had contracted an agreement with Time-Life Corporation that any spectacular finds would be reported to them first, and that they would provide beneficial publicity. Excavation of Burial 10, under Temple 5D-34 on the North Terrace of the Great Plaza, and Burial 116 under the architectural "pin-up" of Tikal, Temple I, were the most notable occasions that prompted articles in *Life* magazine.[9]

It was part of the project organization that each individual staff member received a permanent project number for identification purposes in the record of notes and photographs. Over the course of 15 years of field work, the Tikal Project recorded 113 professional participants, the majority of whom were students from the University of Pennsylvania and elsewhere. It is interesting that while Number 1 was the project's first Director, Ed Shook, Number 113 was allocated to Dr. Payson Sheets, now a prominent archaeologist at the University of Colorado, well-known for his work in El Salvador. Of all these individuals who spent part of their professional and training time at Tikal there were perhaps a dozen who formed the hard-core field force, their work including investigations of central Tikal, peripheral Tikal, and the essential laboratory conservation and analyses.[10]

Naturally, no project on this scale of personnel and time could be free of problems and the Pennsylvania Project was no exception. The difficulties of a variable rainy season, through which work continued, resulted in delays and setbacks. Isolation and illness were indeed factors: injuries on the job, strange diseases unfamiliar to North Americans – malaria, leishmaniasis, meningitis, histo-plasmosis; snake bites by the dreaded fer-de-lance; attacks by army ants on the camp quarters were especially feared, particularly at night. Readings from the medical diagnosis volume, the Merck Manual, came to be a form of unwise entertainment on Saturday nights. Such readings only stirred the imagination. Then, as the project wound down, deeply involved graduate students carried away hefty publishing responsibilities, graduated, and were forced to go on to other jobs. Nevertheless, of 39 projected numbered reports, 18 are already published, while many others are either awaiting the press or in active preparation.

At Christmas 1969, the University Museum officially turned over the site to the Government of Guatemala, and that particular epoch of investigation and restoration came to an end. The goals of the project had been many: to survey the entire site; to gain knowledge through excavation of all levels of society in ancient times at the site, not just of the elite center; to restore and consolidate as much as budgetary limitations would allow for the benefit of future visitors to the site; and to establish a base that could be used by visitors and scholars alike. All these goals were met and publication of these data is now well advanced, although the sheer mass of it, as well as publication costs, have slowed the completion of this phase of the project. To date, the University Museum's Tikal Project is the largest-scale archaeological investigation in the New World.

Proyecto Nacional Tikal

Recognizing both the success of the original Tikal Project as well as the fact that the site was so enormous that its remaining possibilities still demanded investigation, the Government of Guatemala initiated a second project under their own supervision in 1979. The title in Spanish reflected the national control of this venture. The appointed director was Juan Pedro Laporte, a

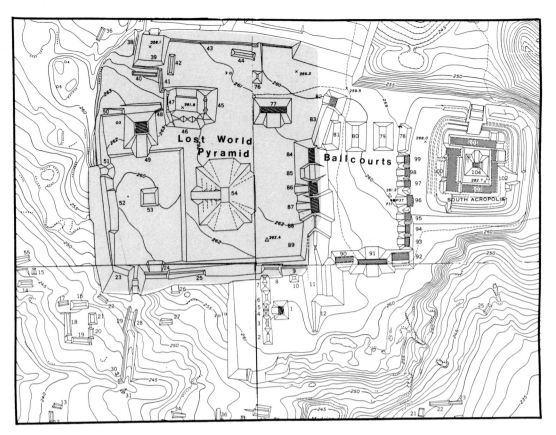

15 Map of the study area of the Guatemalan National Project, with the "Lost World Pyramid" in the center of the group. Three adjacent ballcourts of Late Classic date are found to the east in the plaza known as the "Seven Temples."

Guatemalan archaeologist who had accomplished much of his field experience with the original Tikal Project as project member Number 57.

The new project had a new focus. In addition to furthering the investigations, it was desirable to open up another portion of the site for tourists to visit, and the United States Park Service was consulted for advice on the best locale for such development. The significance of the areas under investigation as well as the need for open space were carefully considered. The zone known affectionately as the "Lost World Pyramid" was chosen as the location for new development and excavation (*ill. 15*). This massive pyramid had been partially explored during the Pennsylvania project, which showed that its origins lay in the Middle Preclassic period (*c.* 600 – 350 BC). It sits in an expansive open plaza surrounded on two sides by numerous temples of various Classic period dates (*ill. 16*). The location exceeded anyone's expectations, revealing yet another royal necropolis that served as an alternative to the North Acropolis excavated by the earlier project.

Also, a zone to the south of the Lost World Pyramid which had appeared to be devoid of any significant surface architecture was given a test-pit series of excavations; the results were expected to be merely routine. Instead, these tests

16 (right) The west face of the Lost World Pyramid (Structure 5C-54) as it appears today, after excavation and restoration. The structure visible is of Early Classic date.

revealed a vast array of buried structures that had been undetected beneath the deceptively flat surface. Excavations in what was called the 5C-XVI Group have revealed an entire buried acropolis dating to the Early Classic period.[11] This discovery has shed much light upon the political activities of the site for this period, as well as suggesting what more may lie undetected in apparently vacant zones of the map. Other planned excavations at Tikal's North Group did not come to completion before the project ended in 1989.

In addition to this zone, the Proyecto Nacional Tikal branched out to work in other areas. Uaxactun, to the north of Tikal, had received no attention from archaeologists since the days of the Carnegie excavations in the 1930s and 1940s. Hence, excavation and restoration were re-commenced here after a road had been constructed to join the two sites.

Both projects, that of Pennsylvania and the National effort demonstrated how much more remains to be learned of Tikal. It is estimated that less than 10 per cent of those structures known by mapping have been excavated. Of the six named "Great Temples," two were excavated by Penn (Temples I and II) and one (Temple V) is presently under a tunneling investigation sponsored by a new joint Guatemala-Spanish project. This leaves three uninvestigated (Temples III, IV, and VI), and these are only of the named great temples. Even in the Central Acropolis, where this author worked for three years, 24 of 46 structures were investigated, a total of 52 percent. We know that the answers to many questions lie beneath the unexcavated portions.

The Guatemalan government has sustained its interest in Tikal through maintenance and consolidation programs in recent years, with new excavations currently taking place and, hopefully, archaeological investigations will

continue. As a laboratory for learning the site offers a virtually bottomless potential. It is a pity that finances for excavation remain difficult to raise, even for this great city that was once a capital of the New World . However, breakthroughs on other fronts of investigation, namely in the translation of hieroglyphic texts both at Tikal and elsewhere, have led to exciting and revealing advances in our knowledge of the history of the lords of Tikal. References to the great central city are found at many other sites in the Peten and even beyond, helping to piece together a sketchy history of Tikal's fortunes, at least for the Classic period.

This volume attempts to summarize what is now known of the site drawing upon the work, not just of the University Museum of Pennsylvania, but of all scholars who have turned their attention to the art, iconography, and especially the hieroglyphic texts which concern the vicissitudes of fortune that marked the site's history in ancient times. No account of Tikal can ever be complete, and this one does not pretend to fulfill such a role. Rather, it is intended to inform the reader and to elucidate the site and its known history to the extent that is currently possible. To do this, I follow the growth of the site from archaeological data prior to the beginning of dynastic rule and the written record. After this record began there is reference to a "founder." This individual was recognized by the Maya of Tikal as an anchor point in their own history. Clearly, the founder was not the first ruler of Tikal, but he is a fixed reference point for the ancient Maya historians who recorded in text Tikal's progress and decline. Following the evidence as presently known, the history of the site is traced through the works and succession of its rulers. The record is not complete, nor might all my colleagues agree with my interpretations of which ruler accomplished which feats and contributions to the development of Tikal. This is the nature of archaeological evidence and scholastic interpretation. The goal of this volume is to present the evidence for interpretation – to flesh out the weathered ruins back into the living entities that they once were – and for the first time to present the story of Tikal as seen through the eyes of its own lords.

Tikal today

The modern pilgrim coming to Tikal today arrives just as did the earliest settlers of the site – at the eastern edge of the city – close to the shore of the Bajo de Santa Fe. No longer can such pilgrims fly directly to the airfield which facilitated the original project. The National Park of Tikal closed the airfield in order to preserve the natural quality of the site and its surroundings. Instead the visitor must take a land route similar to that followed by Modesto Mendez when the ancient city was first visited in 1848. The road now travels directly from the new airport in Santa Elena close to the capital city of Flores and the ancient site of Tayasal.

On arrival at Tikal the visitor is greeted by a cluster of public buildings,

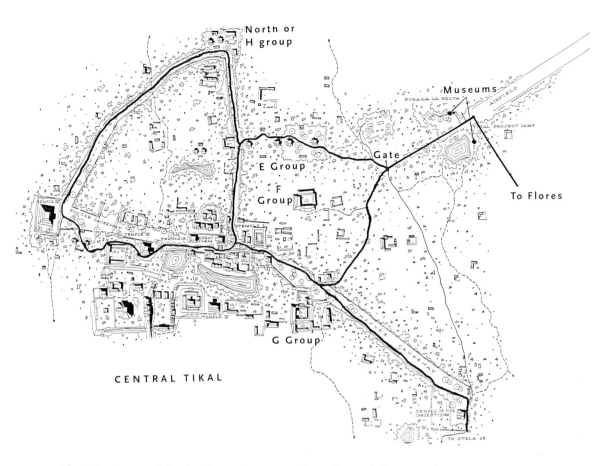

17 The visitor's map of the site shows the entrance from the south, location of museums, and the road routes into the major ruins.

museums and hotels that now cover the space that once was the camp of the archaeological investigators from the 1950s through the 1980s. From this ancient entry way the visitor must walk – as did the original residents – to climb the ridge that attracted the earliest settlers. The single white road leading westward from the modern cluster divides at what is now the Park gate to follow the old roads established by the Pennsylvania project (*ill. 17*). This modern road system is simple and not entirely arbitrary. To the right the road leads to Group E, a pair of twin-pyramid complexes both built by the same ruler on an east–west spine of high ground. From here, the road climbs onto the Maler Causeway which it follows upwards to the East Plaza, immediately adjacent to the Great Plaza, where it joins the top of the southern road right behind Temple I.

The southern road departs from the same gateway close to the "camp." It winds briefly through the forest where no structures are visible from the road and eventually joins the Mendez Causeway at a turning point in the causeway adjacent to a cluster of palaces called "G Group." This interesting complex is partially cleared and the visitor has access to one interior courtyard and a group of surrounding, partially restored palaces. From here, the road follows the Mendez Causeway and one can turn sharply left to the southeast following the lower end of the Causeway until it terminates at Temple VI, called the Temple of the Inscriptions – an important feature of the city. This numbered Great Temple lies at a much lower elevation than the Great Plaza and on the map looks like an urban extension well to the southeast of the city center. Following the Mendez Causeway from G Group towards the Great Plaza, the road rises sharply, climbing onto the ridge to terminate also in the East Plaza where the northern and southern routes meet behind Temple I. Entering the East Plaza, the visitor passes by 5E-38, a substantial temple on the south side of the road. The East Acropolis, the Marketplace and a large ballcourt (where the Mesoamerican ballgame was played) are all hidden in the current growth of forest. A small ceremonial structure with three visible stairs adjoins the great walls of the Central Acropolis and is notable for its Teotihuacan-style decoration. However, the back of Temple I dominates the East Plaza and the first view of it always elicits a gasp of disbelief from the first-time visitor (*ill. 18*).

From the East Plaza, a ramp leads up to the Great Plaza, the heart and center of the city, dominated by Temples I and II facing each other on the east and west sides, with the North Acropolis, a cluster of temples, and the Central Acropolis, a complex of palaces closing the other sides of the plaza. The pilgrim to this place cannot help being awed by this magnificent and sacred space. The Central Acropolis is an elevated complex of six courtyards at differing levels, extending from the middle of the Great Plaza, eastward nearly halfway past the East Plaza.

The roads leading up to the plaza and beyond can only be used by government vehicles and foot traffic today. A bypass behind the North Acropolis now prevents all vehicular traffic from entering the Great Plaza. The old project road continues west from behind Temple II, passing through the West Plaza, next to Temple III, then circles around the "Bat Palace," now called the Palace of the Windows, focusing on a more permanent feature. The formerly resident bats were evicted during restoration of the building. From behind the Palace of the Windows the road curves through N Group, a twin-pyramid group of great significance to the history of the city, and finally reaches Temple IV. The distance from the Great Plaza to Temple IV is 1 km. The tallest aboriginal structure in the New World is not visible at its base due to the growth covering the giant pyramid. The cleared temple above however can be seen from atop a number of structures to the east. From Temple IV, a recently revived road follows the Maudslay Causeway to H Group, the northern focal point of the city.

On the map, the routes of the ancient causeways are clearly revealed, belying the chaotic impression given by the modern roads which only follow bits of the ancient ways. Three of the causeways join together major features of the city in a rough, broken-line right-angled triangle. The Maler Causeway connects the

18 (right) The visitor's first view of Temple I is always from the eastern side. The Great Temple is dramatically framed by the rainforest now growing in the East Plaza.

East Plaza from directly behind Temple I to H Group, the north group, with a bend in the road adjacent to the twin-pyramid group called R Complex. The Maler Causeway is notable for two features. It is broken by a great stairway descending into a ravine just north of R Complex. As the road climbs out of the ravine on the north side and just before arriving at H Group it is interrupted again by a giant exposed rock carving, facing south. This carving once displayed two human figures and three glyph panels. The figures show a seated victor and a standing bound prisoner. The scene is attributed to Yik'in Chan K'awil, the 27th ruler of Tikal who reigned in the middle of the 8th century. The causeway itself may also be his work.

Recent reconstructions in H Group make it well worth a visit. Twin-pyramid P Complex stands to the west of a very large temple (5C-43) which is larger and taller than the Temple of the Inscriptions, but lacks a roof comb, a major feature of Classic temple decoration, and so was not graced with the official term of "Great Temple."

The Tozzer Causeway connects the West Plaza to the base of Temple IV, passing by Temple III, the Palace of the Windows and N Complex (twin-pyramid group) all to the south. Like a drunken hypotenuse connecting the other two Causeways, the Maudslay Causeway twists from Temple IV to the northern H Group, ending at the twin pyramids of P Complex. A cluster of large palace groups north of H Group are not easily accessible.

To the south side of the city center a deep ravine separates another east–west alignment of important architectural groups. On the map parts of this ravine are identified as the Palace Reservoir and the Temple Reservoir. This series of temples, plazas, and monuments extends from opposite the East Plaza almost to Temple IV. The principal features, from east to west, include Temple V, a towering Great Temple presently under restoration and excavation; the South Acropolis, completely unexcavated and facing north; the Plaza of the Seven Temples, including three ballcourts and an elevated palace group; and finally the Lost World Pyramid group with its gigantic four-staired pyramid at the center of a complex of temples and palaces. Although this pyramid offers a difficult climb, the view from the summit is highly photogenic.

Literally thousands of other structures surround the main site, some of them significantly large. The F Group palace complex lies between the East Plaza and E Group and is accessible by trail. However, the group is unexcavated and clearing of the trail is sporadic.

All of the architectural features described in this very brief outline are accessible to the visitor, and require differing amounts of time to explore. For example, due to extensive excavation and restoration, the Central Acropolis alone requires several hours for a thorough examination of its detail. Conversely, the South Acropolis can only be passed at its base on a trail, since neither clearing nor excavation have occurred to date. To visit each of the groups mentioned here would require a minimum of two days for the young and energetic, more for the rest of us.

CHAPTER THREE

VILLAGES AROUND THE RIDGE: THE MIDDLE PRECLASSIC

Birth, dawn, and the color red

Tikal is situated quite favorably on the southern portion of a great divide which runs roughly north–south through the Peten in Guatemala. In the Tikal zone, the spine of this divide is broken by cross arroyos and gullies giving a net effect of a series of irregular hills.

The karstic nature of the Yucatan peninsula remains the delight and mystery of geologists due to the unpredictable quality of this type of land formation. The humps of sharp or blunted hills rise out of plains; underground rivers suddenly surface to appear as open wells; basins of wetland are lined with impermeable clays that cause "perched" water tables that retain water, resulting today in seasonal swamps. All of these features in the varied and advantageously unpredictable lowlands admirably served the ancient Maya who possessed an ingenious ability to adapt to a varied environment. The broken, hilly setting that came to be the city of Tikal is flanked by swampy basins known as "bajos."

Although these basins were uninhabitable they played an enormously important role in the initial settlement and later development of the city. Serving as a source of food production as well as transportation, they also harbored many elements of nature which were incorporated into the ideology and spiritual identity of the city. Crocodiles, frogs, and water lilies are but a few products of the swamps which came to serve as namesakes and ritual elements of the site. The *tinto* or logwood tree from these swampy basins served as wooden lintels or beams that did not deteriorate through time in temples and palaces.

The hills of the site and the swamps that flank it have a physical interplay dependent upon daily temperature fluctuations and air moisture. The rising and setting of the sun effects the temperature change required to produce ground mists that form and gather in the lower parts of the upland, and especially along the flanks of the swamps. Such phenomena were surely not overlooked by the ancient Maya with their deep concern with celestial effects upon the earth. Just before sunrise the air is filled with precipitation – a fog, or thick dew which obstructs the view in the pre-sunrise moments. As the sun breaks the horizon, however, its rays strike the ground moisture and the world turns into liquid gold, announcing the rebirth of Kinich Ahau, the start of a new day, a *kin* in the Maya language. *Kin* means not only "day," but is also the root of the name of the sun god. When the orb of the sun first appears over the horizon it is deep red, the same color it will be when it sinks finally into the west, the direction of death. In the Maya lexicon, red is the color of east, equated with birth, dawn, and a new start (*ill. 19*). It was on the east side of Tikal, on the edge of this great swamp, where the sun rises, that one of the earliest settlements of the site is found. This locale continued to be important to early settlement throughout the Preclassic period. The atmospheric effects in the evening begin shortly before sunset, but they are not as dramatic as the morning display. Today, a number of excellent positions atop ancient architecture offer vantage points for savoring the rising (or setting) of the sun each day, when anyone can appreciate the Maya symbolism of heavenly birth, renewal, and death. With the forest as a factor the highest vantage points now are the top of the Lost World Pyramid (5C-54), the highest points on the North Acropolis (5D-22), and the top of Temple IV. Chronologically, these are structures that date from the Late Preclassic, the Early Classic and the Late Classic respectively. For the earlier settlers, the hilltop that was to become the North Acropolis was likely the best vantage point before the coming millennium of architectural achievements provided better ones.

Sources of settlement

Drainage routes through the great eastern bajo (Bajo de Santa Fe) probably served as the initial entry route from the east – a waterway that may not have been seasonal 3,000 years ago – but rather served to guide canoes of wandering Maya to the broken upland that would become Tikal. The flow is downstream to the east, off the divide, towards other sites which grew along its embankments – Holmul, Nakum and Naranjo.[1] The last-named, at a distance of 40 km from the center of Tikal, would play a prominent role in the fortunes and destinies of the larger site's history, first as a friend and ally, then later as an enemy.

Ultimately, this water drainage which connects a series of sites like beads in a necklace, crosses the modern boundary of Belize, then meanders into larger and greater rivers until it reaches the Caribbean shore. As a trade route, it must have been very significant. Shells, seaweed, the spines of stingrays – all ocean products – assumed a highly significant ritual role for the lowland Maya. Evidence from caches and burials show that the people of Tikal were particularly attracted to this cult of sea-borne objects. As a route of exploration, the eastern water flow likely served to bring the initial settlers to Tikal.

Parts of the southern Yucatan peninsula were settled to both the east and west of Tikal at earlier dates. These include Altar de Sacrificios and Seibal on parts of the western watershed; and the three sites of Cuello, Pulltrouser Swamp, and Colha in Belize, all of which were established by 1200 BC. By contrast, Tikal's earliest recorded settlement occurred near 800 BC, suggesting that this ridge land with its scarcity of permanent water supplies was not a primary

19 Looking east from Temple IV to the direction of settlement of the city of Tikal. This painting by Diana Nobbs invokes the sense of morning and rebirth at Tikal.

site of early settlement. Its many other advantages, discovered later, led to great concentrations of wealth and power.

Tikal's late beginning

Despite extensive searching, no indicators were recovered by archaeology to suggest that there were any residents within the boundaries that now define the site between the years 2000 BC and 800 BC. This is the period identified as the Early Preclassic in the Maya lowlands. This absence of early settlement only says that the ultimate size of a site in terms of land covered and population densities do not necessarily correlate with earliest settlement. This conclusion agrees with recent theories about movement of peoples around the Maya lowlands during the earliest period. The central core of the Peten was not a focus of settlement at this time. Rather, peoples are thought to have moved down from the highlands of both Guatemala and Mexico, across the Gulf Coast and down the coast of Belize. Judging from these sources, settlement apparently spread through a series of lake chains, used as waterways, and moved into the central Peten. Current swamp basins may have been lakes, increasing the number of available waterways into the central Peten. These theories have been most clearly explained by Don Rice of Southern Illinois University, whose reconstruction best fits the known data.[2] Such a pattern of settlement growth could account for Tikal's relatively late appearance in Maya prehistory, and also why there are earlier known dates at smaller sites both to the east and west.

The Middle Preclassic at Tikal

Stages of development (at any site) are identified with blocks of time and by the presence of cultural characteristics such as architecture and artifact types, and sometimes burials. The most commonly available identifier is ceramics, and it is by ceramics that we can interpret where and when the first settlements of Tikal occurred.

In performing his analysis of the massive quantity of ceramic fragments left at the site throughout time, Patrick Culbert sought to identify locations of settlement during the early periods. His strategy of interpretation identified settlement locations by the presence of "pure" middens, that is, garbage dumps which contain discarded and broken ceramics from one period only. Such deposits are rare at Tikal, and even rarer between 800 and 600 BC. These ceramic locations are a first step in defining the characteristics of any given time period. When architecture, burials and other ritual features appear, these too can be added to the assemblages that describe the growth of Tikal.

The Eb sites

The Eb complex was the first to appear at Tikal and is dated at 800–600 BC. Only three locations of "pure" deposits of the Eb complex are known, two close to the center of the site, and one at the edge of the eastern swamp. This distribution of settlement is in itself revealing. It suggests that the first peoples at Tikal had established three separate village units, within reach of each other but in discrete locales, each with its own attraction.

One such locale was found under the North Acropolis, on one of the highest land points encompassed by the site. This spot may well have been venerated as a sacred place before the appearance of architecture, holding meaning for reasons now lost to us. The veneration of sacred hills is known as part of the Maya cosmic belief system. The earliest archaeological activity is a deposit dug into the bedrock that came to be the base of the most sacred royal burial ground, the North Acropolis. The very antiquity of this spot as a primary settlement probably accounts for the quality of ancestral veneration that later led to centuries of royal burials and tombs.

Another locale was found under the structure called the "Lost World Pyramid" (5C-54), a gargantuan building now known to be of Late Preclassic construction (c. 350 BC–AD 250). Again, the primary settlement occurred later in one of the most sacred foci of the city, and incidentally, one of the best places to view the morning and evening atmospheric effects. Structure 5C-54 is central to a larger group of buildings which include the only other known focus of royal burials. The correlation between primary settlement and subsequent royal burials is not likely to be a coincidence, but rather suggests that memory of place was very important to the Maya of Tikal.

The third Eb location of pure ceramic deposit is at the very edge of Bajo de

Santa Fe, a location which at first glance does not seem to fit with the other two on high points of the ridge with the advantage of distant views. However, the swamp-edge locale is only 1 km distant from the North Acropolis location and is at the edge of the water where the sun is seen to rise, adjacent to a food source and easy transportation to the east through the water route. Also, this is not an isolated instance of choosing a swamp-edge for settlement. Similar locations spread along the same bajo border are found right up to the beginning of the Classic period (AD 250). The selection of settlement locations at the edge of the Bajo de Santa Fe was made for important reasons during the earliest phases of site settlement. Turtles, crocodiles, and even fish could inhabit the swamp at least seasonally if the water levels were no lower than they are at present. During the Eb period, all three known settlements were within easy communication of each other, perhaps fulfilling different functions for a unified group. Although the high ridge locations did later develop at a faster rate, the swamp-side locales were not abandoned, and in fact spread in number.

Very little is known about the Eb people due to the scarcity of recovered evidence. The best material derives from the North Acropolis at the heart of the site. Rising 60 m above the eastern bajo, the hill itself was quite impressive. A series of pits were excavated right into the bedrock and mostly filled with trash. Among this trash is a large amount of chert[3] detritus, reflecting the fact that Tikal had access to a good natural source of this material. This is a very important economic consideration. Its presence at this earliest of all settlements indicates that the chert source was another factor in settlement of the site. Also present in these trash pits were fragments of obsidian (volcanic glass) and quartzite, both materials that had to be imported as they do not occur naturally in the vicinity of Tikal. This indication of trade during earliest settlement is significant. A radiocarbon date obtained from charcoal in one pit yielded a date of 588 BC, which is the source of the rounded date of 600 BC ending the course of this particular ceramic occupation. The ceramics themselves consisted of broken vessels in such quantities and sizes that they could be reconstructed on paper. The largest of these bedrock pits contained a pure deposit of Eb ceramics suggesting an adjacent or nearby settlement. Evidence for architecture is totally absent, due largely to enormous amounts of building activity in the same vicinity at a later date which removed the earlier architecture. The quarrying and leveling that took place destroyed whatever construction might have existed in Eb times.

A single human skull complete with articulated jaw was recovered from a nearby trash pit. The combination of skull and jaw preserved together indicate an intentional beheading, or ritual sacrifice since the separation of the head from the body in a single violent act retains the jaw in conjunction with the skull. Had the deposit been a re-location of an old skull from a burial, the jaw (or mandible) would not likely be present. A nearby pit contained a flexed adult skeleton set into the bedrock and is assumed by its proximity to be contemporary with the adjacent Eb activity.

20 Pomacea *shells are a water-dependent species that formed a source of food at Tikal. Their remains have been recovered frequently in food middens at the site.*

Snail shells of a variety native to Tikal (*Pomacea*) occurred in the Eb trash in abundance, indicating not only one food source but also that the damp, marshy conditions which foster this snail were prevalent then as they are now (*ill. 20*).

The other two locations of Eb deposit offer little additional evidence to broaden the picture of life at Tikal during this period. The only architecture consists of *chultuns*, well-shaped excavations in the bedrock whose function at Tikal remains in dispute. Tests have demonstrated that the bedrock is too porous for these bottle-shaped rooms to have held water. Some contain benches and have plastered floors and walls, including Chultun 5D-6, which dated to either the Eb complex or its successor, the Tzec complex. It was excavated into the bedrock on the summit of the hill beneath the North Acropolis and contained a main squared room with a plastered floor and rough hewn bench. Three smaller chambers adjoined the main room at a slightly higher level. The bench and floor suggest living quarters, but such speculation would be difficult to prove. Since chultuns are a fairly common feature at Tikal it is instructive to know that they have their origins during the very earliest phases of occupation.

Characteristics of the pioneer settlement

Little data are available to help in the task of characterizing Tikal in its earliest occupation. That the occupation was small and scattered is clear. The occupation sites either favored the swamp edge, and all that this choice implies; or were hilltop villages that would endure as most sacred places for the entire history of the city.

Ceremonialism, and possibly even sacrifice are indicated by the remains under the North Acropolis. Exploitation of a "home product" is established immediately (chert), and trade of exotic products is already in evidence.

From elsewhere in the lowlands we know that this is a time of small villages with simple ceremonial structures. The presence of chultuns as a characteristic of the site has already appeared. The slash-and-burn system of agriculture called milpa is known to have existed elsewhere at this time and must have been the basis of the economy. The proximity of the swamp with its own special food products, and elements which appear later in the iconography are another source not just of food but of spiritual awareness.

It is the ceramics themselves that are the most eloquent feature for the Eb peoples with a variety of cooking and serving vessels that show a degree of diversity in form and surface finish. The particular vessel types are mostly familiar from other parts of the lowlands but have distinctive qualities which establish their manufacture as local to Tikal, the first of a long series of traditions.

The Tzec ceramic complex

The pioneer settlement of Tikal was followed by the Tzec ceramic complex. The difference lies in a change in the ceramic forms. Despite a scant body of material, enough has been recovered to know that this complex demonstrated a greater variety of vessel shapes and finishes than in the previous complex.

Tzec remains were positioned by stratigraphy above those of the Eb complex, and had been even more thoroughly destroyed in the later modifications to the North Acropolis. As a result, the distribution map for Tzec settlement shows only one known pure deposit as a new location on the bajo edge to the east of the site, even though Tzec material was present on the North Acropolis as well.

Let us consider first those remains that did occur on the North Acropolis, since the continuity of occupation there is obvious even in the absence of an unmixed ceramic deposit. Evidence included a seated human interment enclosed in a bedrock pit (Burial 121), and another group of partially burned bones also in a pit, suggestive of cremation practice. Finally, a single inverted vessel may represent an offering or "cache."

The location of the one certain pure deposit of Tzec ceramics (and implied settlement) lies to the east, on a peninsula of high ground jutting into the Bajo de Santa Fe. While close to the site of the Eb deposit, it is sufficiently separate to argue that a new village had been established. The Tzec locale included a burial (Burial 158) with three intact vessels, a good source for demonstrating the variety of shape and decoration which defines the complex. The range of dishes, plates, and bowls is much better known than that of Eb, simply because a greater quantity was recovered from the site overall. This increase in production implies an increase in population as well as greater spread over the site. During Tzec times, Tikal was gradually becoming a more unified settlement.

During the Middle Preclassic these Maya still clung to two contrasting types of locale to lay the foundations of what would become one of the largest and most celebrated of Maya cities. Settlement at the eastern swamp edge may reflect the point of entry into the site as the pioneers arrived, and it persisted as a preferred location throughout this period. In relation to the city center, this was the direction of the color red, of dawn, of rebirth (*ill. 21*).

21 *Modern thatch huts along the edge of the Camp Aguada evoke the conditions of living at the water's edge which characterized the earliest settlement of Tikal.*

Contrasting settlement on the high ridges had two foci at first, on the North Acropolis ridge, and at the location of the Lost World Pyramid. Both of these continued during the Middle Preclassic, and persisted as sacred burial grounds into the Classic period.

If there was any sense of cosmos at this early time, it manifests itself as position – the Tikal Maya were anchored simultaneously at their eastern boundary and on one of the highest vantage points of the ridges that form Tikal: an east – west axis that followed the daily course of the sun. The shape and size of this cosmos was to change its configuration repeatedly during the generations to come as expansion demanded such change. The north–south dimension was yet to be developed, according to the fortunes and wishes of the individuals who would rule the city. Only part of the story of the early development of Tikal is known, and much of it relies upon inference. During the next major period, the Late Preclassic, the development of a distinct individuality can be discerned together with the first tangible monuments of grandeur. Nevertheless, it was the pioneers of the Eb and Tzec complexes who established Tikal's sense of place, and the rudiments of a sacred cosmos in its layout.

CHAPTER FOUR

THE MOVE INTO GREATNESS: THE LATE PRECLASSIC

Tikal becomes a city

The pioneers of Tikal had established the roots of their civilization at this site with most of its basic characteristics by 350 BC. By the change of eras at AD 1, Tikal exhibited all the attributes of Maya high civilization. A great deal of change affected the people of Tikal during the last three-and-one-half centuries BC and even more change was to come in the next 250 years.

The period that archaeologists call the Late Preclassic lasted from 350 BC until AD 250 at Tikal. The dates of this period vary from one city to another according to the local history of development. It is primarily the ceramics, which are most subject to change, that inform us of these developments, but other artifacts and archaeological features help to define these stages of change and growth at any site.

Excavation data tell that the contours of the city expanded along an east–west axis more than to the north and south of the original settlements. The Maya of Tikal clung to their earliest villages along the edges of the great Bajo de Santa Fe to the east of the city as if fearful of abandoning the direction from which they came. Some locations of villages are those that were first settled, while others are new to this period. The only significant northward expansion was along the shore of the swamp during the earliest part of this period.

The North Acropolis remained the major and constant focus of architectural growth at the site, establishing this ridge as the heart of Tikal, a fixation that was to waver briefly at a later date and then re-affirm itself. The Lost World Pyramid group to the southwest of the North Acropolis was the other location of important growth. The focus here began with the construction of a relatively small group of buildings that had ceremonial and astronomical purpose. This was an example of the architectural grouping known as "E-Groups," named after a configuration of buildings at Uaxactun north of Tikal where this type of group was first recognized. The E-Group functions as an observatory using its four-staired pyramid as a viewing station, looking east, towards a series of three small temple-like structures aligned on a platform. From the viewing pyramid an observer can sight the positions of the rising sun behind the middle of the center temple on the equinoxes; at the far north corner of the north structure on the summer solstice; and at the far south

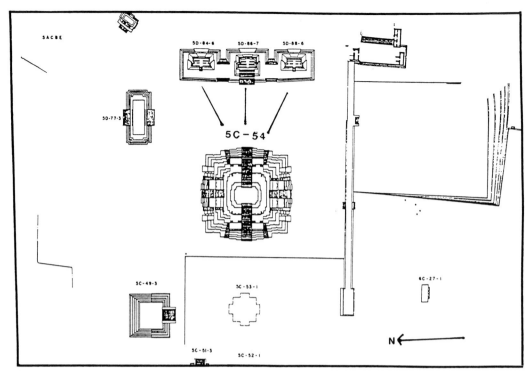

22 *The Lost World Pyramid (Structure 5C-54) was constructed as an observatory building in relation to the three small temples to the east, shown in this map of the plaza.*

23 *One of the small temples which formed part of the observatory group, Structure 5D-84, shows all of the elements that recall Conan Doyle's "Lost World."*

24 *The observatory group of the Lost World is reconstructed here by Juan Pedro Laporte to illustrate the configuration during the Early Classic period, with the radial pyramid on the right and the sighting temples on the left.*

corner of the south structure on the winter solstice. The Lost World Pyramid group began its function as an E-Group when first constructed in the Middle Preclassic and continued this use until the end of the Preclassic period.

Both ceramic deposits and architecture in the Lost World zone show that this location was one of equal development with the North Acropolis throughout the Late Preclassic period. However, their respective functions were quite different at this time. The North Acropolis remained a focus of temple architecture, a place of burial of kings and a growing cosmic expression – a self-contained cosmogram of the world directions, with a strong north–south axis, even though this axis did not meaningfully extend far beyond the confines of the acropolis itself. On the other hand, the Lost World Pyramid group served as an observatory dedicated to marking important solar events for the benefit of recording the seasons.

Pure ceramic deposits from the Late Preclassic period have been found well to the west of the Lost World group and interestingly, far to the southeast of the city center, adjacent to the location of Temple VI which would not be built for another six centuries. Despite some scattered examples of ceramic finds, the city remained spread along its original east–west axis, from the edges of the eastern swamp as far west as Temple IV but clustered in a narrow belt about 750 m wide and 2 km long.

The Lost World Pyramid

The Lost World Pyramid itself is Structure 5C-54 by map designation. It is coupled with 5D-86 to form an east-west axis of ritual and astronomical significance. Structures 5D-84 and 88 flank temple 5D-86 to form the observatory complex (*ill. 22*). The name "Lost World" was ascribed by the original mappers of this area who were strongly impressed by the vision of the great pyramid rising through the jungle growth, and by the wildlife that teemed in the area (*ill. 23*). These explorers of Tikal felt that the setting evoked the imagery of Conan Doyle's primitive world in his book of the same name. The name stuck and has even been translated in the Spanish version of "Mundo Perdido." Juan Pedro Laporte's excavations describe the development through time of what he called the "Commemorative Astronomical Complex."[1]

The main structure began as a small platform from which the other three structures could be faced on the eastern side. These three were aligned north–south, closely together, but so spaced that elements of their architecture marked the visible rising of the sun in the spring to the north of the group at the solstice; in the center on the equinoxes – and to the south at the winter solstice – all viewed from the same central spot on the western platform. This configuration grew in size over the years, with the small western platform finally becoming the Lost World Pyramid itself, a giant pyramid some 32 m high, square in plan with stairways on the four sides. Part way up the stairs are giant stone and sculptured stucco masks, now in a state of severe disintegration (*ill. 16*). Enough detail remained in one or two cases to indicate that these were jaguar masks not unlike those on E-7-Sub, the central structure at Uaxactun that gave its name to this architectural configuration. At Uaxactun the masks were paired vertically, with the one below displaying Night Jaguar and the one above displaying Day Jaguar, the two manifestations of the sun god Kinich Ahau in his night and day appearances. The line between these paired masks was a platform marking the horizon to the east, the point at which an observer needed to stand to view the solar phenomena as they related to the eastern structures. It is likely that the same iconography and function of these jaguar masks pertains to the Lost World Pyramid and its eastern "temple" (*ill. 24*).

The location of the Lost World Pyramid was first occupied in the earliest times of Tikal's settlement. A pyramid with four stairs, one to each side, is called a *radial* pyramid, and the first version was built by 500 BC. The astronomical concept was formalized with new constructions between 500 and 250 BC in the Late Preclassic including a new radial platform and a new eastern platform, both much larger than the prototype from the Middle Preclassic. The importance of the east–west axis was established at this time by the placing of burials and caches along it. There is a contrast between this formal and ritual complex with that of the other major contemporary complex, the North Acropolis in which the ritual axis of importance to burials was north–south.

Further renovation of both the main pyramid and the east platform occurred

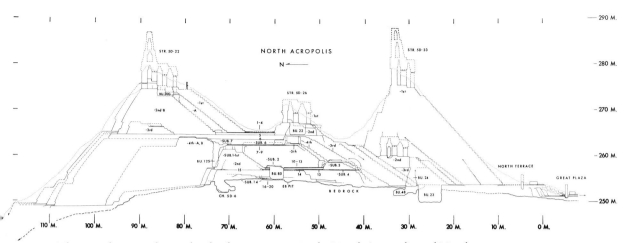

25 *The complexity and time depth of construction in the North Acropolis and North Terrace which form the north side of the Great Plaza was recorded by William R. Coe II, from his excavations in this group.*

between 250 and 100 BC associated with the Chuen ceramic complex. At this point the whole complex increased once again in size but now included for the first time huge masks as central decoration and flanking stairways. The next phase of growth was between 100 BC and AD 250 (the Cauac and Cimi ceramic complexes) when the pyramid grew in size once again, and for the first time small temples were built on the east platform. The central eastern temple even displayed two jaguar masks on the established east–west axis.

Throughout the Late Preclassic burials and offerings were placed on the sacred axis, and although the individuals buried were accompanied by grave goods indicating a moderate degree of wealth, such goods are insufficient in quantity and importance to suggest that they were kings or high-ranking officers. In Cauac times such high individuals were still being interred in the North Acropolis. The end of the Preclassic period did not see the end of growth of the Lost World Pyramid complex. It reached its peak in the next phase during the beginnings of the Early Classic period, as we shall see.

The North Acropolis

Beginning in the Chuen ceramic complex (350 BC–AD 1), burials of men, women, and children had vaulted tombs, a feature normally indicating elite status of the interred. However, the same tombs do not contain the grave goods that would suggest royalty.[2] Few burials are dated to the Chuen complex and although their presence establishes the Acropolis as a cemetery the grave goods are too poor and scarce to suggest that the individuals were especially important. The element of royalty is still missing at this point in the development of the ceremonial hot spot. Coe described the earliest evidence of interment of a clearly important personage beneath a temple building of the later Cauac

57

complex (AD 1–150). Both the structures and the burials of Cauac times begin to define the Tikal style of architecture and burial pattern[3] (*ill. 25*).

Death as a window

It is through the burials of the North Acropolis that we receive a glimpse of the individual style of Tikal as it took form in the Late Preclassic. The Cauac complex tombs tell of attitudes toward death and the ritual placement of the mortal remains. These early burials are all found beneath small temple structures some of which are represented only by their platforms and stubs of torn-out walls, the architectural victims of later and more grandiose construction. The individuals in these tombs are nameless although the ceremony and accompanying precious objects tell us that they were people of substance, leaders – ahaus. The fact that some of these unnamed royalty are women tells us further that women did indeed play a role of some power and influence, even in Late Preclassic times. Their lives had been significant enough to their descendants to allot them a place on the royal necropolis. All these royal burials of Cauac times are known today only by the prosaic designations of burial number as there are no texts to provide a clue to their ancient real names.

Four burials bearing the numbers 166, 167, 128, and 85, are of particular interest. The numbering is based entirely on the chronology of their archaeological discovery and has no relationship to their stratigraphic position in the North Acropolis.

Burial 166 had been placed in a pit through earlier floors as a preparation for the construction of a small east-facing temple. The small, rectangular, and vaulted tomb contained the remains of two individuals. It is their disposition in the tomb that provides some insight into Tikal burial rituals. Both personages were apparently adult females. The central figure had her head placed to the north, a primary pattern at later dates in the North Acropolis for burials of kings. The secondary female had been butchered, with her mixed-up bones placed at the feet of the regal skeleton. The skull of this unfortunate, probably a sacrificial victim, was placed in the lowest of three nested ceramic vessels. Spread around the south end of the tomb, at the feet of the "queen" were 20 excellent examples of the Cauac ceramic complex. The masonry walls of the tomb had been crudely plastered and then painted with red cinnabar – the color of the east, and the color of life. This earliest known effort to decorate a tomb was then further elaborated. Six black-line figures were painted over the red walls on the east, south, and west sides. The blank north wall is a hint at a sexual dichotomy between north and south directions as representing male and female respectively. This unusually well-decorated tomb is our earliest glimpse of the elaborate ceremonial surrounding death and burial at Tikal. It is also significant that this first glimpse is the tomb of a woman. Such female tombs are rare not only at Tikal but at Maya cities in general.

Burial 167 opens the window of death a little further for us. This burial is located under yet another small temple building, this time facing west, across a small plaza formed by structures on a platform of the Cauac period. Another vaulted tomb, this one shows yet other aspects of the burial attitudes at Tikal. This time the main figure is interpreted as an adult male who was laid with his head to the east. In the case of Burial 166, the woman was laid out parallel to the long axis of the temple building. The male in Burial 167, however, is laid at right angles to the long axis of the temple above, an interesting contrast which establishes an eastern orientation of the head. However, the most fascinating features of this burial are in two large ceramic vessels placed one over the head and one over the loins of the main figure. The bowl over the head region contained the cramped skeletal remains of an adult female, while the bowl over his loins held the remains of an infant under a year of age. Who these sacrificial victims might have been raises a plethora of speculations. Could they be his wife and child, cramped into vessels to accompany him in his tomb? The grave goods accompanying the main male figure indicate his high, and likely royal, status. Shell bracelets with bone clasps surrounded his wrists. A necklace of shell beads with pendants graced his neck and chest. A greenstone figurine, which may have related to his namesake, lay in the pelvic region. Similar carved figurines recovered from later Classic period tombs at Tikal proved to bear a relationship to the name of the king. Nine fine Cauac vessels were clustered in the northwest corner of the burial chamber and two red-painted stuccoed gourds were an unusual addition to the lexicon of goods usually accompanying deceased rulers. The walls of this tomb were plastered, but not painted. For all his glory and the grisly ritual of his interment, the man in Burial 167 did not receive quite the same level of decoration as did the lady in Burial 166, but since we do not know their relationship to each other, such comparison means little. It is of further interest that the small shrine built above the ruler in Burial 167 was indeed elaborately decorated with polychrome frescoes painted on the sides and rear of the structure, in hues of black, yellow, red, and pink over a cream-colored plaster.

Burial 128, the next burial of interest in the range of Tikal techniques for dealing with death, does not come from the North Acropolis but from a large, low platform located 1.5 km to the southeast of the North Acropolis. It is west of the future location of Temple VI, not to be built for at least six more centuries. Burial 128 was discovered during excavation of a housemound and is one of the pure ceramic deposits described in the next section. The burial did not include a vaulted chamber but yielded eight Cauac vessels, one of which was extremely large and contained the remains of the burial figure. This first example of a "pot burial" contained an adult female, showing clear head deformation, a mark of beauty among the ancient Maya achieved by strapping the infant's skull to a headboard during the years of skull growth. She wore shell and bone bracelets, similar to those found in the male burial of 167. The similarities of the grave goods are so strong that the dates of Burials 167 and 128 are believed to be the same. This additional example of graves with female figures included during this phase of Tikal's development suggests that women played a more important role than is to be found in later Classic period burials. The predominance of Classic period male royal burials has indicated that patrilineal descent was the norm in the Classic period. The tomb contents from Burials 166, 167, and 128 suggest that maternal relationships may well have played a major role during the more developmental phases of Tikal's growth.

Burial 85 brings us back to the North Acropolis. This vaulted tomb was placed below another small temple structure on the south side of the acropolis and directly on the critically important north–south axis of the acropolis itself. In Classic times this axis was to take on the sacred properties of a ley line. As the generations passed, the central axis of the North Acropolis grew steadily as it became increasingly sanctified by the burials of kings. This is in contrast to the east–west axis described earlier of the Lost World Pyramid group and indeed the axis of growth by which the city was settled.

Once again, death's window is opened a little more for us with new grisly details of Tikal burial practices. The first known ruler to be buried on the sacred axis was an adult male who had been dismembered following death. His skull and thigh bones were not included in the burial. We now know that these important parts of the body were occasionally omitted from a royal burial. This occurs not just at Tikal but at other major sites as well, most notably Palenque far to the west in the realm of the Usumacinta River. It is a matter of speculation just why specific parts of the human body were sometimes retained and not included in a burial. Was it a matter of parts missing in action, lost in war, or retained by the enemy as trophies? Or was this the result of familial retention of these parts for much the same reason? Reverence of the dead, and even for specific body parts of the dead is clearly indicated, whether or not this reverence came from enemies or friends.

In Burial 85 what remained of the ruler was bundled together, probably with textiles, and placed in a seated position in a chamber otherwise filled with splendid ceramics. Included within the bundle was a stingray spine used in bloodletting ceremonies, and a prepared *spondylus* shell, both imported from the sea. The spondylus, or spiny oyster, was a favorite trade item for the Maya of Tikal and is commonly found in caches and burials throughout the Classic period. Interestingly, this bi-valve shell is found in both the Caribbean and Pacific Oceans. The Maya of the central Peten, far from either ocean, traded for both species, which can be individually identified. The closest source for Tikal lies in the reefs just off the coast of nearby Belize. The Maya loved to scrape the white lining from the shell to reveal the orange-red underlayer – a color sacred to their cosmology – the color of the east, of rebirth, the direction of the great swamp east of Tikal and also of the distant Caribbean, nearest source of these precious shells.

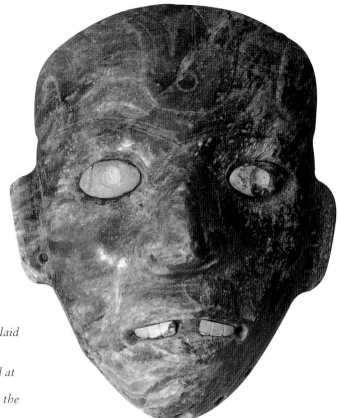

26 This mask of greenstone with inlaid eyes and teeth of shell is one of the treasures placed in Burial 85, a Late Preclassic tomb of the Cauac period at Tikal. The mask may have been a replacement for the missing head of the buried lord.

The most endearing object retrieved from this burial was a small greenstone mask with inlaid eyes and teeth of shell (*ill. 26*). This gem may have been attached to the bundle itself in place of the missing skull, evoking images of the mummy bundles of the Inca civilization. This object also recalls the small carving found with the male ruler in Burial 167. It seems that such greenstone carvings are not found in the royal ladies' tombs.

Ceramics of the Late Preclassic: an art form and time marker

The Late Preclassic period spans three different ceramic complexes at Tikal over 600 years dating from 350 BC to AD 250. Ceramics are extremely important to any site chronology and are not merely the dry stuff of archaeological analysis. They are an art form which often achieves rare beauty. Ceramics are a plastic art and because of this plasticity are subject to rapid change and individual expression. Each major Maya site has its own artistic expression in the rendering of details in their locally made ceramics. The overall style which emerges at a single city contains a combination of the shapes and finishes of vessels and the individual characteristics of painted decoration developed by the artisans of that city. In the Preclassic period there is no painted decoration *per se*, but there are distinctive shapes and colors. For example the chamber-pot-like wide-mouthed vessels of the Eb complex are distinctive at Tikal (see below). Similarly, spouted, flaring-mouthed vessels and fire-hydrant shapes are also part of the Tikal style during the Cauac complex. However, all vessels found at any given site were not necessarily made there, especially those that are found in royal tombs. This is true for two reasons: the Maya traded extensively among themselves and royal funerals often included gifts of respect from other rulers. We assume that such mortuary presents arose from inter-city alliances made either by marriage or for purely political reasons. Such gifts brought by outsiders to be included among the burial paraphernalia of the dead king cannot always be identified as items that were introduced – a situation which presents problems for accurate description of a given city's style. The alliances which resulted in gift exchange were more common and significant in the later periods of Maya history, but undoubtedly were already at play during the Late Preclassic at Tikal.

It is the variation in individual style of ceramic production that makes ceramics so important to archaeologists. Ceramic shape and decoration change with time across the Maya region and this allows the division by style into specific periods for each given major site or city.

The three ceramic complexes that characterize the Late Preclassic phase at Tikal are called Chuen (350 BC–AD 1), Cauac (AD 1–150), and Cimi (AD 150–250). The number of complexes that can be discerned at any given site will vary according to several factors. The amount of excavation that has been realized in proportion to the size of the site is certainly a major factor. The complexity of the site's history as it interacted with other surrounding realms will affect the influences on home-made pottery as well as the introduction of outside styles.

Chuen times at Tikal

One indicator of how the population of the site was growing through time is found in the comparison of the incidence of pure deposits of ceramics in the Chuen complex with those of the preceding Tzec complex (Middle Preclassic). Only one deposit is known in Tzec times, whereas there are seven such deposits from Chuen times. Their occurrence shows the site spreading out over the ridgetops, expanding outward from the central area, but still maintaining a village population near the edges of the great swamp to the east. As well as the expected deposits in the North Acropolis, there are now also deposits in the Central Acropolis to the south indicating a location of residence occupied by the elite social stratum. Other deposits were found to the west of the Great Plaza; in the Seven Temples group (near the Lost World Pyramid); beneath the Lost World group itself; far to the south of the Great Plaza in a residential platform; as well as at two locations at the swamp edge.

27 (right) *Some Cauac period vessels were designed with side spouts, showing that the period had developed a greater variety of shapes and finishes than before.*

28 (below) *The shaded zone on this composite map of the site, shows the approximate limits of Tikal at the end of the Cauac Preclassic ceramic period at circa AD 150.*

Cauac times at Tikal

This phase of development shows a great step forward, with a burst of growth and variation in the cultural component associated with Cauac ceramics. The forms are more varied than ever before and quite specific to Tikal. The "fire-hydrant" shape mentioned above and several kinds of spouted vessels are particularly characteristic. Ceremonial ceramics recovered from royal burials, mostly in the North Acropolis, are larger than any found to date, and the complexity of shapes suggests that more leisure time was available to be devoted to artistic and ceremonial pursuits (*pl. III* and *ill. 27*).

While there are fewer actual occurrences of pure ceramic deposits than during the previous Chuen complex, the quantity of Cauac ceramics is far

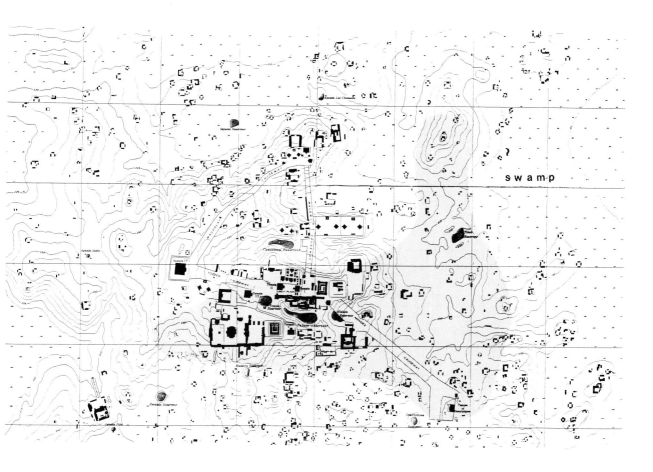

swamp

greater and distributed over larger parts of the site. Of the four known pure deposits, two are in the North Acropolis, one being from the north terrace, abutting the south side of the acropolis. The other two deposits are interesting for their locations: one from the swamp edge, but in a new settlement unrelated to those found here at earlier times; and one close to the present location of the Temple of the Inscriptions (Temple VI), described above as Burial 168. The establishment of a Late Preclassic center in this location near Temple VI is suggestive of the ceremonial origins of a sacred place that would become highly significant much later in time (*ill. 28*). The swamp edge site shows that this particular environment remained one of great importance to the people of Tikal, probably for economic reasons such as the on-going exploitation of the swamp as a source of food, either of aquatic lifeforms, or by intensive agriculture – a possibility by this date (AD 1–150).

Cimi times at Tikal

The last ceramic complex belonging to this period is called Cimi and dates to its last century (AD 150–250). The pure ceramic deposits only tell us that the population of Tikal was spreading even further westward, while still clinging to residential bases at the swamp edge. Occupation of the North Acropolis continued to become more elaborate with ever more complex architecture and burials, as described elsewhere.

The ceramics of this phase are sometimes called Protoclassic and include the four-footed dishes with mammiform feet that had their origins in the southeastern regions of the Maya area.[4]

The Late Preclassic at Tikal witnessed the first large spurt of growth in the city. This growth is evidenced by vastly increased quantities of ceramics and a new vision in scale of architecture. A threshold had been passed: the entry into greatness. No longer was Tikal a cluster of amalgamated villages or even the sizeable town it had become by the beginning of this period. Rather it was a city with differentiated zones of residence, high ritual, and royal burial. The only missing piece of the formula for Classicism is the written language. No inscriptions exist from Tikal for this period, although many scholars today believe that the written form of Maya did already exist by this time. The city had an elongated east–west configuration by this period, stretching from the ever-important eastern swamp to the approximate eventual western limit where Temple IV now stands. Between the eastern and western limits were two points of high ritual punctuated by the highest elevations of architecture at the site at the time: the North Acropolis, marking the longest occupied location of the city; and the Lost World Pyramid, not yet at its fullest, present height, but nevertheless breaking the horizon as a rival to the royal burial acropolis in the city center. Trade items already show that the city had made its mark on the landscape and begun to form inter-city relationships. This spurt of growth was a taste of what was to come.

CHAPTER FIVE

THE BIRTH OF DYNASTIES: THE EARLY CLASSIC EMERGES

The same features that gave Preclassic Tikal the image of an urban center preoccupied with ritual and death, wealth, and beauty continue and are magnified in the Classic period. Everything gets bigger – the size of the population and hence of the city; the size of the architecture; the elaborateness of the ceramics. In addition, the culture of the great highland city of Teotihuacan, a contemporary of Tikal, wielded enormous influence on its art, and to a certain extent on its burial customs.

As well as the changes in scale and artistic expression there is the extremely important appearance of written texts. For the first time in Tikal's story we have available a written history in the form of the hieroglyphic texts inscribed in stone on royal monuments and painted on ceramic vessels. The texts are a little late in appearing in the archaeological record, with an earliest date for Tikal at AD 292[1] (Stela 29, *ill. 30*), almost half a century after the recognized change of cultural periods which occurred at AD 250. However, later texts concerned with lineage and historical descent reach back in time to fill in some of the early gaps. The addition of a written history is the greatest breakthrough in knowing the story of Tikal.

Only in the last decade have archaeologists begun to understand the intricacies of the Tikal dynastic systems through the great strides made in the translation of texts. Inscriptions occur in two distinct bodies of material: one is calendrical, involving the numerical counts of time, the names of days, months, and other time cycles which the Maya observed and recorded; the other consists of narrative texts telling of events in the lives of individual rulers and their families. The whole body of known texts from Tikal is still, as of this date, not fully translated.

29 The founder of the Tikal dynasty was named Yax Ch'actel Xok whose name glyph is cited frequently throughout Tikal history.

The texts tell of a dynastic founder recognized by all subsequent rulers of Tikal, even though this personage was clearly not the first leader of the city since he does not appear until the second century AD, and perhaps died around

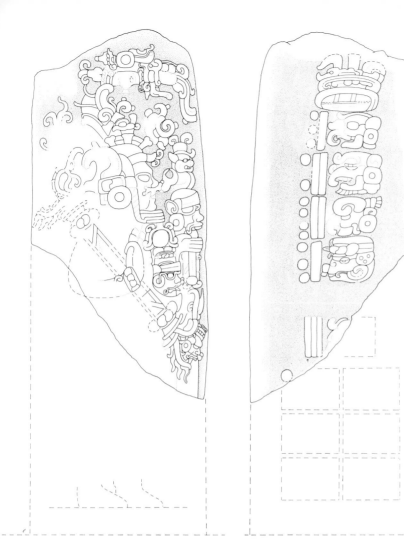

AD 200, a full millennium after the city site was first occupied. Nevertheless, the Maya themselves counted all subsequent rulers as successors from this man's reign. His name in Maya reads "Yax Ch'aktel Xok" (First Scaffold Shark),[2] and this name is repeated often throughout the next several centuries as the starting point of the count of the rulers of Tikal (*ill. 29*). Another reading of the Maya glyphs for this man's name is "Chaac Xok." The "Xok" part of his name is universally agreed to be the Maya word for "shark" – probably the origin of this word in English.[3]

Over a period of almost six centuries the hieroglyphic texts of Tikal (and elsewhere) tell us that there were 31 known rulers of Tikal after the founder. Not all have been identified by name, nor is it known whether this number represents all of Tikal's rulers after the founder. The earliest inscription at Tikal is set in AD 292, while the last known ruler is mentioned in inscriptions of AD 869, after which there are no more texts as the written record for the city slips into oblivion. Therefore, there are 577 years of recorded history. However, the time span between known rulers is from AD 200 until AD 869, i.e. 669 years even though no contemporary inscription is known for the earliest dynastic ruler. Of the 31 known rulers only 18 of them are known by name glyphs, including the founder.

An important aspect of rulers' names at Tikal is their repetition through time. Whether this was based upon admiration of an earlier ruler who achieved greatness during his rule, or by means of some other cultural selection system is not known to us, and cannot be determined from the existing evidence. The hieroglyphic record is spotty, yielding a great deal of information about certain individuals, a little about others, and none at all about still others. It is suggested that rulers who performed the greatest exploits wrote more texts and left a fuller record of the events in their lives, and that these people were honored by their descendants who later recycled their names. However, the Maya of Tikal had no system for recording the succession of a re-used name. There is no usage such as "George I, II, and III" and so forth. We can only tell from associated dates how the the same names succeed each other, and this analysis allows us to dub these names as "Jaguar Claw I, II, and III." The Maya of Tikal themselves made no such distinction.

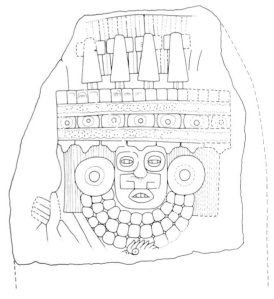

31 (left) The influence from the highland city of Teotihuacan is strong at Tikal during the Early Classic period. This lidded tripod vessel is typical of the imported style, although the vessel was likely made at Tikal.

32 (above) Stela 32 shows a pure Teotihuacan face, a Tlaloc image, the rain god of the highlands. Its presence at Tikal where it was carved demonstrates the strength of foreign influence.

The time of Yax Ch'aktel Xok falls within the late part of the Cimi ceramic complex at Tikal which extended from AD 150 to 250. This was a time of many changes for the city. Along with influence on the ceramic forms and styles that came from the Highland Mexican city of Teotihuacan, there also came a focus on warfare, and possibly new ways to make warfare more effective. Now we find evidence not just of grisly burial practices but of new ways to shed blood in conflict – Maya against Maya, city against city. The influence of distant Teotihuacan was so important to the trajectory of Tikal's cultural development that it deserves some attention here. Many clues to the relationship between Tikal and Teotihuacan have been found. They show themselves in the shapes of ceramics made at Tikal, most specifically the tripod, lidded cylinder vessel (*ill. 31*), which is usually also decorated with designs that originated in the Mexican capital and in other expressions of art (*ill. 32*). The presence of green obsidian which comes only from the region of Teotihuacan shows that Tikal was trading directly or indirectly with that city. The styles of its art, ceramics, and mythology were copied at Tikal and it is quite likely that individuals from Teotihuacan even came to Tikal, lived there, and may have ruled the city for a while during the Manik ceramic phase. Conversely, one or more lords of Tikal may have visited Teotihuacan and brought home ideas as well as objects. Influence from Teotihuacan began very early in the Early Classic period and continued at Tikal through the reigns of several of the earliest known rulers – in fact, until AD 550.

There are a number of unidentified burials from the North Acropolis for this time and it is likely that one of these is the burial of the founder. Recently,[4] Christopher Jones has proposed Burial 125 in the North Acropolis as the probable grave of the founder. It is a curious burial indeed in that it was devoid of any associated grave material, suggesting that the corpse was laid in the tomb naked. In most tombs traces or layers of organic materials lie beneath the bones of the interred indicating the rotted presence of clothing, costume, or shrouding animal skins. In Burial 125 such organic traces were absent. The skeleton was that of a tall adult male, measuring 1.7 m (5 ft 7 in) in stature. The interment was located directly on the original sacred north–south axis of the North Acropolis. However, our understanding of this strange burial is complicated by another contemporary feature that lies some 6 m to the east of the tomb's spartan chamber. This is a buried deposit containing the very kinds of goods that would be expected to be found in the tomb of a king of this period: fine ceramics, shells, the bones of probable sacrificial victims. This strange deposit looks like the contents of a ravaged tomb in which the grave goods were deposited separately from the main figure. It is an inference that these curiously divided deposits, one human, the other of goods, both pertained to the same individual – possibly the founder of the great dynasty of Tikal. The connection between these two deposits is that their locations precisely mark the original and new axes of the North Acropolis. The peculiar deposit of goods without a main figure was placed on a new axis line resulting from an eastern expansion of the North Acropolis. This new axis remained valid for the duration of the usage of the architectural complex throughout the Classic period. No further lateral expansions caused a change in the location of the central axis. It is an acceptable interpretation that the new axis was established by the dynastic founder himself and that his burial was divided in this fashion, with his bones marking the old axis and his grave goods marking the new.

The founder, Yax Ch'aktel Xok, established a dynasty more than one millennium after the site was first settled. The Maya of Tikal seem to have been aware of this distinction. Several inscriptions stand out at Tikal for their extreme importance to the site's history. Among these is the very long inscription on the back of the roof-comb of the Temple of the Inscriptions (Temple VI), an outstanding historical text which purports to reveal the history of Tikal up to the point of its carving (about AD 790). This "history" takes the reader well back before the time of the founder, right back, in fact, to the time of first entry into the site. It is an account of this quality that tells us that Tikal's own historians knew the difference between the founder and the founding.

The count of known kings

Foliated Jaguar (Hunal Balam)

Discussion of any king/ruler of Tikal must be tempered by reference to the problem of identification of these human beings by name. Positive identification depends upon the existing level of confidence in the translation of known texts. Most such translations are still tentative, so that it is not possible in the late 1990s to give a consistent reading in English translation versus Maya reading of the glyphs for all known rulers. While this inconsistency may be of some inconvenience to the reader, it reflects the excitement that characterizes the on-going study of Maya archaeology. Descriptive names in English frequently found in the literature are "nicknames" based upon a subjective interpretation of certain glyphs' outward appearances. Usually, when more study has been accomplished, such nicknames are discarded in favor of a real translation. Furthermore, the current state of translation is such that the scholar may be able to confidently convert the ideogram to a Maya word or phrase, without being able to take the next step of translating the Maya phrase into English. This is because the ancient Maya spoken language in use as the base for conversion into glyphs is not perfectly understood. As we try to reverse the process we run into barriers of understanding. The ancient spoken language was Cholti, a now extinct language not recorded in Colonial times. Given these limitations, the names of Tikal kings have to be presented in three different ways: an English descriptive phrase which only says what the glyph looks like (and may be wrong); a true (or tentative) Maya translation; and best of all, a translation into English of the true Maya translation. The last is available for only a few of Tikal's recorded kings.[5]

33 The name glyph of Foliated Jaguar or Hunal Balam is the earliest recovered name of a Tikal lord after the founder.

This problem arises immediately with the next known king. Emphasis here must be on the word "known" because Foliated Jaguar (Hunal Balam) is certainly not the next king in line after the founder, but the next known king by name, probably the 6th or 7th in line given the time span available. Reference to Hunal Balam is made on Stela 31, one of the most important texts so far recovered from Tikal. Its date of carving is approximately AD 445,[6] but it refers backwards in time to earlier rulers. Unfortunately, on Stela 31 the name glyph for Hunal Balam has lost its associated date (*ill. 33*). Interpretation of the name glyph has variously been presented as "Foliated Jaguar" as used here, and "Scroll Jaguar." Peter Mathews has suggested[7] that the same name glyph appears as an object held in the hand of the ruler shown on Stela 29, the earliest dated monument of Tikal at AD 292[8] and that this monument may indeed depict Hunal Balam himself. The surviving text on the monument does not tell us which numbered successor after the founder the personage shown might be, denying us any further clue to the identification.

Zero Moon Bird[9]

Much of the written record about Tikal comes from outside Tikal, from other cities which recorded events concerning their interaction with the rulers of this obviously important capital. During the troubled beginnings of the Classic period, in the early 4th century, an object called the "Leiden Plaque" was made: a carved jade plate that was found outside Tikal and which later surfaced in the European city of Leiden. Both sides are incised: one side bears a drawing of a ruler in the contemporary style of Tikal art; on the other is an inscription mentioning the city and stating that the ruler named "Zero Moon Bird" was seated as king in the year AD 320. Since this date conflicts with the recorded dates for the king named "Jaguar Claw" as listed on Stela 31 at Tikal, two possible interpretations must be allowed. One is that Zero Moon Bird was a ruler at Tikal between two rulers, both named "Jaguar Claw," or else that Zero Moon Bird was a collateral "ruler" near or at Tikal fulfilling a rulership function that was different from that of Jaguar Claw. If this interpretation is true, then he would have been ruling at AD 300. The Maya texts from Tikal have told us that there are differing levels of rulership that operate at the same time. This fact alone is a fascinating aspect of the socio-political structure of the city. References to these differences in leadership level occur later in the story of Tikal, but this is the first time that it presents interpretive importance of who was ruling when and in what capacity. The recorded facts could mean that Zero Moon Bird, referred to only twice in the known hieroglyphic record for Tikal, was in fact serving as a regent while the infant Jaguar Claw I was too young to rule. He would have been the 7th or 8th lord of Tikal. Alternatively, he could have been an important noble from another city who had allegiance with Tikal at this time. In addition to the reference to Zero Moon Bird on the Leiden Plaque, a second reference comes from Altar 13 at Tikal. This is a fragment of a sculpted altar found together with Stela 29, the stela with the earliest known date from Tikal, which refers to ruler Hunal Balam. Found together, the two monuments show a style of sculpture that is nearly identical, and the altar's artistic design includes a glyph identical to Zero Moon Bird's patronymic glyph. Together, all this information suggests that Zero Moon Bird lived at Tikal and somehow formed a bridge between the reign of Foliated Jaguar and Jaguar Claw I.[10]

34 Jaguar Claw I was also known as Jaguar Claw the Great, because of his attributed exploits. His name glyph occurs frequently in the texts of Tikal.

Jaguar Claw I (Chak Toh Ich'ak I)[11]

Chak Toh Ich'ak I is one of several Tikal rulers whose dates and role are known from the enormous text of Stela 31 (*ills. 34 and 35*). This long inscription contains the most detailed exposition of historical events covering the early part of Tikal's dynastic history and helps to reconstruct the early part of the Classic period for which there are few other monuments. Fortunately, the Maya occasionally made reference to their own distant heritage. From these rare texts emerges some sense of identification of the first 10 rulers of the dynasty following the founder. Faulty and full of gaps as they are, these written clues are all we have to date. From the text of Stela 31 we encounter the first difficulty in deciding how many rulers were named "Jaguar Claw" over a period of 61 years. The events recorded do not make clear whether there were one or two such rulers of the same name. Here, a single ruler is assumed, named Jaguar Claw I.

Events were moving quickly as city centers close to each other struggled for supremacy. For Tikal the rival city was Uaxactun, just 18 km to the north. The relationship between Tikal and its nearest neighbor remains one of the intriguing mysteries of the Maya, and the tension between the two cities reached a peak in the first half of the 4th century during the reign of one of the rulers known as "Jaguar Claw." The two dates associated with the same name are

35 The text carved on the back of Stela 31 is one of the most extensive historic records so far recovered at Tikal. The stela was found in a redeposited position inside the buried temple of 5D-33-2nd on the North Terrace.

AD 317 and AD 378. It is possible that they both refer to the same ruler despite the 61-year gap in the dates, but this cannot be proven. It is known with certainty that he was the 9th ruler of Tikal. He presently is often referred to as "Great Jaguar Claw" in deference to his exploits and length of rule. The conquest of Uaxactun in January of AD 378 was until recently associated with the rule of this man at Tikal, even though the warrior responsible was named K'ak' Sih or "Fire-Born" (see below). The date of the conquest is the same year as the recorded death on Stela 31 of Jaguar Claw I. Any connection between the conquest battles and the death of Jaguar Claw I is not known since Fire-Born received the glory and apparently went on to rule over Uaxactun.[12] In a recent paper by David Stuart,[13] new readings have shed some light on his "arrival" at Tikal on 16 January AD 378. Fire-Born, presumed a warrior from "the west" is thought to have come from Teotihuacan, and the death of Jaguar Claw I on the same day is significant. The subsequent "conquest" (if that is what it really was) of the city of Uaxactun was under the auspices of this foreign warrior of whom more will be said below.

Royal settlement and defense systems

Royal social life in 4th-century Tikal centered around the Great Plaza. The North Acropolis teemed with a cluster of temples and served as the cosmic center of the city (*ills.* 36 and 37), the place of burial of its kings. Its north–south axis likely was perceived by the 4th-century Maya as the axis of their world. On the south side of the Great Plaza that fronted the North Acropolis was another acropolis, a complex of palaces and administrative buildings called the Central Acropolis. By the 8th century this architectural complex occupied 4 acres. In the Preclassic period, we know that there were scattered residential structures in this area but they did not form a cohesive group. As early as the 4th century this area had emerged as a complex of palaces that were not entirely residential, not just the homes of the elite and certainly not the only places in Tikal where the elite lived. By this time palaces in Tikal had evolved into structures of complex function. Some of these structures were family residences while others served solely ceremonial and administrative uses, such as retreat houses, reception places and houses of judgement.[14] Even those palaces that were built as family houses had other uses if the family head was a member of the elite royal court. Then his house had also to serve administrative functions, and such royal houses would likely also have contained rooms set aside solely for religious functions, comparable to our concept of a royal chapel. Of all the known Early Classic palaces, those that front directly on the Great Plaza are not residences, but rather serve ceremonial purposes such as the south side of a cosmic space, the Great Plaza itself. Further east, in the Central Acropolis, beyond the space of the Great Plaza, the Maya built other palaces that were residential. While the courtyards of the whole complex integrated with the ceremonial palaces that do face the Great Plaza, the

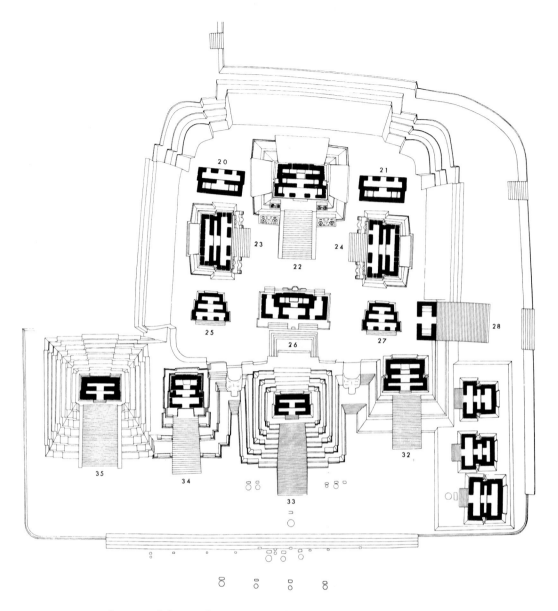

36 The map of the North Acropolis and North Terrace show the complexity and density of temple construction that formed the heavenly axis of a cosmic grouping in its final Late Classic stage.

residential palaces all lie physically east of the plaza itself and south of the East Plaza. The Central Acropolis was the place of the high royal court for centuries, but not the only place of socio-political power and wealth at Tikal.

Looking back to the time of settlement in 800 BC of the region that would become the city of Tikal, we noted that the site was settled as a series of villages – small settlements scattered over the landscape. This quality of scattered settlement persisted throughout the history of Tikal and is still reflected during the beginnings of classicism in the 4th century AD. Elite family residences did not occur only in the Central Acropolis close to the cosmic center of the Great

Plaza. Rather they are found scattered around outlying parts of the city in a fashion that suggests that there was a conscious dispersal, or de-centralization of the elite power. The more "rural" groups of palaces would have served ceremonial and administrative functions as well as those of a wealthy family residence just like the ones close to the city center. The de-centralization was itself probably a strategy of internal control, rather than a defense against outside attack. However, such attack was part of life and there was an effect upon settlement at Tikal.

We know conclusively from the texts, not just from Tikal but from a large number of other Peten sites, that warfare was a prominent feature of life in the Early Classic period. Politically, a city the size of Tikal had to be concerned about two different forms of aggression: one from within, the control of which is represented by the scattering of elite centers around the physical boundaries of the city; and one from without, which is represented by an increasing amount of subtle fortification inside the site, as well as the very real fortifications that appear at this time as wall/moat constructions to both the north and south sides of the city.

37 Seen from Temple II, the temples that line the edge of the North Terrace seem to obscure their earlier counterparts in the North Acropolis.

Aside from the city settlement patterns, the rise of warfare had other effects upon the 4th-century Maya. A system of allegiances and enmities had already come into being. Tikal's relationships with its neighbors, near and far, were fragile and mutable. An ally under one king could shift quickly to an enemy under the next, or even under the same leader. One explanation of the source of conflict lies in Tikal's strategic location and control over trade routes. During the early phases of the Early Classic we have only hints of the troubles that were brewing. The specifics become clearer toward the end of the Early Classic, when they virtually boil over, heralding the major cultural shift into the Late Classic period. That warfare played a significant role in the cultural shift now is beyond doubt.[15]

The sacred clan house of the Jaguar Claw family

At the eastern end of the Central Acropolis there is a very special structure that had an extraordinary history. This building is now known as 5D-46, but when it was built around AD 350, or earlier, it was the clan house of the Jaguar Claw family whose name identified a bloodline and dynasty lasting through to the very demise of Tikal. The dynasty did not endure all those centuries without difficulty, and it is the ups and downs of this extraordinary family that tells the story of Tikal. As if it represented the fortunes of the family line, Structure 5D-46 survived, unlike any other elite house of the period, up to present times (*ill. 38* and *pl. IX*).

38 At the beginning of excavations, the earth mound that was to be revealed as a palace complex was overgrown by trees at the site of 5D-46 the home of Jaguar Claw I.

39 (right) This polished black, carved cache vessel was excavated under the west stair of 5D-46 in 1965. Its text was not translated until 20 years later.

40 (below) The carving and text on the dedicatory cache vessel from 5D-46 was finally translated by Linda Schele in 1985 who revealed that it declared the building to be the house of Jaguar Claw I.

Built by the king known as Jaguar Claw I (Great Jaguar Claw), this building is one of a very few that has been positively identified as a family residence within the Central Acropolis. Further, it is the only Early Classic residence that was not partially demolished and covered by a later structure in central Tikal. This evident reverence for the building extended not only to the dynastic residents of the city, but to its enemies as well, during times of defeat and domination. This building was considered so sacred and so important to the identity of the city that no one dared touch it, other than to make additions and embellishments over time, and certainly, such additions were made. Even at the time of excavation a variety of features of the building identified it as a probable family residence in the analysis of my own excavation.[16] However, in a very rare case of corroboration of academic interpretation, the discovery of a cache under a ceremonial stair of the original building served at a later date to confirm the function and sanctity of this building. The cache had been buried beneath the western stair – the direction of death – not a direction normally dedicated to a doorway to living quarters. It was a broad and high staircase resembling the stair to a temple. The cache included an extraordinary vessel of carved and polished blackware, a cylinder with a lid. A carved inscription surrounded the lid of the vessel. The text revealed that this was the house of the ahau named Great Jaguar Claw, the 9th ruler in the succession since the founder Yax Ch'aktel Xok (*ills. 39* and *40*). The work of Linda Schele and David Freidel has been seminal in re-working and understanding the relationships between Tikal and Uaxactun during the reign of Jaguar Claw I. Schele translated the text on the cache vessel, which I had recovered in 1965, some 20 years after the excavation, confirming my hypothesis that this was indeed a royal residence.

In its original form the building had seven rooms on the ground floor and was oriented equally to both east and west, with three doorways on each side. The central western room was approached by the grand staircase above the dedicatory cache and its identifying inscription. The central room had no interior access to any other of the residential rooms of the building and likely served as a household shrine. Thus the household was protected from any malevolent influences from the open-sided western approach by an unconnected sacred room.

As time passed, the palace grew in size and changed in character. Stratigraphic evidence shows that the second story of the building and its interior staircase, unique at Tikal, were added at a slightly later date, but still well within the architectural building traditions of the Early Classic period. Addition of the second story may have been made toward the end of the 4th century, or even in the 5th century AD. Much later, probably in the late 8th century, and likely during the reign of the 29th ruler of Tikal, a number of large additions were made to the main building. These included raised patios to the north and south ends surrounded by residential rooms probably accommodating a much expanded royal family. By this time the orientation of the structure had changed considerably and access to the western side had been restricted from the outside. When these additions were made, the house was already over 400 years old. The newly built patios and their residential rooms were reached exclusively from the eastern side of the palace now totally enclosed by a private courtyard . In other words, the structure built as the sacred clan or lineage house of the Jaguar Claw dynasty enjoyed over 400 years of continuous occupation during which time it suffered no known damage. Knowledge from written texts of the history of Tikal tells us that there were a number of occasions during almost half a millennium when interlopers and even conquerors were in charge of the city, often resulting in damage to public and sacred buildings and monuments. However, this particular structure held such a sacred aura, that not even the interlopers dared do it harm. These same interlopers joined themselves to the count of Tikal lords, appropriating the very same founder as his legitimate heirs. Thus they too had to cherish the house of one of their greatest ancestors.

The significance of royal titles at Tikal

The royal titles used at Tikal are an essential part of the city's history and of its social structure. Each title is represented by a known hieroglyph. *Chacte* or *kalomte*[17] is the highest rank used at the site, and is likely comparable to the European understanding of "emperor." It denotes the supreme leader of highest possible rank whose domain was greater than a single city such as Tikal, and encompassed the area that such a large city dominated outside its own boundaries. For example, the nearby city of Uaxactun, dominated by Tikal at one point in its history, would be included in the domain of a kalomte.

The next highest rank is *ahau* which bears the literal translation of "lord" and signifies a leader whose domain may include the whole, or just part of a very large city like Tikal. More than one ahau could be in office at Tikal at the same time, but there could be only one kalomte. The evidence is that the importance and meaning of this title changed over time at Tikal. Originally it meant supreme ruler, leader, or king, but as the city itself grew to resemble a kingdom, a grander title became needed – hence the appearance of "chacte" or "kalomte" in a newer reading. The earliest leaders of the city are cited with the title "ahau" with the apparent meaning of "king or lord of Tikal". During the Early Classic period (AD 250–550), this concept changed and ahau came to denote a lesser rank, or a leader who had given allegiance and loyalty to the reigning kalomte of Tikal.

Batab is another known title used by the Maya but may have been an office less active at Tikal than at other cities. Tikal's diplomatic relationships with batabs at other cities are cited in hieroglyphic texts both at Tikal and elsewhere. Similarly, *sahal* is a recognized title denoting a noble of high rank which is more commonly used outside Tikal, although it was recognized there as well. A bowl belonging to the king "Animal Skull" (see below) makes reference to this title.[18]

After the reign of Jaguar Claw I there were always two officials who ruled together, kalomte and ahau. When the kalomte died, the reigning ahau usually succeeded to his title, while another lord, the next in line, moved up into the position of ahau. Thus we find in the known, named individuals whose histories are described here, there is frequently a surviving record of this succession, but not always.

"Fire-Born" (K'ak' Sih)

Just as Hunal Balam was a shadowy figure in the lineage and politics of early Tikal, another character, known originally as "Smoking Frog" (from his glyphic representation, *ill. 41*), but now known as "Fire-Born," played a role at Tikal during the reign of Jaguar Claw I and overlapped in time with the next documented ruler of the city, "First Crocodile" whose dossier follows. This shadowy character (Fire-Born) might have remained nothing more than that, but in 1983, Juan Pedro Laporte's workers pulled an extraordinary object from

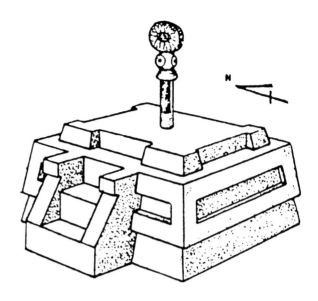

41 *One of the most mysterious figures in the Early Classic history of Tikal was named Fire-Born, known for many years as "Smoking Frog." His name glyph has been found in several different contexts at the site.*

42 *(above) This drawing of the "marcador" or ballcourt marker reconstructs the object in its original architectural setting, as found in the excavation of Laporte.*

43 *(left) The personage called "Spearthrower Owl" is now thought to be the father of the 10th ruler of Tikal, and likely never came to the city. His name glyph occurs in a number of contexts.*

rubble in the Lost World complex. Although the powerful influence of Teotihuacan had long been recognized at Tikal, Laporte found the first sculpture in pure Teotihuacan style. The texts inscribed upon it allow a few alternative understandings of the role played by Fire-Born. He was a warrior of great strength and was directly connected to the interaction between Tikal and Uaxactun, which was thought to be a conquest by Tikal, enacted by Fire-Born in AD 378. The newest interpretation made by Stuart (see above) says that the Tikal ruler called "First Crocodile" "arrived" (as the texts euphemistically put it) at Tikal in the company of Fire-Born. References to a higher order personage, not of Tikal, by the name of "Spearthrower Owl" suggest that this latter person was a ruler of Teotihuacan and that he sent his son (First Crocodile) to Tikal. The "arrival" of this pair from the west was anticipated at Tikal and coincided with the death of the reigning king, Great Jaguar Claw. The death of Fire-Born, who apparently stayed in the Tikal region, is recorded on Stela 31 at AD 402. Great Jaguar Claw I had already died in AD 378 (on Stela 31), and the next year, AD 379, is the recorded date for his successor coming to power. The difference is once again that of kalomte and ahau. Fire-Born was a high kalomte, but the dimensions of his domain are not known other than that they included Tikal.

Fire-Born became more important to the history of Tikal upon the discovery by Laporte[19] of an extraordinary object in Group 6C-XVI south of the Lost

World Pyramid. This group proved to be a buried Early Classic complex of palaces and other ceremonial structures and one such structure yielded an object now known as the "marcador." This was a columnar decorated stone piece known by its form from Teotihuacan as a ballcourt marker (*ills. 42 and 43*). The inscribed text on the column mentions Fire-Born twice in relation to his action against Uaxactun. The artwork on one side of the upper flange shows a representation of Tlaloc, the rain god important to Teotihuacan. On the reverse is a bearded owl crossed by a drawing of a human left hand holding an *atlatl* or spear thrower, an instrument of war. No other ballcourt markers of this kind have been found at Tikal and it is thought that this object displays evidence that new war methods were introduced to Tikal at the time of its conflict with Uaxactun and perhaps through the agency of Fire-Born, a warrior, a kalomte.

A turning point

By the middle of the Early Classic period at AD 370 the base for Tikal's culture and family lineage had been set. However, there were still more changes and influence from Teotihuacan yet to come. The concept of a scattered power base with a strong control center emanating from the Great Plaza and its environs had been established. Tikal had become a center for trade and distribution of its own art style. A new element that had not been prominent in the Preclassic emerged. This was warfare, and Tikal became a center for its vicissitudes.

Changes, and worse, were coming.

Table 2

Chronology of the early part of the Early Classic at Tikal

Time span AD 200–402 (202 years)

Name	Date	Event	Source	Ruler No
Yax Ch'aktel Xok (First Scaffold Shark)	c. AD 200	ruling		Founder (1st)
Hunal Balam (Foliated Jaguar)	AD 292	ruling	Stela 29	6th or 7th
Zero Moon Bird	AD 300(?)	ruling(?)	Leiden	7th or 8th
Chak Toh Ich'ak (Jaguar Claw I)	AD 317	ruling	Stela 31	9th
	AD 378	death	Stela 31	
K'ak' Sih (Fire-Born)	AD 378	kalomte	Stela 31	Not of Tikal
	AD 402	death	Stela 31	

CHAPTER SIX

CHANGE AND CHALLENGE: THE END OF THE EARLY CLASSIC

First Crocodile I (Yax Ain I)

Accession to power of the ruler known as "First Crocodile" brought further change to Tikal (*ill. 44*). Not only was influence from Teotihuacan increased, but there was most likely a change in the actual lineage at this point. Until the appearance of this ruler, the lineage in power was that of Jaguar Claw – a lineage that will re-appear at a later date. Moreover, it is possible, and even probable that First Crocodile was a nobleman from the Mexican highlands – from Teotihuacan itself as has been argued by a number of scholars.[1] In order to enter peacefully into the hierarchy of a city of such wealth and power, he must have married into the ruling line. Present knowledge from archaeological and glyphic evidence is not able to tell exactly what relationship permitted an outsider to take rulership of the city.

44 *The name glyph of Yax Ain I is very important as he may have been a foreigner who came to rule Tikal from the highlands. It translates as "First Crocodile" and his tomb, Burial 10, contained a crocodile skeleton.*

First Crocodile has had many names in the progress of study of Tikal. Previously known as "Curl Nose" or "Curl Snout," the image of his name glyph was not recognized as the head of a crocodile until recently. He is the next true successor after Jaguar Claw I and he became ahau of Tikal in AD 379, as 10th ruler in the succession after the founder. As usual, what we know about his life comes largely from the commemorations and inscriptions that followed his death. The contents of his tomb are not just revealing, they are among some of the finest art works to emerge from the city. In Maya his name is Yax Ain. The word "ain" means "crocodile" in Maya.

Twenty-three years after First Crocodile's accession as ahau of Tikal, the death of the lord Fire-Born, the kalomte in power in Tikal, is recorded in AD 402. First Crocodile then acceded to the most exalted position. Reference to First Crocodile's death in AD 420 is found on Stela 5, not of Tikal, but of the site of El Zapote, a small regional city that owed allegiance to Tikal. By this time the distinction between ahau and kalomte had been formalized at Tikal

82

and the documentation for both offices is in the comprehensive inscriptions of Stela 31, one of two of the city's major known historical records.[2]

The American crocodile (*Crocodylus acutus*) was not thought to inhabit Guatemala until the late 1980s, when one was killed in the camp water-hole at Tikal (see *ill. 8*). They are now known to be quite widely distributed throughout the Peten. In ancient times the swamps that bounded Tikal with their slow-moving waters were a perfect habitat for this species of meat-eating man-killing saurian. As an animal spirit for the Maya, the power of the crocodile must have rivaled that of the jaguar – one a spirit of the water, the other a spirit of the forest.

The ruler named Yax Ain I (First Crocodile) was indeed the first known ruler of Tikal to bear this distinguished name, but by no means the last, and his influence on Tikal was formidable. Coggins[3] has argued that he probably was not a native of the city, and that he may have come to Tikal by way of the Guatemalan highland site of Kaminaljuyu which at this time period was closely affiliated to the civilization of Teotihuacan in Mexico. Others have suggested that he came directly from Teotihuacan, possibly as a resident diplomat. At any rate the influence he brought from Teotihuacan upon architecture, ceramic style and decoration is especially strong and is perfectly exemplified by the contents of his tomb. This crypt is known as Burial 10 (*ills. 45 and 46*) and

45 Burial 10 was excavated by Edwin Shook, the first Director of the Project. Here archaeologist Stuart Scott, who aided in the excavation, observes the progress of exposing the riches of the tomb.

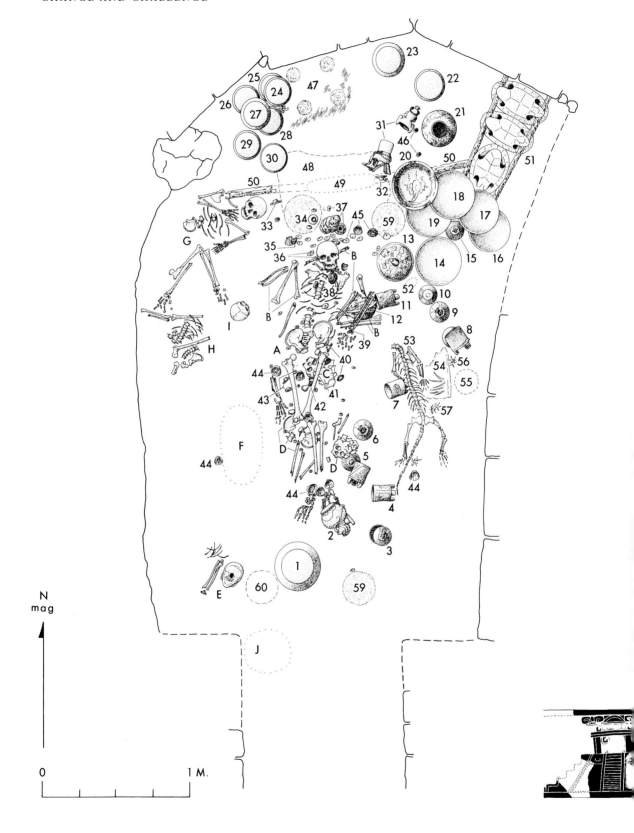

46 (left) Burial 10 was the tomb of Yax Ain I, and contained many pieces of strong Teotihuacan influence. The lord's namesake in the form of a crocodile skeleton was included among the many burial riches.

47 (right) This complex sculpture of a parrot morphing into a conch shell holds the symbol of song in his beak. The piece may have originated in Teotihuacan and been imported as part of Yax Ain I's personal treasure.

48 (below) A painted vessel lid from Burial 10 depicts a pure art style from Teotihuacan. The vivid paint was applied to a stucco coating over the surface of the vessel.

49 (below) One of the most revealing pieces of art from the Early Classic Period shows the arrival at Tikal of Teotihuacan peoples bearing the new technology of war – the atlatl.

was found beneath the temple 5D-34 on the North Terrace fronting the North Acropolis. I was fortunate enough to be present during the excavation of this extraordinary tomb in 1959.[4] The tomb was unique, we now know, because so many of the grave goods it contained have a foreign flavor, influenced by, or imported directly from the distant Mexican city of Teotihuacan. The temple above the burial was First Crocodile's commemorative temple and remained intact until the abandonment of Tikal.

Despite the influence from Teotihuacan upon the art contained in First Crocodile's tomb, the pieces are still Maya in their nature and rendition. As in the tomb of the lesser Egyptian king Tutankhamun, Yax Ain I's tomb contained "wonderful things." But Yax Ain I was not a lesser king at Tikal. His role determined the direction of thought, art, and warfare at the city for decades to come.

Some interesting items in the funerary material of Burial 10 include three turtle carapaces and one headless crocodile skeleton. The latter was doubtless a personification of the tomb owner's name, but why this dead saurian was presented headless we can only guess. The evidence of birds as funerary equipment appears here for the first time at Tikal. With First Crocodile's body were included the remains of two pygmy owls, green jays and an ant tanager. Coggins sees the addition of birds and their feathers to the much older trappings of jaguar skins and snake motifs as an influence from Teotihuacan where feathers and birds were very prominent in artistic symbolism. Ironically, while the Teotihuacanos had to import their bird feathers from the Maya lowlands, the Maya themselves had paid little attention to the use of such feathers until their culture was influenced by the Teotihuacan customs evident in First Crocodile's tomb.

Stingray spines and spondylus shells were also part of the tomb goods, ritual items imported from the Maya sea coasts. Also of great interest was a jade ornament depicting the same stylized crocodile head that is part of Yax Ain's name. Such an object recalls similar greenstone carvings found in the tombs of male royal burials at earlier dates, apparently a custom at Tikal.

Three effigy vessels among the grave contents are quite remarkable for their iconography and probable history. The so-called "Old God" deity figure, made in two parts, depicts the deity seated on a tripod of human bones and holding a human head in his extended hands (*pl. II*). The details of the imagery of the head contain references to the sun god (Kinich Ahau) in his Sun-in-the-Underworld/Night Jaguar guise.

A second effigy vessel was made of fine creamy paste with a bridge spout, and was covered in painted stucco. The figure represented a fantastic blend of a bird bonded into a conch shell (*ill. 47*). This extraordinary piece had been coated with stucco several times and repainted each time. Coggins suggested that it may have been an heirloom piece brought to Tikal by First Crocodile from either Kaminaljuyu in highland Guatemala or even from Teotihuacan itself. The iconography of bird/conch shell images is prevalent in the Tetitla zone of Teotihuacan where the tabbed fillet held in the bird's beak obviously represents a speech scroll indicating song, and possibly doubling as the sound of the conch trumpet as well. One of the bird's wings becomes the conch shell trumpet. This sensual blend of sight and sound in visual punning is something that the Maya would very much appreciate in their culture, even if the piece originated from another civilization. It may have been this meeting of values that made the rich iconography from Teotihuacan so appealing to the Maya. These elements suggest a strong and perhaps direct trade alliance with the highlands of Mexico at this particular time in Tikal's history. Shells and feathers of local Tikal origin are also included with the grave goods paralleling the bird/shell imagery of this amazing effigy vessel.

A third important vessel from the tomb is a blackware cylinder tripod with a "diving god" figurine depicted as the handle of the lid. The iconographic concept is very Maya in design even though the tripod cylinder form originates in Teotihuacan. Of particular interest are the projections from the legs and hips of the diving figure in the form of *cacao* pods, a crop known to be of great importance to later Maya economy, but apparently already valued at this time.

It is in the treatment of the ceramics, the painting style and presence of stucco undercoat that demonstrates the most direct influence from Teotihuacan. The Tlaloc (rain god) faces and motifs that occur on the vessels from Burial 10 could have been copied directly from painted murals at the highland city. The survival of this fragile surface treatment over the centuries is remarkable (*ill. 48*).

Another important vessel that helps us to understand this period of transition comes from a contemporary deposit of a large number of ceramics that looks a lot like the contents of a tomb that was re-located. The most prominent item in this strange deposit was a whole tripod blackware vessel with an incised scene (*ill. 49*). The scene depicts a royal personage standing on a palace platform, drawn with details that identify him as a Maya. He is receiving a procession of six figures in dress that is obviously derived from highland Mexico. The setting includes a combination of Maya and Mexican architecture. The weapons, spears and atlatls (spearthrowers) being carried by the apparently friendly Mexicans have been interpreted as the introduction of highland warfare techniques to the Maya. Be that as it may, the scene does represent exactly what was happening at Tikal at this time. Representatives of a foreign culture were received in a friendly manner by the Maya of Tikal. Yax Ain I himself may have been one of these people. While the deposit cannot be directly dated, it is certainly within the range of his 41 years of rule. As noted, we know from Stela 5 at El Zapote that Yax Ain I (First Crocodile) died in AD 420, suggesting the date of his tomb.

Stormy Sky (Siyah Chan K'awil)
The next ruler, the 11th in succession since the founder, has been called "Stormy Sky," a name describing his patronymic glyph which shows a sky band

rent by lightning (*ill. 50*). He is most assuredly the son of First Crocodile and ruled both as ahau and kalomte of Tikal. His rule is most noted for the creation of Stela 31 which shows the king's carved portrait on the front (*ill. 51*), while the extremely long and informative text on the reverse (*ill. 35*) provides the single most detailed lineage account from the time of the founder until his own rule. Unfortunately, the account does not provide the entire lineage for this long period of about 165 years and 11 rulers. The phonetic reading of his name glyph is quite different from our subjective interpretation of a "stormy sky." Phonetically it reads Siyah Chan K'awil, for which an extremely loose translation might be "Sky-born K'awil."[5] Two interesting features can be noted on the carving of Stormy Sky's image on Stela 31. One is that his name glyph is incorporated into the headdress that he wears. The other is that an ancestor figure hovers over the main figure peering down from the sky. This ancestor figure bears all the attributes of Stormy Sky's father, First Crocodile.

50 Claimed to be the son of Yax Ain I, Stormy Sky, or Siyah Chan K'awil, was the 11th successor in the line of Lords of Tikal.

Stelae associated with Stormy Sky's name include Stelae 1, 2, 28, 31 and now also 40. There are two dates associated with his accession to power, one in AD 411[6] to the title of ahau, and the other in AD 426[7] to the title of kalomte. Since his father, First Crocodile, died in AD 420, Stormy Sky became ahau of Tikal nine years before his father's death, but did not become kalomte until six years after that death. This suggests that a son did not automatically and immediately succeed to a title following the death of the father who bore it.

A date associated with Stormy Sky's death was painted on the walls of the tomb believed to be his burial in the North Acropolis (*Burial 48, ill. 52*). A single date painted on a tomb wall in AD 457 was assumed to mark the date of interment, but turned out not to be the case. The discovery of Stela 40 in 1996 suggested new dates for his demise and new detail for the succession of his son K'an Ak. Thus we know that Siyah (Stormy Sky) died on 19 February, AD 456 and was not finally interred until 9 August, AD 458.[8] Therefore, the painted date in the tomb, at 9 March , AD 457 lies 383 days after the actual death and 515 days before final interment. One can only wonder about the stages of funerary rites that fell between these dates, and whether or not the same interval applied to the deaths of all rulers. In the absence of better information the assumption is generally made that the date of the death of one ruler conforms fairly closely to the accession date for the next in line. Given his date of accession in AD 411 and death in AD 456 Siyah Chan K'awil held power in Tikal for 45 years.

*51 Stormy Sky recorded his own visage as well as that of his parentage on the front of Stela 31,
one of the most exquisitely carved monuments at Tikal.*

In life, the rule of Siyah Chan K'awil continued to foster the Mexican influence that was so apparent in his father's time. Figures on the side of Stela 31 flank the ruler in Mexican battle dress, and are identified as his father, First Crocodile, holding the shield and spearthrowers of warfare. Texts for this time period say that Tikal cemented a friendly relationship with its northern neighbor Uaxactun. It was a period of great positive activity at these two sites, with Tikal emerging as a pre-eminent power over the region.[9]

In death, this ruler further presented his devotion to the Mexican style. Burial 48 was placed on the sacred north–south axis of the North Acropolis in front of the small temple called Structure 5D-26, in a location that would be buried more than two centuries later by the construction of 5D-33-1st, a great monument destined to mark a major turning point in Tikal's history. The tomb chamber was small, much smaller than his father's tomb. The walls were painted with strange, rather abstract figures as well as the aforementioned date in hieroglyphs. This is 11 years after the dedicatory date on his most famous monument, Stela 31. It is all but the last of several major burials of rulers to be placed on the sacred axis of the North Acropolis. Subsequent burials occur beneath temples on the North Terrace, fronting the Acropolis or elsewhere in the Lost World Pyramid group.

Stormy Sky himself, like a number of his predecessors, was not buried as an intact corpse. The head and hands are missing, and the presence of organic material indicates that his body was wrapped in cloth as in a bundle burial. Poignantly, a single blade of obsidian was placed where the head should have been. The significance of this substitution is not known. He was flanked by the skeletons of two young adolescent males, apparent sacrificial victims sent to accompany the great warrior.

Apart from the painted date, the east and west walls were decorated with painted glyph-like emblems, forty-five of them in all. Many forms can be recognized, but they do not form a coherent text. Coggins suggested that they may represent a ritual chant, possibly part of the funeral ceremony.[10]

Among the grave goods were 30 ceramic vessels, including several that were stuccoed and painted in the Teotihuacan style so well known from First Crocodile's tomb. The usual spondylus shells and stingray spines are present along with green obsidian imported from Teotihuacan, and more bird remains. In all, the contents are quite similar to those of Burial 10, believed to be Stormy Sky's father. One notable grave object was a magnificent carved bowl of alabaster with an inscription, as yet untranslated, around the outside of the bowl. The form and content of the carved and stuccoed vessels in the tomb show a continued central Mexican influence but also a definite trend toward Mayanization.

Almost 140 years remain from the death of Stormy Sky until the end of the period called the Early Classic. During this time there are six known, named rulers at Tikal as well as evidence that others whose names are unknown also existed. Of the six only two are known by burial, while the rest emerge from the hieroglyphic record.

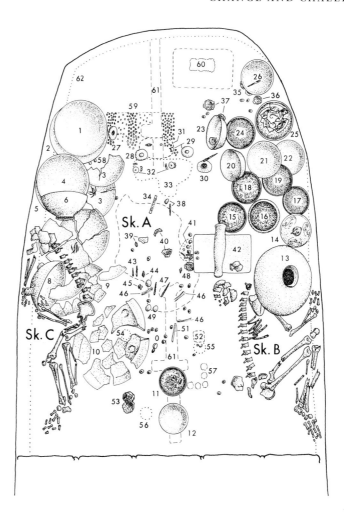

52 Plan of Burial 48 found in the North Acropolis and thought to be the tomb of Siyah Chan K'awil. This burial is located on the sacred north–south axis of the North Acropolis.

There is one other burial of related interest because of its location and time period. This is Burial 177 found in Court 1 of the Central Acropolis on the south side of the Great Plaza. The style of ceramic decoration is slightly later than the time of Stormy Sky, and Coggins has suggested a date of AD 475, based on style. The burial consisted of a small crypt that had been built into the fill of Court 1 during a major architectural expansion of that courtyard. The individual has been identified as probably female, young, and was placed seated in a tiny chamber facing west. The most interesting feature of Burial 177 is that it is located precisely on the sacred north–south axis, even though it is far to the south of the North Acropolis itself. The crypt had been covered over at the foot of the south stair of Structure 5D-71, a ritual three-doorway palace that faced the North Acropolis on the opposite side from the burial. Both the location and the grave contents suggest that this was a relative of Stormy Sky's, perhaps a daughter or younger sister, given the honor of burial on the sacred axis, but far to the south which has been suggested earlier (during the Late Preclassic, Chapter Four) as a direction pertinent to women.

Troubled times: the Early Classic Dark Ages

From the beginning of the written record with Stela 29 attributed to Hunal Balam in AD 292 until the death of Stormy Sky in AD 456 is a span of 164 years. Despite an incomplete record there is sufficient information to infer the patterns of development at Tikal, including the growth of a Tikal Maya style in art and ceramics, followed by influence of Mexican art motifs and styles of warfare, and finally a trend towards the Mayanization of these styles under Stormy Sky. During this same period warfare had become more prevalent with growing rivalry between sites. Following the death of Stormy Sky, the 11th ruler in the succession, there is a period of 137 years which spans the next 11 rulers ending with Ruler 22, whose name is Lizard Head (E Te II[11]) and who was interred in Burial 195 on the North Terrace.

This period is one of increased warfare and a developing animosity towards Tikal on the part of another great city to the north, Calakmul. There is a saga of alliances and enmities which led to a number of defeats for Tikal. Such defeats are not recorded at the city itself and must be either inferred from texts at other sites or from other kinds of evidence at the site. The very lack of texts is one result of the turmoil, since conquering enemies tended to destroy, deface or otherwise eliminate the record of a defeated city. This undoubtedly accounts in part for the relative lack of a written record at Tikal for the 137 years that bring the Early Classic to an end. The sparse record provides us with the names of seven of the 11 rulers of this period. The record is found on 16 different stelae at Tikal,[12] including one belonging to the 17th successor whose own name is not known. The names of the seven known rulers, in chronological order are: Yellow Peccary (K'an Ak), Jaguar Claw II (Chak Toh Ich'ak II), Lizard Head I (E Te I), Curl Head (no Maya reading), Jaguar Claw III (Chak Toh Ich'ak III), Double Bird (Yax K'uk' Mo'[13]), and Lizard Head II (E Te II). An outline of this troubled period of nearly fourteen decades follows.

Yellow Peccary

Yellow Peccary (K'an Ak)[14]

The 12th successor is mentioned on two stelae (9 and 13) both located close to the front of temple Structure 5D-34 where First Crocodile was buried. K'an Ak's name glyph shows the head of a peccary with a *kan* cross in its eye and a trefoil device above the eye which identifies the beast positively as the peccary as opposed to other wild porcine species that live in the Tikal environment. Jones interpreted the eroded "father" glyph in Stela 13 as reading Stormy Sky, making Yellow Peccary the direct line 12th successor. The iconographic style of Yellow Peccary's two monuments bears no resemblance to the carved works of his father, specifically Stela 31. However, this perception was completely changed by the dramatic discovery in July 1996 of a new carved stela, Stela 40[15] (*ills. 53* and *54*). This stela was dedicated by K'an Ak and contains a stunning new series of dates for the lives of both his father, Siyah Chan K'awil and of himself. New facts and dates in the lives of both rulers were revealed as

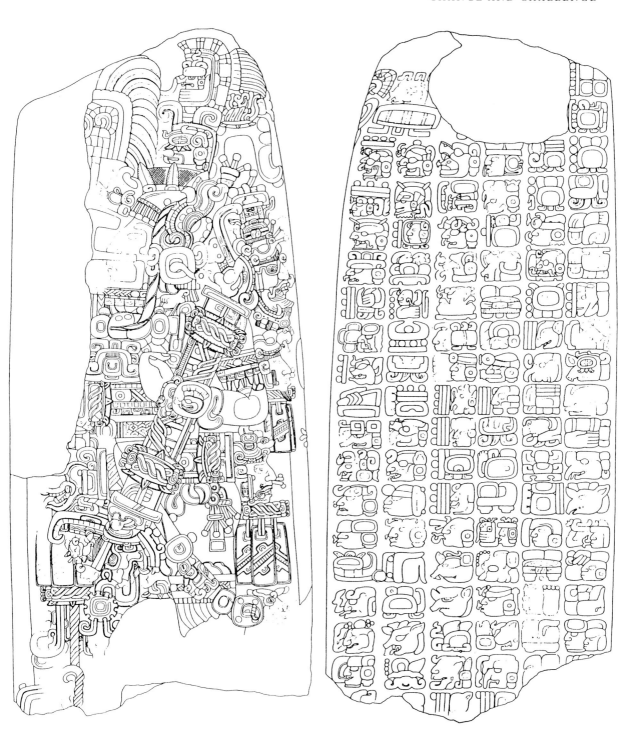

53 *Drawing of the front of Stela 40 made by Federico Fahsen showing the personage of Yellow Peccary or K'an Ak, the 12th Lord of Tikal and son of Stormy Sky.*

54 *The complex text from the back of Stela 40 deals with the succession history of the period. Its style suggests that the monument was carved by the same hand as Stela 31. Stela 40 was carved in* AD 468.

described above. The text goes on to say that K'an Ak acceded to power in Tikal on 24 August AD 458, 15 days following his father's final interment and that the Stela 40 itself was dedicated by K'an Ak on 20 June AD 468.[16] The dedication date is set at only 23 years after the dedication of Stela 31 and the styles are so closely shared as to suggest the same hand carving them. This is extremely helpful in understanding the succession as the inscriptions referring to K'an Ak on Stelae 9 and 13 are short and offer little information with few dates, in stark contrast to the historic record on Stela 31. Some change in manner of presentation took place even though the descent line is intact. From a date on Stela 9, we know that K'an Ak was still ruling in AD 475[17] but no other dates for his reign are secure.

While the 14th ruler is firmly established as a direct line son of Yellow Peccary, named Jaguar Claw II, the identity of the 13th ruler in between is less clear. There are two contenders.

The 13th successor

Because of the importance in the calendar of the number 13, this should have been an important position in the dynastic descendancy, a ritual feature of which the Maya would surely have been acutely aware. Yet this ruler remains obscure with only one associated monument.

Stela 3 refers to a son of Yellow Peccary (the 12th ruler) as reigning king of Tikal. The unread name is only known not to be that of Jaguar Claw II (the 14th ruler) and furthermore, the date at AD 488[18] falls neatly between the known dates of the reigns of Yellow Peccary and Jaguar Claw II. This reference on Stela 3 could be to the unidentified 13th ruler. According to the detailed reconstruction made by Genevieve Michel[19] for the difficult succession of this part of the Early Classic, K'an Ak was a prolific father. His five sons all served as rulers of Tikal, and of these, the 13th ruler likely was the older brother of Jaguar Claw II, who is known to come next.

Jaguar Claw II (Chak Toh Ich'ak II)[20]

Jaguar Claw II

There is no doubt surrounding the 14th successor whose position is described on Stelae 7, 15 and 27. From each of these monuments we know that he was ruling in AD 495[21]. As noted, the Maya do not have a means of denoting the re-use of a name. Although the Jaguar Claw lineage was likely broken shortly after the reign of Jaguar Claw I, it is now re-established with the revival of his name nearly a century and a half later. Just how the continuity of succession was maintained while the lineages changed remains one of the mysteries of Tikal politics.

Lizard Head I (E Te I)

Although problematical because of the difficulties in reading an eroded text, it is likely that Stela 8 from the Great Plaza represents the 15th ruler. The name glyph shows the head of a saurian, either lizard or frog, holding the Maya *te* sign in its mouth. The same name glyph was found in a painted inscription of a looted vessel from the correct time period. The date on Stela 8 is AD 497[22] a mere two years after the date recorded for the reign of Jaguar Claw II. The best interpretation is that these two men were brothers, both sons of Yellow Peccary, and ruling in sequence of their ages.

Lizard Head I

The succession from 16th to 18th rulers

While the only known date for the 15th ruler was set at AD 497, the next firm date for any known successor is in the reign of the 19th ruler at AD 527. This period spans only 30 years but accounts for the reigns of three largely unknown rulers at Tikal.

A painted inscription found on an unprovenanced vessel appears to refer to the 16th ruler at Tikal, including the ruler's name.[23] However, no phonetic value is yet proposed for this name. Michel refers to him as the "black pot ruler."

The 17th ruler is likely the figure shown on Stela 6 with a date of AD 514.[24] This stela is fragmentary but was originally placed at the east end of the North Terrace near temple Structure 5D-32. The carving style shows that this was the last in a series of similarly carved stelae depicting the ruler holding a prominent and elaborate staff.

Despite these glaring gaps of knowledge in the succession there are some other events that are known during this same time period that hint at the strange doings and interruptions that plagued this chapter of Tikal's history.

The 18th ruler

A blend of archaeological evidence, hieroglyphic texts, dates and iconography reveals a fascinating and unresolved mystery revolving around a woman. Once known as "Woman of Tikal" or simply "Lady Tikal" she is another example of the power of women that prevailed throughout the history of this city. Her name glyph combines the sign for "woman" and the emblem glyph for "Tikal." Her role was important enough to involve two carved stelae in association with the tomb of a very prominent male in Burial 160.

Woman of Tikal

The importance of the man in the burial hinges on the identity and parentage of the woman associated with him through the inscriptions on Stelae 23 and 25, both located near the pyramidal structure under which the male was buried. Adjacent to the pyramid was an added platform that covered the burial of a woman (Burial 162). This small temple and its associated stelae were located in the distant forest far from the city center, far from the North Acropolis, burial place of kings, and yet the male burial is clearly as rich as any royal grave. The stelae both refer to the woman.[25] Stela 23 was dedicated to Lady Tikal and was probably commissioned and erected by her. It is one of the very few monuments at Tikal dedicated directly to a woman and the only one in the Early Classic period. The monument states that she was born in AD 504.[26] The stela suffered severe defacement, likely at the hands of Tikal's invaders. Flanking figures on the sides depict a male and female, probably parent figures for the main figure on the front. The text also includes a probable accession date at AD 511. These dates suggest that a member of the reigning lineage (female?) was seated at the age of six years as an ahau, but not necessarily as a king (or queen).

Stela 25 was located about 200 m distant from structure 7F-30 which covers the royal burials. It had been badly mutilated and fragmented. Flanking portraits of a male and female are barely visible on the sides while the main figure is too badly disfigured to discern its sex. Of the lengthy text on the rear only the dedication date remains telling us that this stela at least was placed in AD 517. This may also be the date of placement for Stela 23 as well.

It is the tomb in Burial 160 that fires the imagination in this group. The main figure is clearly an adult male accompanied by rich burial goods. These are highlighted by a mosaic mask (ill. 56), an artifact made of greenstone, shell and bitumen that has come to herald the high quality of artistic achievement at Tikal. A number of features in the tomb lead to this man's identification as "Lord Quetzal" (K'uk' Ahau). Grave goods included the skeleton of a quetzal bird laid between his legs. Also the hooked bill on the headdress of his mask

55 This rare photograph shows Burial 160, taken by Edward Crocker who assisted in the excavation. Bones, jade and predominant red cinnabar are typical of a royal burial.

56 (right) The mortuary mask from Burial 160 was made of jade, shell, and bitumen. Probably that of the 18th ruler of Tikal, the burial dates to the early 6th century.

resembles the same bird. Just as First Crocodile had a crocodile skeleton in his tomb, reflecting his name, the lord in Burial 160 may have used the quetzal (*k'uk'*) as his name emblem. The identity of this man is not known. He may have married into the Jaguar Claw clan through his wife (Woman of Tikal?) and have been a foreigner to the city. He may also have served as a ruler – the missing ruler 18 would fit into the time scheme. Coggins suggested that having wealth and power through marriage with a member of the direct dynastic line, that he was buried by his wife with the ceremony due his station but at a location removed from the city center, perhaps at the insistence of other members of the family.[27] His demise by murder has even been suggested. Eventually this noble woman had herself buried (Burial 162?) in the same locality, adjacent to her husband, but without ceremony. It is of note that this group is located in the far southeastern quarter of the city, a location which Jones has argued was on a trade route entry to Tikal. It may have held some special economic or personal significance to the "royal" members of the family who have not left their clear mark as members of the Jaguar Claw lineage. The monuments that accompany the grave site were probably destroyed during a raid upon the city – from Caracol perhaps, which lies in this direction – and then subsequently reset with reverence in their damaged condition. The precise explanation of the roles of these obvious members of the royal family remains unresolved.

One final mystery surrounds this mini-saga. The stela numbered 14 was found set on the North Terrace. It was a bottom fragment with carving on all four sides that seem to match the style of Stela 25, but had been reset backwards with the glyphic text facing outwards. It is possible that this is the missing base of Stela 25 transported by someone all the way from Tikal's southeast quarter back to the city center for a ceremonial, but incorrect, setting. The suggestion of long memory and attempt at reparation is strong. Despite all the unanswered questions this cluster of evidence, Stelae 23, 25 and 14 as well as Burial 160 (*ill. 55*) are now all associated with the 18th ruler of Tikal.

Curl Head

Curl Head

The 19th ruler bears the name of "Curl Head," which was established by Jones for lack of any other reading and has remained in the literature so far. Martin and Grube feel that the Curl Head glyph is a generic title and that the true name of this ruler is Kalomte Balam[28] ("Ruler" Jaguar). Known from both Stelae 10 and 12, this personage's only securely known date is AD 527 which has been taken as the date of dedication for both stelae as well as for his probable date of accession to power. There is a question as to his claim of legitimacy to the Jaguar Claw lineage. He may indeed have been a usurper. Both monuments stood on the North Terrace fronting the Great Plaza and exhibit the very deep relief that had come to be fashionable at this time at Tikal. On Stela 10 (*ill. 57*) the king stands facing the front with head turned to the viewer's left and holds his right hand aloft displaying a now eroded object in the fashion of Stormy

57 The lord known as "Curl Head" or Kalomte Balam displays his glory on Stela 10. It was carved in the deep relief style of the late part of the Early Classic period facing the viewer's left. The date is AD 527.

Sky's gesture on Stela 31. The text on Stela 10 also refers to a "cutting and chopping" of the seat of title that refers to Calakmul. This may be a definite reference to a skirmish in the growing animosity between the polities of Calakmul and Tikal which took place under this man's rule.

Jaguar Claw III (Chak Toh Ich'ak III)[29]

A parentage statement on Stela 17 states that the father of ruler 21 was Jaguar Claw III, making him the 20th ruler and hence next in succession after Curl Head. There is no stela firmly associated with this ruler, which leads us to fall back on chronology to seek possible information about him. A clue comes from a very important and beautifully carved monument, Stela 26 (*ill. 58*).

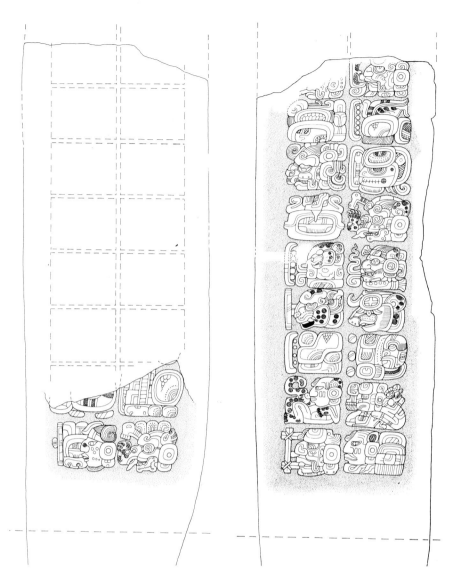

58 Texts on the sides of Stela 26 are carved in careful relief, but the incomplete state of preservation prevents positive identification of the ruler who ordered it to be made. Probably it was commissioned by Jaguar Claw III.

The carving that remains on Stela 26 is exquisite, in deep relief and well preserved. It is a great pity that so much of the stela is lost – only a basal fragment has survived. No dates have survived on this monument. Records from other stelae suggest that the fragmentary inscription deals with a parentage statement preceding the announcement of accession to power of the next in line. The next available date at Tikal is from Stela 17 associated with the next, the 21st ruler, named Double Bird (see below). The earliest date on Stela 17 is AD 537[30] and is interesting as the date of Double Bird's accession. This same date would fit well for Jaguar Claw III as his probable death date in the same year. Such a reconstruction is made by deduction and not from any direct evidence.

Called the Red Stela, Stela 26 was excavated by Edwin Shook in 1958 inside the temple of Structure 5D-34 above the tomb of First Crocodile (Yax Ain I). Reconstructing the history of this strange location from what is known for this chapter of Tikal's misfortunes, it is assumed that a major raid, possibly from Caracol resulted in the breaking up of Stela 26. Later, the recovered pieces were re-assembled and buried with ceremony under a masonry altar in the temple of 5D-34. Much later, in Postclassic times, the altar was itself desecrated, at which time more pieces of the stela may have been lost. These events testify to the increasing violence of the latter half of the Early Classic period. The power and cohesion of Tikal was coming under dire stress and test, and the physical evidence of this stress is apparent in the destruction of the public record of carved monuments. This evidence for the reign of Jaguar Claw III is secondary and tenuous, all that remains due to the violence of the times.

Double Bird (Yax K'uk' Mo')

Double Bird is reported on Stela 17 as the 21st ruler of Tikal, assumed to have acceded on the earliest stela date at AD 537. The same inscription reports that Jaguar Claw III was his father. This is the first time in the Early Classic period that a succession from father to son is directly recorded since Stormy Sky reported that First Crocodile was his father some 10 rulers in the past and now we know from Stela 40 that K'an Ak claimed Stormy Sky as his father extending that known father-son connection one more generation. Succeeding relationships have had to be inferred from the dates and the succession statements. Double Bird's date of accession to power is recorded at AD 537 presumably as ahau of Tikal.

Double Bird

Double Bird's name has not been translated in Maya as yet, and it is interesting to note that a highly similar name glyph for the founder of the city of Copan, one of Tikal's allies represents an intertwined quetzal and macaw. This "double bird" combination is translated at Copan as Yax K'uk' Mo'. The founder of Copan died in AD 435, one hundred and two years prior to Double Bird's accession in Tikal. Indications of a strong alliance between the two cities have emerged by this time. A sharing of a ruler's patronymic would be one way of expressing that alliance and the suggestion here is that this ruler of Tikal assumed the name of Copan's founder in a gesture of solidarity. The two birds in the 21st ruler's name glyph are not clearly enough preserved to identify their species, but the probability seems good that we have another Yax K'uk' Mo' in this personage.

The inscription on Stela 17 is very long, with a total of 108 original glyphs. However, most of it has been lost to defacement and erosion. One of the most interesting bits of information left to us is the statement of conflict at a place called "Flint Mountain." We know that this connotes a region in or around the city of Caracol with which Tikal engaged in a long and severe conflict. The last date on the stela is AD 557[31] and this is taken to be the dedicatory date for the erection of the monument. This is 1 katun, or 20 years to the day, after the accession of Double Bird to power in Tikal. It is also the last date to be recorded at Tikal for the next century and a quarter. This long block of time with no recorded dates is known as the "Hiatus" and is discussed in the next chapter. The Hiatus spans the change from the Early to Late Classic and so it is very important to the history of Tikal, as well as to the lowland Maya in general.

The final date on Stela 17 is not likely the date of Double Bird's death. However, the great conflict between Tikal and Caracol intervenes in the record. It is from the record of Caracol that we find the claim that they defeated Tikal in AD 562[32] some five years later. Apparently this was a very protracted war, and the consequences for Tikal were severe. The war apparently began under the rule of Double Bird. The event in which Caracol won against Tikal is the first record in the Maya lowlands of a "star war,"[33] a war whose timing is determined by the positions of the planets, especially Venus. It is ironic that Tikal was the victim in this momentous event since Tikal itself would engage actively in many "star wars" in its future.

Lizard Head II (E Te II)[34]

The 22nd ruler of Tikal has been identified as lying in Burial 195 on the North Terrace, beneath temple Structure 5D-32. His name glyph has been described as a jawless reptilian head with the *te* sign in its mouth and is repeated after the 15th ruler. The name occurs in painted texts on two polychrome tripod plates accompanying the burial.

Lizard Head's succession follows the death of Double Bird sometime after his dedicatory stela in AD 557. The defeat of Tikal by Caracol in AD 562 may have prompted Double Bird's death, and hence the succession of Lizard Head. His tomb under 5D-32 follows the pattern of the previous North Terrace temple burials established by First Crocodile and Stormy Sky with a placement progression from west to east through time, but not in an unbroken succession, since ten rulers intervene between Stormy Sky and Lizard Head.

Lizard Head's name has been reported from a number of other painted vessels, not from his tomb and these may be references to the Tikal ruler in some other context from outside the city. The ceramics and other contents of his grave complex are from the beginning of the Ik ceramic phase but show a continuing interest in stuccoed and painted objects (*ill. 59*). New kinds of objects emerged from this tomb, objects of perishable material that had been treated with a stucco/paint surfacing. These included four carved figurines of the deity K'awil (*ill. 60*), whose name is used by many Tikal rulers; a wooden yoke (from the Maya ballgame); and stuccoed gourds. The fragility of such items makes their archaeological recovery quite rare.

While the contents of Lizard Head's tomb tell us little about who he was and who his parents were, they do tell us that the Early Classic period at Tikal had reached a climax of artistic style and that this style was distinctive to the city (*pl. IV* and *ill 61*).

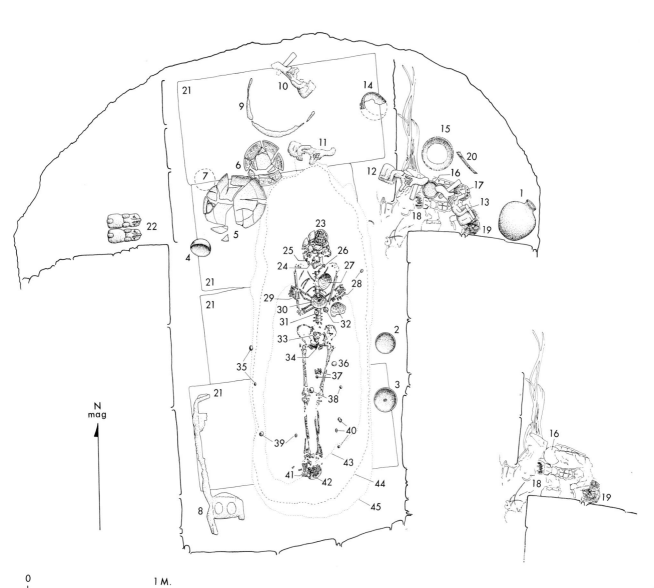

59 (above) Burial 195 was discovered beneath
Temple 5D-32 on the North Terrace and is
attributed to the 22nd Lord of Tikal, Lizard
Head II. The burial contained many complex
wooden and stuccoed objects.

60 (right) Four wooden figurines were found
in the tomb as a set. Three of them were
preserved sufficiently to display as shown
here. Originally identified as the four chacs,
they are now called k'awils, the deities of
power.

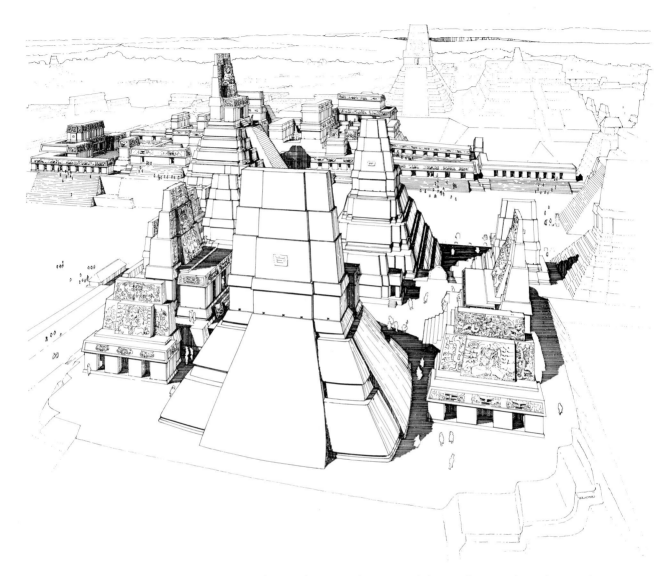

61 *Reconstruction drawing by H. Stanley Loten of the North Acropolis and Great Plaza with the Central Acropolis in the background. The time period is in the early 9th century.*

The later half of the Early Classic at Tikal saw a shift from artistic influence from the Mexican Highlands back into a distinctive Maya style. However, the influence of warfare that came from the highlands had a disastrous effect. The animosity between Tikal and Calakmul shifted through a series of alliances alternating with attacks upon a variety of cities, almost all of which is known from outside Tikal. This great metropolis fell silent as it suffered a major defeat.

Table 3
Chronology of Early Classic Tikal kings
Time span AD 402 – AD 562 (160 years)

Name	Date	Event	Source	Ruler No
Yax Ain I	AD 402 (?)	kalomte	Stela 31	10th
(First Crocodile)	AD 420	died	Stela 5, El Zotz	
Siyah Chan K'awil	AD 411	ahau	Stela 31	11th
(Stormy Sky)	AD 426	kalomte	Stela 31	
	AD 456	died	Stela 40	
	AD 457	tomb painting	Burial 48	
	AD 458	buried	Stela 40	
K'an Ak	AD 458	ahau	Stela 40	12th
(Yellow Peccary)	AD 468	dedicated Stela 40	Stela 40	
	AD 475	ruling	Stela 9	
	AD 488?	died?	Stela 3	
13th ruler (no name)	AD 488?	accession?	Stela 3	13th
Chak Toh Ich'ak II	AD 495	ruling	Stela 7, 15	14th
(Jaguar Claw II)				
E Te I	AD 497	ruling	Stela 8	15th
(Lizard Head I)				
16th ruler (no name)	no dates		"black pot"	16th
17th ruler (no name)	AD 514	ruling	Stela 6	17th
K'uk' Ahau?	AD 511?	accession as ahau?	Stela 23	18th
(Lord Quetzal?)				
Kalomte Balam?	AD 527	accession?	Stela 10	19th
(Curl Head)				
Chak Toh Ich'ak III	AD 537	probable death	Stela 17	20th
(Jaguar Claw III)				
Yax K'uk' Mo'?	AD 537	accession	Stela 17	21st
(Double Bird)	AD 537	Stela 17 dedication	Stela 17	
E Te II?	AD 562?	accession?	Caracol Altar 21	22nd
(Lizard Head II)	no date	Burial 195 (5D-32)		

62 *For several centuries the Lost World Pyramid was the tallest structure at Tikal, seen here from the north side following excavation and partial reconstruction.*

CHAPTER SEVEN

ARCHITECTURE AT TIKAL

Preclassic through Early Classic

Architecture at Tikal is a subject worthy of a volume of its own which cannot be overlooked here. The subject is divided into two parts because of its complexity. This chapter deals in a cursory fashion with styles and shapes from the initial settlement in the Middle Preclassic until the end of the Early Classic (800 BC–AD 550). The even more complex but better known Late Classic styles are discussed in Chapter Twelve.

A major spurt of physical and conceptual growth occurred in the Late Preclassic period at Tikal both in terms of the size of the population and in the ambitions of architectural size. For the first time we find monumentality in the architecture at a level that demands recognition of a high civilization. Large work forces had to be free from the pursuit of food production in order to construct projects on the scale that was achieved both in the North Acropolis and the Lost World Pyramid group. A population of several thousand must have enlivened this city in order to produce an independent kingdom capable of creating such grand architectural towers. The Lost World Pyramid, up to its last phase of construction in the Early Classic period, remained the highest structure in Tikal until the end of the 7th century AD, at over 30 m in height being slightly higher than Structure 5D-22 on the North Acropolis. For half a millennium, it was this structure that first broke the horizon for visitors as they approached the city of Tikal from any direction (*ill. 62*).

The Classic style of Tikal architecture was born during this period. To some analysts this style has appeared severe by comparison to the baroque ornateness devised at other Maya cities such as Palenque with its florid arches and pagoda-like roof lines. The distinctive style of the Puuc region in Mexico covered exterior wall spaces with masks in a litany of prayer by architectural decoration. By comparison, the Tikal style is indeed severe, but not one bit less impressive. The architectural style of Tikal plays with light and shadow, emphasizing change of plane in both horizontal and vertical surfaces. Corners are seldom single sharp angles. Instead the plan line has an inset – a false corner – that emphasizes the real corner with a bracket on both sides (*ill. 63*). Jain architecture in the 10th to 14th centuries in India utilized the same device to decorate and emphasize corners. Vertically, the change of plane toyed with opposites. The slope of a terrace that characterizes the stepped pyramid was broken into vertical parts, representing elements from a simple thatched structure (*ill. 64*). Where the basal platform of a house would be, now there was an

63 *(left)* The addition of shadow planes through the use of corner insets can be seen on the multiple platform corners of Temple II. This feature is most common with temple structures and may be a functional identifier.

64 *(below)* A group of thatched houses in San Jose, Peten, showing the use of rock platforms as the house base, a practice that is several millennia old. Also note the horizontal, functional wall dividers showing through the daub.

65 *(right)* The interior rooms in Structure 5D-63 from the Central Acropolis show the effect of a plastered, finished roof vault.

66 *(far right)* The use of side insets, on the otherwise plain sides of temples, creates an interplay of horizontal and vertical lines and planes producing a complex shadow and light pattern that adds liveliness to the structure.

inset, as if the step were real. Above that is a recessed panel, and then an over-hang breaking the sloped line of the platform surface. The Maya introduced these features as compressions of the vertical profile of the most ancient primi-tive house and thus created a series of shadow-lines that had iconographic meaning (*ill. 65*). These two devices, the vertical and the horizontal line breaks, utilized clean lines of architectural construction to create a play of light and shadow over the surfaces of a temple or palace, in addition to decoration with masks and sculptures (*ill. 66*). The horizontal and vertical line breaks were devised during the Preclassic period and remained throughout time, with embellishment, a defining feature of the Tikal style. This style has come to be recognized as the "Central Peten style" in architecture, characterizing a much larger geographic area than just Tikal itself, where it was apparently invented (*ill. 67*).

During the Preclassic and also into the early part of the Early Classic period, masks were used to adorn the facades of platforms, as on the supportive

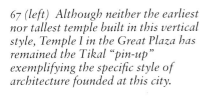

67 (left) Although neither the earliest nor tallest temple built in this vertical style, Temple I in the Great Plaza has remained the Tikal "pin-up" exemplifying the specific style of architecture founded at this city.

68 This reconstruction of a decorative panel on the upper zone of Temple II shows that even though such decoration was limited to certain parts of public buildings, it was nonetheless elaborate.

pyramid of the Lost World structure, and this use seems to go back to the earliest of times. Unlike other parts of the Maya lowlands, the architecture of Tikal utilized vertical surface decoration only on the supportive platforms, the upper zones and the roof combs of a structure (*ills. 68* and *69*). Decoration on the surface of the walls of a temple or palace was very rare at Tikal. Mask decoration below the level of a structure's upper zone fell into disuse in the Late Classic Period, when the Tikal style is best defined and at its most austere.

69 (left) The upper zone and roof comb of Temple IV is likely the physically largest spread of decoration at Tikal. The seated king facing east in the center of the roof comb is barely visible.

Architecture and style at Tikal

An architectural style goes much beyond such questions of surface treatment. A brief outline here of the variability in architectural styles at Tikal may be useful to the reader at this point, since it becomes increasingly important in the progression of the city's history.

The story of architectural development of the ancient Maya reaches far beyond the limits of Tikal. The forms and variations of architecture had their origins in the lowly Maya house, a thatched-roofed structure made of perishable materials, usually known as wattle-and-daub in the Old World. The Maya version of wattle-and-daub was a simple building with walls of sticks, woven together by vines and then covered by mud and stucco, and finally whitewashed (see *ill. 64*). The roof was the most complicated affair. A series of beams and trusses were held together by vines and then covered with a series of layers of palm thatch (*ill. 70*). The type of palm used varied by region. In Tikal it is called "guano" palm which has nothing to do with bat dung (the other meaning of the word), but is simply a local variant of the fan palm (*ill. 71*). The elements that make up a stone structure are all derived from the basic wattle-and-daub house. The way in which these elements are used varied from region to region. The Tikal variety of style is one of the most elegantly simple in the Maya area.

Structures built entirely of stone, mortar, and fill comprise only a small portion of Maya architecture, since the thatched perishable building was numerically far more common in ancient times and is still with us today. In theory, the perishable version was developed around the same time as agriculture was introduced in the area, around 1500 BC or earlier. Its form has changed little, and can still be seen today in all parts of the Maya area. It is the stone structures that evolved differently in different areas, which brings us to the question of local style.

A major distinction is made between *platforms* and *structures*. We have used both words up to now without an explanation. Some platforms are very large and were designed to support more than one structure. The North Acropolis, for example, embodies a number of such platforms, causing it to be raised above the surrounding terrain, and justifying the use of the term "acropolis" or "high place" borrowed from the Classical world. Other platforms are relatively small and are designed to support and raise a single structure. A structure may have more than one elevating platform, stacked in diminishing size, creating the effect of a pyramid. This was the case with the Lost World Pyramid and with all buildings described as pyramids at Tikal (*pl. VIII*).

On the other hand, structures have a number of separate components when the profile is considered. At the base there is usually a "building platform" which is conceptualized as an integral part of the whole structure, and different from other larger platforms described above. The building itself is vertically divided between a lower and upper zone. The lower zone includes the building

70 (right) The truss-and-beam structure required to create a house roof is a complex and very ancient technique. Tied only with vines, and entirely created from local products of the forest, this system is still used today. This house was under construction in the Tikal village in 1959.

71 (below) The process of roof thatching can be seen in its various stages in the Tikal village, as it was being built in 1959.

walls, while the upper zone is an exterior reflection of the stone corbeled vault that supports the interior. This vault is a "corbeled arch," not a true arch, which the Maya did not achieve. The difference lies in a "key stone" set between the two sides of corbeling. The Greeks and Romans realized the role of a pressure receiver in this position while the Maya did not.Instead, Maya architecture relies upon the cantilever principle with a capstone instead of the key stone of the true arch.

The three vertical components of a structure – the building platform, the lower zone walls, and the upper zone – in turn reflect the same parts on a primitive perishable structure: namely the stone platform that served as the building's base; the stick and plaster walls, and the thatched roof, respectively.

Because the prototype roof was necessarily slanted, the stone version is usually also slanted. In the Tikal style the degree of roof slant (in the upper zone) is very slight, and sometimes even vertical. The Tikal architects were always frugal in their interpretation of life forms. At other regional style sites, such as Palenque, the roof slant is very steep, more closely reflecting the slant of a thatched roof.

It is common for the upper zone to be decorated at Tikal while the lower zone very rarely supports decoration. This is an item of style which separates the Central Peten style of regional architecture from other regions, where decoration of the lower zone is common, especially in the northern Maya regions.

On the roof of the structure there may be another level of decorative construction called a "roof comb," which itself may be plain or decorated. At Tikal the presence of a tall roof comb is usually an identifier of the function of a "temple," although its use is not restricted to them. There are other identifying features to help distinguish between structures functioning as temples, palaces, or something else.

This question gives rise to another archaeological problem in identifying the function of a structure. At Tikal there is a gradual metamorphosis through time in the shape of temples. In the earliest stages of development the buildings that we call temples are wide and low in proportion, with three frontal doorways. The simplest statement, always subject to exceptions, is that by the Late Classic period (and we will talk about this much more in a later chapter) temples became taller and narrower in proportion, with a single frontal doorway. The effect of elevating the temple structure so that its single doorway appears to be located in the heavens to the viewer on the ground below was a style that was initiated in Tikal and limited to a rather narrow distribution of imitators in the central Peten region (*see ill. 67*).

Structures that are called "palaces" are even more complex in their variation of form. Because of the Maya habit of razing old structures to build new ones, little is known about palace structures in the Preclassic period. Remnants of the basal platforms tell us that they existed, but details above this vertical level are scant.

Palaces have been re-named as "range-type structures" in an effort at objectivity which recognizes that most of these buildings have numerous rooms that are ranged in a variety of ways.[1] The Central Acropolis of Tikal is a complex of range-type structures that grew from the Late Preclassic until the collapse and abandonment of the city. Most, but not all, of its buildings are of the palace type, although there are very many differing functions involved, reflecting the daily life of a royal court. Only a handful of these buildings have been identified by function with any confidence, and only one served as a family residence. This one, Structure 5D-46, was the clan house of the Jaguar Claw family as described in Chapter Five.

More common than the elaborate stone structures that make Tikal so

spectacular are the much smaller and barely noticeable "housemounds," so-called because there is seldom standing architecture. These buildings were not constructed entirely of stone, but incorporated varying amounts of perishable materials as described earlier. Depending upon the wealth of the house builder, a simple house platform can have its own range of complexity. At the very simplest level is a low, crude platform of earth and stone often leaving little physical evidence on the surface (*ill. 72*). From this lowest level the complexity increases to include several tiers of platforms with well-faced stones and plaster finish. Walls were sometimes built with low stone footings, and sometimes had stone construction right up to the vault, which was still made of thatch. For a house structure, the vault was always of perishable material. These were the houses of the people, ranging in cost of construction from the very poor for the peasant farmer to quite elaborate for the wealthy merchant or ranking officer in the hierarchy of the society.

72 (above) Archaeologist Bennet Bronson excavates house structures that had no visible surface dimension, and thus do not appear on the Tikal ruins map. Test excavations in the forest showed that such "invisible" structures were a common feature of the city.

73 (right) The small ballcourt adjacent to Temple I (Structure 5D-74) shows the elements of this type of building: two parallel structures with sloping benches on the interior of the "court." The Central Acropolis is in the background.

There exist other kinds of specialized structures whose functions are identifiable by their equally specialized shapes. Examples include the sweat bath with low roof, fire pit and benches. Ballcourts are a common and specialized type of structure requiring the special features demanded by the ballgame – a major feature of Classic Maya ceremonial life (*ill. 73*). These features include sloping side benches that bounce a struck ball back into the court, and scoring markers which may or may not still be present. At Tikal the greatest number of examples of these special function structures are known from the Late Classic period. An Early Classic mural showing ballplayers was found near the Lost World complex by Laporte, associated with the ravaged palace complex in Group 6C-XVI.

Twin-pyramid groups are another architecturally specialized, local feature of Tikal and will be reserved for later description due to their importance to Late Classic growth of the city.

VIII *A series of stacked platforms creates the pyramid effect, which is most easily seen on Temple I with its nine platforms and elegant proportions. From below the temple itself appears to be in the heavens.*

IX *After excavation and partial restoration, the palace complex of Jaguar Claw I is revealed to be a noble and royal household now known prosaically as 5D-46.*

VIII, IX

CHAPTER EIGHT

THE HIATUS:
WAR AND OUTSIDE DOMINANCE

The prevalence of warfare at Tikal is a feature throughout the most of the life of the city for which records are available. Virtually the entire Classic period is characterized by escalating warfare. Researchers[1] have argued that the introduction of the Mexican spearthrower known as the *atlatl* had an important effect on the way warfare was conducted at Tikal. Before its introduction skirmishes in the forest with short-distance spears and hand-held weapons limited the amount of damage suffered by the opposing forces. The spearthrower (or more properly dart-thrower) changed all that and made long-distance thrusts a matter of deadly accuracy. This instrument had been introduced to Tikal during the time of Jaguar Claw I. The personage known as Spearthrower Owl,[2] a contemporary and possible relative of Jaguar Claw I, even used the instrument as part of his name glyph (*see ill. 43*). The first great event that is likely to have been affected by this instrument was the conflict between Tikal and Uaxactun in the mid-4th century described in Chapter Five in connection with the character Fire-Born.

The role of warfare clearly escalated from this early date. The causes of alliance and enmity are presumed to rise from either economic sources or disputes rooted in familial dissent. Alliance was often achieved by the device of marrying women of one city's royal family into that of another city. Tikal had such marriage-based alliances with a number of its neighbors, near and far. They did not prevent a breakdown of the friendly relationship which often ended in armed conflict between former allies. We know a little about these relationships that led up to and continued during the Hiatus at Tikal.

The traditional date for the end of the Early Classic period falls between AD 550 and 600. At Tikal the date of this major cultural transition depended upon local events which have been blurred by the prevalence of warfare. A major defeat of Tikal is recorded in the year AD 562 at the hands of the city of Caracol, working in conjunction with Tikal's age-old enemy Calakmul. This claim of defeat of the great capital of the Maya comes from a carved altar at Caracol while other inscriptions from this southeastern city tell us of the alliance with Calakmul.

With this definitive defeat, Tikal fell silent. There are no known carved monuments, no inscriptions of any kind recorded at the city for a period of 125 years. Nor were any structures dedicated or lintels installed for the glory of a ruler. Because the silence falls precisely during the transition between cultural

X *Reconstruction by Terry Rutledge of Hasaw in his glory, based upon the image on Stela 16, but shown in front of his first Temple project, 5D-33-1st in the Great Plaza.*

periods, the problem of analysis of events is especially difficult. The Hiatus itself is unique to the city of Tikal.

However, the written voice from other sectors of the Maya lowlands is not silent during this period. Whatever horrors were happening at Tikal did not occur in the same way at other Maya cities in the lowlands. The fact that inscriptions are lacking at Tikal over this long period of time does not mean that they had not been made. Monuments may well have been erected with texts, but are now lost. Christopher Jones considers that this was a period of intense monument destruction. Warfare was prevalent in the lowlands in general although Tikal was a particular focus – an uncharacteristic loser – during this silent time. The absence of surviving monuments and texts is assumed to be the result of domination or the intense conflict of the period.

The tomb of Lizard Head II (Burial 195) is associated with the transition from the Early to Late Classic periods as known by the contents of the grave, although the exact date of the burial is not known. It is quite possible that this ruler and his burial post-date the defeat of Tikal, in which case Lizard Head II may not be of direct genealogical descent from a Tikal lineage at all. He is one of the earliest rulers of the Late Classic period at the site. This vagueness and uncertainty is characteristic of the change from the Early to Late Classic at Tikal – it remains shrouded in mystery.

The Hiatus at Tikal spans from AD 557, the last recorded date on Stela 17, until AD 682,[3] the first date recorded for the activities of the 26th ruler, Hasaw Chan K'awil. While this ruler was not the first ruler known to hold sway over Tikal at the start of the Late Classic period, he was the first to restore a written record to the city.

The fact that the Hiatus of Tikal spans the change from one major cultural period into the next is surely not a coincidence. One has to ask why a unified cultural system like that exhibited in the Early Classic period, which had already endured some three-and-a-half centuries, should undergo such profound changes as we see in the Late Classic period.

The explanation in part for such change may be that the cultural shifts were not as profound to the ancient Maya as they seem to us. These changes consist primarily of the abandonment of old shapes and influences in the ceramics – the most plastic medium of Maya art. There are also changes in architectural forms. These shifts of style may represent merely a fading of the influence of Teotihuacan in the midst of internal conflicts and warfare. By the time of the Hiatus, the highland civilization itself had dissolved into oblivion. What emerged at Tikal was a very positive Maya form of art and architecture with little outside influence. One could interpret the Early Classic period as a time when Tikal succumbed to the influence of another culture which it viewed as superior, adopting its art forms and its methods and philosophies of warfare. Teotihuacan's influence had led to a brief period of glory for the city. However, the focus of warfare took over the structure of society and escalated throughout the lowlands. For Tikal this ended in a nasty defeat. While rebirth would come later, one of the results of the influence of Teotihuacan was a period of subjugation for Tikal.

The record of the final battle that led to Tikal's Hiatus is sparse at the site itself. The onset of the strife was recorded on Stela 17, in which Double Bird told of a "chopping/cutting" event taking place at a location known as "Flint Mountain" at the hands of Tikal. This location is now identified in the center of the city of Caracol, and the event marked the beginning of a long conflict between the two cities.

Information about Tikal's ensuing fortunes and misfortunes is gleaned from inscriptions at other cities that had not been similarly beaten. Simon Martin and Nikolai Grube[4] have provided the scenario by way of readings of texts from outside Tikal (*see ill. 74*).

Caracol entered into warfare with Tikal after an earlier period of alliance based upon familial interaction. The events leading up to the war with Tikal provide a textbook diagram of political intrigue. We know, for example, that a ruler was installed at the city of Naranjo, lying 42 km to the east of Tikal, under the auspices of the reigning king of Calakmul in AD 546[5] (Naranjo Stela 25). Furthermore, conflict with Calakmul had been in progress for quite some time in the power play between the two cities that may have been rooted in the rivalry for dominance over trade routes. We have to remember that Tikal and Calakmul both sit astride the peninsular divide and thus are alternative places where trade routes could cross in the lucrative overland east–west route that connected the Caribbean to the Usumacinta drainage.

Iconography suggests that these two rival cities had a lot in common. They shared the same protector deity in the form of the jaguar god and both cities had dynastic leaders with related lineage names, Jaguar Claw at Tikal and Fire Jaguar Claw at Calakmul. These convergences suggest an even closer affiliation, perhaps based on family ties that may have once connected the patrons of the two cities. It would not be the only time that enmity between cities was based on an earlier family connection. Not enough information is available yet from Calakmul to point to a common dynastic origin for the two opposing polities. Even if deteriorated family ties had been a factor, the most likely explanation for a rivalry that escalated into bloody warfare lasting a couple of centuries is commercial: competition for control of trade routes.

Meanwhile, Caracol, some 70 km to the southeast of Tikal, had installed a new king under the aegis of Tikal's ruler of the time in AD 553 (dates from Caracol Altar 21 and Stela 6). This must have been the Tikal ruler, Double Bird, according to the record of known dates. This installation of a king at Caracol by Tikal took place only three years before Tikal was at war with the same city. The installation was likely a failed attempt at control without warfare. The texts suggest that this act on Tikal's part was a response to the defection of their neighbor, the city of Naranjo, lying dangerously close to Tikal's eastern flank. The geography is important. Naranjo is only 42 km east of Tikal, and, while not in a straight line, is located between Tikal and Caracol.

Then in AD 556[6] Tikal enacted a formal "axe war" against its former ally Caracol.[7] This type of war, symbolized by an axe, indicates a serious attack with intent to destroy, but unlike a "star war" was not determined by ritual or astronomical timing. The attack was apparently unexpected and hurt Caracol. Then, just six years later in AD 562,[8] Caracol retaliated against Tikal with the first recorded "star war" known in the Maya lowlands. This date is taken as the date of Tikal's fall to Caracol. A "star war" is a full-scale war planned in accordance with specific astronomical events, usually the first appearance in the morning sky of the planet Venus. The heliacal rising of the brilliant "star" in the pre-dawn sky was considered by the Maya as a highly evil portent. As such it was an appropriate herald of warfare, at least on the part of the attacker.

Caracol's act of aggression initiated a type of intensive war that was to be repeated a number of times in the future, between many different cities in the lowlands. Noting the dates of these particular conflicts between Tikal and Caracol we can see that they are a prelude to the end of the Early Classic period as a cultural marker, but the conflicts continue on an accelerated scale during the Late Classic. It would be easy to interpret warfare as the stimulus of change that brought about the end of the Early Classic, and just as easy to see the same cause as slowly building up to the collapse of the Classic culture in the lowlands as a whole.

Altar 21 at Caracol records the defeat of Tikal, and this claim coincides with the Hiatus at Tikal, and therefore bears credence. Although eroded, the text on this important altar includes a reference to Calakmul, the northern capital already known to have been in conflict with Tikal for some time. The reference on Altar 21 suggests that Calakmul was behind or at least in support of this particular and seminal "star war" against Tikal. Calakmul had won a political victory in the struggle for Caracol's allegiance, probably in hurt retaliation for the surprise "axe war" that Tikal had enacted against the disputed city, its former ally. Further reference to an ahau of Calakmul, and his personal emblem glyph, is found on Caracol Stela 3 at the date of AD 572,[9] confirming that the shift in allegiance by Caracol from Tikal to Calakmul was complete. All of these events were critical to both kinds of change that were occurring in the lowlands: in the cultural landmarks that distinguish the Early from the Late Classic; and in the shifts of the political landscape.

Further, in AD 588[10] the birth of a Lord of Caracol is recorded on Panel 1 at Naranjo, suggesting a friendly affiliation between these cities by this time. That a former ally of Tikal displayed friendship with an enemy of Tikal indicates a change in the relationship between these nearest neighbors. This minor event did not bode well for Tikal. It indicated a tightening military presence, slowly but surely encircling the City of Lords, in a classic military pincer movement. Simon Martin's eloquent illustration of these relationships shows graphically what was happening at this time (*ill. 74*).

Inscriptions falling between AD 593 and 672[11] occur at sites both to the west and to the east of Tikal and these indicate that business as usual was being

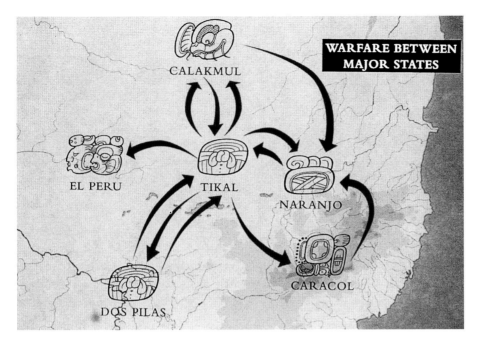

74 *This diagram of the interaction between major sites of the Peten including Tikal was made by Simon Martin and Nikolai Grube.*

conducted on a friendly basis outside Tikal, while they remained hostile towards the great city. Notably, Tikal remains in silence during this entire period. Domination from Caracol, or possibly from a number of sites in collaboration, including Calakmul, seems as good an explanation as any currently available for this silence.

In AD 672[12] the site of Dos Pilas raised a new presence in the political landscape, leading to more speculation about what had been happening at Tikal. At this date, Dos Pilas recorded its own defeat by a "star war" event launched from Tikal, showing that Tikal had revived enough to effect this aggressive attack. As it happened Dos Pilas was a new site with roots in Tikal, but nevertheless, a hostile rival. The evidence substantiates this kind of connection, pointing towards an origin in Tikal for the founders of not just Dos Pilas but its entire political enclave including three other sites: Aguateca, Tamarindito, and Punto de Chimino.[13] One interpretation of the connection between the Dos Pilas polity and Tikal is that collateral members of the royal family at Tikal, realizing that they could never aspire to rulership of the central capital, defected from the city and established a new base to the west toward the end of the Early Classic period. Evidence that this splinter hegemony established a new kingdom at Dos Pilas out of Tikal is found in the dates themselves and the respective site emblem glyphs. The dates for the beginnings of the Dos Pilas group coincide with Tikal's time of intense conflict with surrounding powers.

Also, Dos Pilas itself adopted the Tikal emblem glyph as its own, as if calling itself "New Tikal". To our Western way of thinking this suggests most strongly that a disgruntled member of the Jaguar Claw clan at Tikal defected, realizing that he/she had little hope of power at the central capital, already under serious political and military siege. This personage (or personages) claimed the emblem glyph of the mother site for him/herself and proceeded to establish new allegiances, particularly with cities already hostile to Tikal.

The site of Dos Pilas had come into existence about AD 625,[14] some 47 years before it recorded its own defeat by Tikal. Its establishment apparently occurred under the auspices and support of Calakmul, already well into conflict with Tikal at this time and all too ready to assist defectors.

This assumed dissension and defection from within the royal family must have been a blow to the current ruler already under severe siege by surrounding sites. The piracy of the Tikal city emblem glyph probably would never have succeeded without the support of a powerful ally like Calakmul.

These events have been argued convincingly by Schele, Grube, and Martin. By AD 588 Tikal found itself threatened by Caracol in the southeast, by Naranjo to the nearby east, by the giant Calakmul to the north, and even by the Dos Pilas hegemony to the west. Tikal was virtually surrounded by enemies. The beleaguered city's best allies lay far away, Palenque to the far west and Copan to the far south.

We know that the leader of the attack on Dos Pilas in AD 672 was Shield Skull I (Nu Bak Chak I[15]) of Tikal, the 25th ruler in Tikal's succession, and this event fell within Tikal's period of silence. The record of the event is at Dos Pilas. The last ruler with a written record at Tikal was Lizard Head II, the 22nd ruler. This leaves a gap of two unknown rulers, the 23rd and 24th in the succession. As Genevieve Michel has noted, this is a very murky period with few clues to the identity of these missing rulers.

The clues that do exist come from painted inscriptions on ceramic vessels, one from Tikal and two of unknown provenance. These refer to a minor lord who lived at Tikal under the reign of Lizard Head II.[16] This minor lord, a sahal, was named "Star Jaguar"[17] and he may have become the 23rd ruler. This person's son was called "Long Snout"[18] and he may, in turn, have become the missing 24th ruler. These observations, however, are speculation filling in a cloudy gap. Because of the warfare and defeat of Tikal the rulers of this period could have been interlopers from Caracol, unrelated conquerors from Calakmul, or even suppressed descendants of the Jaguar Claw family itself. We simply do not know. The passage and transformation from the Early to the Late Classic at Tikal was a difficult time.

CHAPTER NINE

RETURN OF THE CLAN JAGUAR CLAW – THE GENIUS OF HASAW CHAN K'AWIL

The Hiatus of silence at Tikal spanned the end of the Early Classic and the beginning of the Late Classic periods at the city. The literary darkness finally came to an end with the raising of monuments by the 26th ruler, Hasaw Chan K'awil. At the time of this writing the name of this "great man" is translated loosely as "Standard Bearer of the Great Sky," or possibly "Heavenly Standard Bearer." On 15 March AD 692[1] this great ruler ended the silence at Tikal by erecting his first pair of monuments, Stela 30 and Altar 14. However, before the long silence was ended some important events took place during the first decades of the Late Classic period. This overlap of the Hiatus into the Late Classic is described in this chapter because of the father-son relationship that existed between an early lord of the Late Classic and the subsequent return to glory effected by Hasaw Chan K'awil.

Texts at other sites as well as later texts at Tikal tell the story of the earliest years of an early ruler of the Late Classic period. This ruler, the 25th in the succession, was called Nu Bak Chak I[2] with the modern nickname of "Shield Skull." There have been no inscriptions found yet at Tikal that are attributable to him directly.

Shield Skull (Nu Bak Chak I[3])

Shield Skull's Maya name has been translated by Schele and Grube as "Oracle Bone Chak," a translation still subject to revision. This king not only had a long period of rule, he fought for the revival of Tikal on both diplomatic and military fronts. Texts from Piedras Negras, Yaxchilan, Palenque, and Dos Pilas tell some of the story. He engaged in battle well to the west of his base city, taking captives in Yaxchilan in August AD 659.[4] This must have been quite difficult for several reasons – the great distance from Tikal; the logistical needs of troops so far afield; and the unsettled state of affairs back home in Tikal. This victory at Yaxchilan was recorded at Piedras Negras, at the time an ally of Calakmul, while Yaxchilan was under the domination of Piedras Negras. Therefore, Shield Skull's attack on Yaxchilan was in line with the established ranks of alliance and enmity.

Texts describing the campaigns of Shield Skull against Yaxchilan and those of Pacal of Palenque against the site of Pomona (near Palenque) suggest an

Shield Skull

alliance between these two important rulers – even a companion-at-arms kind of relationship. These western battles represented the height of allegiance between Tikal and Palenque. On 13 August AD 659,[5] just six days after the Yax-chilan skirmish, Shield Skull's arrival at Palenque was celebrated on a panel of the Temple of the Inscriptions itself. This location was one of Palenque's most important sources of public record, testifying to the significance that Pacal placed upon Shield Skull's friendship.

While Pacal of Palenque was successful in his local campaigns against Pomona, Shield Skull went on to battles against Dos Pilas, a protectorate of Calakmul, and the defector group from Tikal. On 8 December AD 672[6] he led a battle against Dos Pilas. Two subsequent battles engaged combined forces of Dos Pilas and Calakmul and ended in two defeats for Shield Skull on 20 December AD 677 and on 30 April AD 679[7] respectively. During this last skirmish Shield Skull either died or was taken captive and this is the last firm date associated with his name. We know that Shield Skull's successor was Hasaw Chan K'awil, his son, and we guess that the succession in AD 682 must have occurred shortly after Shield Skull's death.

There are a few other mentions of Shield Skull's name from later texts at Tikal written by his son Hasaw Chan K'awil, which lend a curious note to his identification. Hasaw refers to his predecessor with the term "father" in a lineage statement and even names "Lady Jaguar Throne" as Hasaw's mother and Shield Skull's wife. This has all the appearance of a very definite lineage statement. However, Shield Skull is also referred to in the same text as the "man from the west," and there can be no doubt from his history that he spent a great deal, if not most of his time away, far to the west of Tikal.

The tomb of Shield Skull is identified as the individual in Burial 23 beneath the temple Structure 5D-33-1st, on the North Terrace and fronting the North Acropolis because of the construction date of the tomb. This building dominated the Great Plaza when it was constructed by Hasaw Chan K'awil, changing the cosmic configuration of the Great Plaza forever, and leading the way for the future development of the Great Plaza's triad of Great Temples. The building of his father's memorial and his reaction to the political events that led to his father's death are part of the story of Hasaw Chan K'awil, which follows.

Hasaw Chan K'awil (Heavenly Standard Bearer)[8]

The 26th ruler in the Tikal succession can be characterized as the "great man" in the history of the city. He acceded to power on 3 May AD 682,[9] a time of year when the heat is building and the clouds form in the east every day, heralding the coming of the summer rains. He was inaugurated at this time into the role of kalomte of the city, the highest rank of ruler. Not for another ten years did the king erect a carved monument with the inscriptions that ended the literary hiatus of the city. During these years he was extremely busy re-building the prestige that had been lost during the years of domination. One of his activities was the construction of Structure 5D-33-1st, which covered his father's tomb.

Heavenly Standard Bearer
(Hasaw Chan K'awil)

There are no firm dates for this building project, the first truly great temple to be raised at the site and the first to herald a new style of architecture for the Maya lowlands (*ill. 75*). The raising of this building signified the reversal of fortune for Tikal and the event was surrounded by ceremony that can be reconstructed from the stratigraphy of burials deep beneath it and caches enclosed within it. Before Hasaw's construction project began there existed an earlier temple built over the tomb of Stormy Sky, one of his ancestors. This latter tomb and its temple were centered on the sacred axis of the North Acropolis. Stormy Sky's temple was beautifully decorated with masks flanking the stair on two levels of terraces, but was still low enough not to obscure the grandeur of Temple 22, the highest structure looming above the north side of the Acropolis.

Until the higher building was created above 5D-33-2nd, the architectural configuration of the North Acropolis served as its own cosmogram, a realm of the dead, a realm of kings ruling as gods, focused on its own high point, Temple 22. The original temple of 5D-33, below which Stormy Sky lay in state, was lower in height but on the same sacred axis as 5D-22.

Hasaw Chan K'awil changed all that. He selected the site of Temple 33 as the place to begin a new cosmogram and began with his father's burial. Burial 23 was excavated deep into the bed rock of the very ridge that had become the most sacred place in Tikal, a little south of the tomb of Stormy Sky. The tomb builders had to excavate down through the existing temple to create Shield Skull's final resting place. Part of the ritual of the construction of the new temple was the sacred burial of Stormy Sky's most important monument, Stela 31. This stela had been desecrated during the occupation of the usurpers from Caracol. Now it was reverentially placed into the old temple itself, treating both the temple and the old stela as if they were themselves deceased ancestors to be buried under the new architectural wonder. First the stela was set into a pit inside the back room of the old temple. The roof of the temple was then razed as was customary for temple renewal, covering the stela as if it were a cache dedicating the new structure that would rise above it. Construction of the mighty new temple proceeded above the revered ancestral cache.

At the same time a similar ceremony was conducted for Stela 26, the "Red Stela" that had declared the glory of either the 20th or 21st ruler, we still don't know which. This stela had suffered the same fate as that of Stormy Sky's Stela 31 and Hasaw tended to its reparation at the same time, but without completely burying the stela or razing the temple. He was honoring and restoring the glory of the defaced ancestors, whether they were direct lineage ancestors or merely predecessors in the holy succession. It was a time of renewal and restoration for the City of Lords.

With the temple called 5D-33-1st, built as a memorial above his father's tomb, Hasaw introduced a new style of architecture to the lowland region. A high, soaring series of stepped platforms supported a temple structure with a single doorway. The visual effect for the viewer on the plaza floor was to emphasize the vertical dimensions such that the temple seemed to be lifted into the heavens. From the time of Hasaw's accession to power until the estimated time of his grandson's death is a span of 118 years. During this period, this new Tikal temple style, introduced by Structure 5D-33-1st, developed and flourished, marking the city's peak of achievement.

In the short period of a mere four years, three political events took place in the Maya lowlands that were to shape Tikal's future. These were: the accession to power at Tikal of Hasaw Chan K'awil in AD 682, already noted; the death of Pacal of Palenque, Tikal's great ally, late in the year of AD 683;[10] and finally, the accession to power of a young man named "Fire Jaguar Claw" as king of Calakmul on 3 April AD 686.[11] These events represented the appearance of the strongest power in the Late Classic period at Tikal; loss of a powerful ally in the west for Tikal; and the rise to office of a virulent ruler-king at Tikal's most powerful rival city. The stage was set for major upheaval in the Maya lowlands.

Hasaw's first major construction and round of ceremonies honored death and restoration, but his second work focused on the honor of time. On 15 March AD 692[12] a new architectural group was dedicated with the inscription that broke the silence of the Hiatus. This inscription is found on Altar 14 accompanying Stela 30 in the twin-pyramid group known as "M Group" or Group 3D-1. One of Tikal's many twin-pyramid groups, this one followed an earlier sequence of structures that marked the end of the sacred katun, the 20-year period in the Maya calendar. Curiously, Altar 14 which bears the important date is carved with a giant ahau face in the style of Caracol, a style that presumably was introduced to Tikal under its period of domination. The curiosity is that the restorer of the ancient family lineage would still utilize this foreign symbol of defeat. The Tikalenos may have become accustomed to this "style" during the long Hiatus.

The chronology of Hasaw's life and the extraordinary events that colored it are known from a variety of sources, not all of them from Tikal. The construction of Temple 5D-33-1st and of the twin-pyramid M-Group have already been mentioned. Other major monuments that were built or planned by this unusual ruler include the Great Temples numbered I and II, facing each other across the Great Plaza, and creating the most recognized landmarks of Tikal; another twin-pyramid configuration called N-Group, with significance that will be explained below; and Structure 5D-57, a decorated palace in the Central Acropolis which likely served as his personal house and the location of the royal court of Tikal during his reign. There are doubtless many other

75 (right) Structure 5D-33-1st was the first temple built in the Tikal style and the first temple of Hasaw Chan K'awil, designed to cover the tomb of his father, Shield Skull. It is on the North Terrace, facing the Great Plaza.

monumental architectural achievements that were built by Hasaw, but to date they remain unidentified. Each of these buildings played a role in the development of Tikal as a leading capital in the Maya lowlands. The effect of these public works combined with Hasaw's military conquests changed in a positive manner both the physical appearance of the city and its role in the context of the political landscape of the times. These changes were pivotal to the history of the city and Hasaw's rule can be characterized as the most important of the city's known 31 rulers.[13] The last king to have had such a profound effect on the fortunes of the city was Jaguar Claw I who built the family clan house in the Central Acropolis that was to be occupied until the very abandonment of the city. Hasaw's known works, the six major buildings described above, all survived until the collapse as well.

A number of specific, significant events that marked Hasaw's life are known from a variety of sources. The events include certain important ceremonies, construction projects, and wars. The sequence of their occurrence has been reconstructed from hieroglyphic texts most of which were not contemporaneous with the event recorded. Rather they are retrospective, telling of events in the past, in some cases after his death. The primary sources include the long text on Lintel 3 of Temple I, the temple that was dedicated to the ruler's memory and housed his burial chamber; and from objects that were included in his tomb. The events are described here in their sequence of occurrence, which is often different from their sequence of being recorded.

Hasaw Chan K'awil acceded to power in the role of supreme kalomte on 3 May AD 682. Less than a year later, on 28 August AD 683, the greatest ruler of Palenque, Hanab Pacal, died. Since Palenque had been an important political ally of Tikal, the western anchor, as it were, this death must have had a profound effect on the leadership of Tikal.

In a flash-forward, many years later, a king of Copan called 18 Rabbit recorded the titles of rulers of Copan, Palenque, Tikal, and Calakmul in AD 731 on Stela A. Hasaw was the contemporary ruler king of Tikal at the time, and by then he was very close to death. Of the four cities cited in that famous Copan text identifying the cornerstones of the Maya world, three were friendly and only was in hostile relationship to the others. That one was Calakmul.

The defeat of Calakmul

It was a war event that reversed Tikal's fortunes and changed forever the political landscape of the lowlands. This event was recorded by Hasaw on Lintel 3 of his mortuary building, Temple I, as having happened on 5 August AD 695.[14] This war was a major event, following in the tradition established by Caracol's attack on Tikal 133 years earlier. Determined in its timing by the position of the planet Venus, this engagement was launched against the long-established rival Calakmul, which for many katuns had been harassing Tikal and encircling the city with allies. It was under the patronage of Calakmul that Caracol

76 Drawing of an orthostat panel on the lower zone of one end wall of Structure 5D-57, a palace built by Hasaw Chan K'awil in the Central Acropolis. It depicts the lord in his battle armor.

had been able to defeat Tikal before the Hiatus, so this enmity began in earnest in AD 562. For the intervening 13 decades Tikal had been in a cultural eclipse, engaged in both hot and cold wars with Calakmul. The event recorded by Hasaw definitively terminated Tikal's period of anguish at the hands its antagonist. The defeat was accomplished at an unspecified location outside Calakmul and against the ruler of that city, one Fire Jaguar Claw[15] (Yich'ak K'ak). The possible significance of this name, likely related to that of a Tikal dynasty, now turning up at the enemy city is discussed below. From Tikal's point of view this defeat of a Calakmul ruler was a cause for celebration, and it gave rise to a whole series of related ceremonial events at the victorious city. The leaders of Tikal were not about to let such a long-awaited glory pass unnoticed.

Thirteen days after the official conquest of Calakmul's ruler, it was recorded that an official of that city named Ah Bolon was captured on 18 August AD 695.[16] This minor event related to the enormously important overthrow of the Calakmul overlord was recorded on a decorated upper zone of a palace structure in the Central Acropolis, Structure 5D-57, believed to be a house built by Hasaw. Although minor, the event occurred exactly 13 days after the victory itself. Two depictions of Hasaw himself were found on Structure 5D-57 (ill. 76), in full battle armor in both cases. The house was probably built in commemoration of the great victory. The capture scene with text telling the details is found on the upper zone of the east end of the building. The highly stylized plate-like appearance of the armor is related to the old-fashioned Teotihuacan

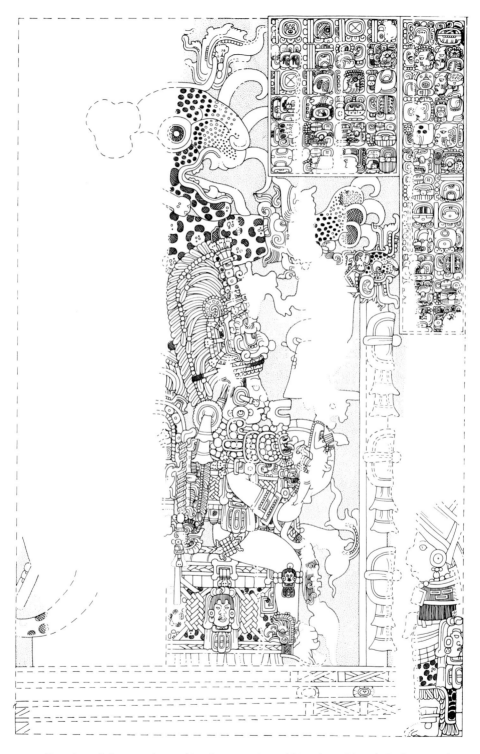

77 *Drawing of the complex and intricate carving of Lintel 3 in Temple I, showing the lord seated on a throne.*

style of body armor. This may well be the last remnant of the highland style to occur at Tikal. The fact that capture of this miserable individual occurred 13 days after the main victory could well be a ceremonial re-telling of the event couched in a sacred time distance, rather than a reflection of reality.

Forty days after the capture and killing of Fire Jaguar Claw[17] of Calakmul, three more events took place. These events were commemorated on Lintel 3 of Temple I and all took place on 14 September AD 695.[18] In their recorded sequence these events were: firstly, Hasaw sat upon the captured palanquin, symbol of the city of Calakmul, a sacred object which bore its own identifying name – Nu Balam Chacmal[19] (*ill. 77*); secondly, a bloodletting ceremony was observed by the "Holy Lord of Tikal" that is, Hasaw;[20] and thirdly, a dedication ceremony took place. While the text does not indicate where this dedication occurred, it is possible that it was a re-dedication of Temple 33, or at some other location. The stela buried there honored Hasaw's direct ancestor, "Stormy Sky." The actor in this ceremony is described as the child of "Lady Jaguar Throne" and "Shield Skull" (Nu Bak Chak), known to be Hasaw's parents.

The next recorded event in the life of Hasaw occurred on 30 November AD 695,[21] 117 days after the victory over Calakmul. This event was recorded on an incised bone contained among the burial treasures accompanying Hasaw in his tomb under Temple I, and named Burial 116. The text proclaimed that a captive was defeated by a person named "Split Earth," whose place emblem closely resembles that of Calakmul. The indication is that a person close to Hasaw had been defeated by someone from Calakmul – a possible retaliation for the earlier defeat of the latter city.[22]

Royal sorrow: the story on Altar V

As time progressed, the next important thing we know about Hasaw's life is the dedication of another twin-pyramid group marking the end of katun 14 in the Maya calendar. This group was constructed close to the present location of Temple IV, but well before that highest of all temples at Tikal had been built. The group is identified on the maps of the site as "N Group" or "Group 5C-1." Excavation of the group showed that the north boundary of the complex was built against the wall of a pre-existing causeway which led to a point unknown, but probably to an earlier version of Temple IV, as we know it.[23] This intriguing bit of evidence suggests that when N Group was built it was not the westernmost point of the city center. The twin-pyramid complex was built to celebrate the closing of katun 14 under the reign of Hasaw, on 1 December AD 711.[24] Although it is an archaeological convention to consider this date as the date of the group, the structures obviously took time to build, so that its dedication in AD 711 recorded the culmination of the construction process. This is true of all major architectural monuments.

As with all twin-pyramid groups, the northern enclosure contained a royal stela and accompanying altar. Here, they are Stela 16 depicting Hasaw in full ceremonial livery, and Altar 5 which lay at his feet. However, the contents of the depiction on the altar are unique among twin-pyramid groups at Tikal, and indeed of all altars in the city (*ills. 78–80*). The scene on Altar 5 is totally different from any carved before or after. This altar has an importance likely greater than any other at the site because of its multiple roles, recording a complex segment of Hasaw's life and carefully positioned so that the location itself supplements the story contained. The altar would later determine an axial line that would define the alignment of Temples I and II in the Great Plaza itself.[25]

The ring of glyphs surrounding the edge of the altar could not contain the whole story that had to be told.[26] There are supplementary panels within the background on which the narrative continues. The scene depicts two men shown either in kneeling position, or standing behind a flat object, facing each other, dressed in quite distinctive livery, both in the heraldry of their headdress designs, and in the objects of symbolic rank held in their hands. Between them is a neat arrangement of human bones, apparently piled in a quadrant and surmounted by a jawless human skull. The text speaks of a woman who was Hasaw's wife and it is presumed that the bones are hers. The name given for the woman is not the same name recorded elsewhere in the city as the mother of Hasaw's son Yik'in Chan K'awil (Ruler B). There is a mystery here regarding the various names ascribed to Hasaw's wife (or wives, as the case may be). The inscription on Altar 5 is very complex but Grube and Schele have worked out a decipherment of the sequence of glyphs and the strange story which they tell. The figure on the left is interpreted as that of Hasaw himself, while the figure on the right is a nobleman, probably from Calakmul.[27] At the time, Tikal and Calakmul were still in a state of high hostility, since Hasaw had killed the king of Calakmul 16 years before. The bones are thought to be those of Hasaw's wife who had died on 24 May AD 703,[28] some eight years before the dedication of this altar. The interpretation followed here suggests that this woman had been buried at the site of Topoxte, a small city to the southwest of Tikal on a lake of the same name. Presumably, this was her place of birth and her remains were returned there for burial. This small city had come under the domination of Calakmul in its campaign of expansion in the region now known as the Peten. Under such domination, royal burials were in danger of desecration, and because of Hasaw's role in the overthrow of Calakmul, any relative of his would be a direct target for such desecration. The complex text of Altar 5 indicates that the lord of Calakmul escorted Hasaw with safe passage into the enemy-held territory of Topoxte in order to collect and retrieve the bones of this royal lady.[29] The implication is that the lord from Calakmul was also related to her by blood rather than marriage, and for this reason co-operated under truce with Hasaw to save the lady's remains from desecration. All of this action took place shortly before the end of the katun, so that the dates involved lead up to the katun dedication itself (*ill. 81*).

XI *The mosaic jade vessel from Burial 196 bears a strong resemblance to a similar one found in Burial 116 (ill. 87) but portrays a woman (Hasaw's wife?).*

XII

XIII

The mystery of the woman's identity revolves around the use of names. On Altar 5 the name given initially is Na Tunte Kaywak. Later in the context of removing the bones a different name is given. Neither name is the same as that given elsewhere as the name of Hasaw's wife (Lady Twelve Macaw). Explanations of these multiple names include: the possibility that Hasaw had more than one wife; that the woman's Topoxte name and her Tikal name were different; or that two of the names were titles rather than proper names.

Grube and Schele also noted that while we know little about the rules of diplomacy of the 8th-century Maya, this interpretation suggests that royal bones and their continuing care was important and that an arrangement to retrieve them from enemy territory was a possibility. This further suggests that major polities were in communication with each other even in times of hostility and that truces were negotiable. Further, it was to Hasaw's advantage to record this exploit and display it in a public place, a place usually reserved for exhibition of a bound prisoner.

In addition to the unique quality of the content of the decoration on Altar 5, analysis suggests that the surface configuration of the figures and their accoutrements are laid out according to geometric rules of integral right triangles.[30] This same principle of artistic planning by geometric rules is important also to the layout of architecture in Tikal, and particularly to the placement of Altar 5, in its physical relationship to Temples I and II of the Great Plaza (see Chapter Twelve).

The completion of the 14th katun is recorded on Stela 16 at 1 December AD 711. This date also terminates the narrative on Altar 5. Christopher Jones noted[31] that although the cache beneath Stela 16 had been looted at an unknown date, Ledyard Smith had retrieved one of the frequently found incised obsidians from this cache, a discovery that allowed W. R. Coe to reconstruct the contents of Cache 32 from beneath Stela 16, showing that they were similar to other stela caches at Tikal. During his investigations of twin-pyramid groups, Jones penetrated deeper beneath the stela butt and found a number of bones as additional and highly unusual cache material.

On the stela face itself, Hasaw is shown in full war livery including a back mask, full headdress, heavy necklace and a pectoral that probably included the very jade beads found in his burial, a skirt with crossed bone symbols and a waistband with human trophy heads and high decorative sandals and anklets. Hasaw holds the ceremonial bar in a horizontal position across his mid-torso, while his head is turned fully to the right side. The regalia and the pose are typical of the Late Classic period at Tikal.

XII *Rollout scene from a Late Classic vessel found in Structure 5C-49 of the Lost World group. The presentation of tribute in the form of a jaguar skin is typical of administrative functions of palaces.*

XIII *The painting by Carlos Vierra made in 1915 depicts Tikal in the years following its abandonment. Despite never having visited the city, Vierra's reconstruction is quite accurate.*

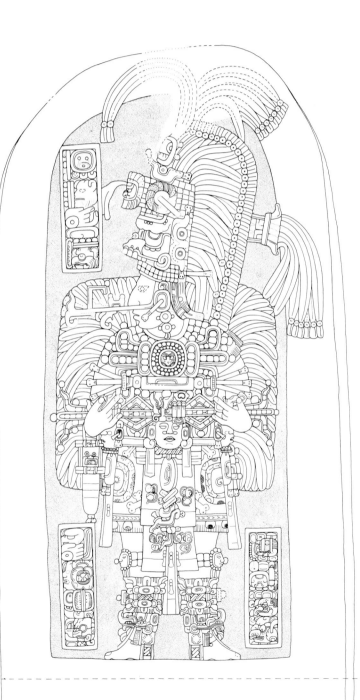

78 (above) Stela 16 was raised by Hasaw Chan K'awil in the twin-pyramid Group N in AD 711 commemorating the 14th katun. The Altar in front commemorates his deceased wife.

79 (right) Detailed drawing of the carving on Stela 16. Hasaw Chan K'awil is depicted in full ceremonial dress, with feathered headdress and back mask. By this date he had been kalomte of Tikal for 29 years.

80 (above) Drawing of the scene and inscription on Altar 5, which accompanied Stela 16. The individual on the left is thought to be Hasaw while the lord on the right is from Calakmul.

81 (left) Reconstruction drawing of the scene on Altar 5 by Terry Rutledge. It is now thought that the scene depicts the exhumation of Hasaw's deceased wife's bones shown between the two lords.

Other known dates and events in Hasaw's life

A number of beautifully carved bones were part of the funerary equipment in Hasaw's tomb. One of these depicts a scene in which Hasaw is being transported in a canoe with "paddler gods" propelling the craft. This scene has been variously interpreted as a death scene in which the king is being taken to the underworld or as a celestial event commemorating the Maya day of creation. As there is no evidence that Hasaw had died by the date carved on the bone, the latter interpretation seems more likely (*ill. 82*).

Another incised bone bears the date 22 October AD 726.[32] The accompanying text honors the death of Ruler 2 at the city of Dos Pilas who was an enemy of Hasaw according to other texts of this time. Hasaw may have been celebrating the death of an enemy, or, enemy or not, of a relative.

On the same bone, another date, about three months later, at 24 January AD 727[33] records the death of an important woman, possibly from the site of Cancuen. This site is perceived as hostile, allied with the large hegemony of Calakmul, but once again, the protagonist could have been a relative of Hasaw.

The ending of the next katun occurred on 18 August AD 731[34] and was commemorated by the construction of the twin-pyramid group Complex O, with a plain stela. The omission of a carved scene and inscription for such an important event while Hasaw should still have been alive suggests that he was too weak, old or ill to attend the dedication. This assumption is supported by the fact that the next recorded date at Tikal is the accession to power of the next king, Hasaw's son, on 8 December AD 734.[35] While this is three years later than the last recorded event in Hasaw's life, we have to remember that his last public date was that on Stela 16 at the end of the 14th katun, some 20 years earlier. The intervening dates come from objects in Hasaw's tomb that likely were among his personal possessions, not used for public display.

The two grandest architectural contributions made by Hasaw to his city were the construction of Temple II and the planning of Temple I (*pl. I*). Their respective dates of construction have not been solved, but both buildings are so important to the ritual and visual presentation of the city that they demand some discussion. The two great temples may have been built simultaneously, or at least partly so, since they were conceived to satisfy more than one cosmic relationship with pre-existing buildings in the city. For example, the two great

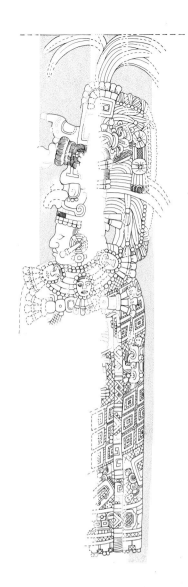

82 (left) Drawing of a canoe scene from one of several incised bones found in Burial 116, the grave of Hasaw Chan K'awil. "Paddler" gods transport the dead lord to the underworld.

83 (right) Drawing of the remains of the carved Lintel 2 from Temple II showing Lady Twelve Macaw, Hasaw's wife in her ceremonial robe. The images carved on the lintels of Temples I and II of the Lord and his wife faced each other.

temples facing each other across the Great Plaza actually define the new cosmic center of the city, replacing the North Acropolis, the older architectural cosmos – the necropolis of kings. Temples I and II form a triad with the temple Structure 5D-33-1st on the North terrace. This triadic formation was the largest yet built at Tikal, observing the classic configuration with temple structures bounding the north, east and west sides of a sacred space. Structure 33-1st became the northern synonym for the North Acropolis itself, representing the heavens where the kings resided. Temples I and II were constructed for their part in such a manner that their physical position aligned with Altar 5, the commemorative stone of Hasaw's wife, as well as in specific configuration with other pre-existing structures in the city. All of this had to be carefully planned, and these plans were clearly made by Hasaw.

Clemency Coggins[36] first suggested that Temple II was constructed in honor of Hasaw's wife. The name assumed for this wife is "Lady Twelve Macaw," the name recorded as the mother of Hasaw's son (Ruler B or Yik'in Chan K'awil). The relationship of this woman to the names recorded on Altar 5 remains a mystery, although the specific alignment formed by Temples I, II and Altar 5 strongly corroborates the interpretation that the woman on the altar and the woman on Temple II are the same. Lintel 2 of Temple II was carved, and the surviving remnant shows the figure of a royally garbed woman, but no text has survived (*ill. 83*). The carved beam of this lintel now resides in the American Museum of Natural History in New York. In his excavations of the Great Plaza, W. R. Coe (Tikal Report 14) determined by the stratigraphy that the beginning of construction of Temple II preceded the beginning of construction of Temple I by a few years. This is significant for a number of reasons. The dates on Altar 5 indicate that Hasaw's wife had died in AD 703, 31 years before the accession of her son in AD 734, presumed to be close to the date of Hasaw's death which is not recorded anywhere yet known. Given this long gap in time, it is likely that Temple II, if indeed dedicated to Hasaw's wife would have begun to be constructed before the even more monumental work of Hasaw's own mortuary temple, Temple I (*ill. 84*).

There has been much speculation about the date of construction of Temple I. We do not know for certain if it was constructed during his final years in preparation for his death in the Egyptian manner, or if it was built after his death by his son. The clues provided by the texts, especially those included on the lintel suggest that he prepared his own monument. Further, as noted above, the sequence of events shows placement of Altar 5 first, followed by the construction of Temple II, and finally construction of Temple I, and that all were planned by the same person according to a coordinated design that linked the woman to the man for eternity. Certainly the image of the woman on Temple II and that of the man known to be Hasaw on Temple I were set to face each other across the expanse of the Great Plaza throughout time. Seldom in archaeology does the dry evidence of dates, inscriptions, and tombs give the opportunity to glimpse the human side of the ancient royal players. In this case love and loyalty are testified in stone and wooden monuments.

Excavations below Temple II failed to reveal any evidence that a tomb ever existed under this structure. This negative evidence further supports Coggins' interpretation that the temple was built to honor the woman, not house her bones which lay elsewhere, as stated on Altar 5. Coggins also pointed out that certain temples at Tikal likely served as cenotaphs, much like our monuments to fallen soldiers in public parks. Temple II could be such a monument.

The last resting place of Hasaw was recovered in Burial 116 under his greatest architectural achievement, Temple I. The possibility exists that the tomb was prepared in readiness for death with a tunnel left open as access for the funeral rites. The great king of Palenque, Hanab Pacal, had readied his own tomb before his death half a century earlier and one year after Hasaw had acceded to power. Hasaw could have attended that funeral and, remembering 50 years later, prepared his own tomb in a similar fashion.

If Hasaw died in the same year that his son acceded to the throne, then the reign of this great ruler had lasted 52 years, coincidentally the same as a full cycle of the calendar. Comparing his reign with that of Pacal of Palenque who had ruled for 68 years and died in his early 80s, the two rulers each fulfilled the role of "great man" to their respective cities.

Hasaw's tomb was discovered in the spring of 1962 as a result of tunneling excavations into the core of Temple I. The tomb was not located on the central axis of the structure which commemorated it, an unusual fact which delayed discovery. Eventually, the presence of dense layers of flint and obsidian – chips, flakes and cores – in the construction fill indicated the nearby presence of a major burial to the north of the central axis. A sealed capstone was finally located in the "floor" of the tunnel. In November 1962, the tomb of Hasaw was opened with some formality and considerable care, approximately 1,228 years after its closing (ill. 85).

The stone, when lifted, proved to be the central capstone of a large vaulted chamber. The capstone was painted with a large circular spot in red cinnabar, perhaps representing the sun disk shining forever over Hasaw's mortal remains. Parts of the chamber's walls and vault had collapsed, obscuring the contents upon first entry into the tomb. The chamber was large and rich in content by the standards of previously excavated tombs at Tikal. The single male was laid out on a raised dais "richly adorned with unusual quantities of jade, pearls, and shells, and surrounded by grave furniture." Aubrey Trik's description[37] imparts the sense of awe experienced by the excavators: "The jade, some of exceptionally fine color and quality, consisted of headdress plaques, tubular necklace beads, bracelets, anklets, and earplugs. Many well preserved pea-shaped and baroque pearls were found in the neck and chest area, probably originally part of the jade necklace. Across the lower chest was a surprising 'collar' composed of 114 spherical jade beads, graduated in size from one-half to two inches in diameter and weighing a total of eight and one-half pounds" (ill. 86). In addition to a vast array of painted ceramic vessels, there was a lidded cylinder vase made of jade mosaic (ill. 87), an alabaster dish in the form of a conch shell, many shells, slate plaques, stingray spines and the remains of organic materials.

The jade mosaic vessel was constructed of fitted jade plates for which the binding had disintegrated, requiring painstaking reconstruction. On the apron lid of the vessel was an inscription of 12 glyphs, naming Hasaw, and identifying him as a "four-katun" batab. The batab title at Tikal is a substitute for "ahau," meaning "lord." The knob handle was in the form of a human head, presumably a portrait made of intricate, tiny fragments of jade representing the lord himself.

A coverlet of jaguar skin lay beneath the ruler, under which had been a straw mat. The aforementioned incised bones were an unusual and highly informative feature of this tomb, providing both chronological information as well as some remarkable iconography.

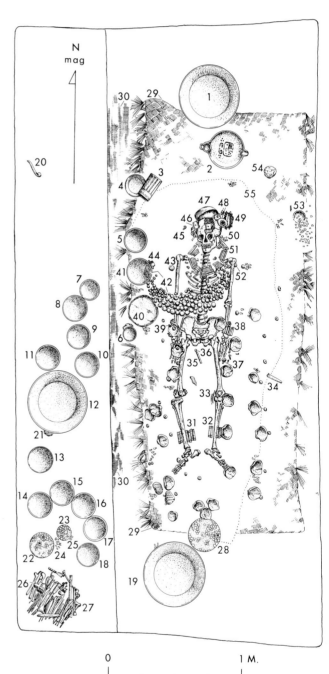

84 (left) The view from the room of Lady Twelve Macaw's lintel in Temple II framing Temple I across the Great Plaza and to the east.

85 (right) Drawing of the contents of Burial 116, the tomb of Hasaw Chan K'awil under Temple I. Note the richness of vessels, jade beads and other treasures which accompanied the "great man" to the underworld.

86 (below) Aubrey Trik, Field Director at the time of discovery of Hasaw's tomb, works on the intricate task of uncovering the delicate grave goods.

87 One of the most spectacular pieces from Hasaw's tomb was this mosaic lidded vessel made from tiny pieces of jade. The inscription on the lid bears Hasaw's name and so it is assumed that the image on the lid is his portrait.

The contents of his tomb and those details known to us of Hasaw's life and influence will continue to be a subject of analysis and discussion for many decades to come. As we shall see, his descendants continued the work he began for another 66 years, based upon the estimated time of death of Hasaw's grandson in AD 800. Although he did not build the tallest structure in Tikal, Hasaw made more changes and contributed more to style and restoration of power than any known ruler at Tikal. In recognition of that style, his own monument, Temple I, became the symbol of the city in modern times.

One final feature about Hasaw's contribution to Tikal is found in the physical layout of Temples I and II. Besides forming a new triadic cosmic group around the Great Plaza, with 5D-33 as the northern focal point, other conditions were satisfied by their construction. The axial line between Temples I and II form an alignment with the Stela 16/Altar 5 enclosure of N Group. This alignment establishes a connection between the temples and the altar which tells the story of Lady Twelve Macaw. Further, this baseline forms a perfect 3-4-5 integral right triangle with Structure 3D-43, an Early Classic temple known to contain an important burial. In this way, Hasaw used a geometric configuration to connect himself and his wife to an ancestor, either a real or a politically motivated connection (*pl. X*).

Table 4
Chronology of the beginning of the Late Classic at Tikal
Time span AD 659 – AD 734 (75 years)

Name	Date	Event	Ruler No
23rd and 24th Rulers	lost in the Hiatus:	No data	23rd/24th
Nu Bak Chak I			25th
(Shield Skull I)	August AD 659	Victory in battle with Yaxchilan	
	August AD 659	Visits Pacal at Palenque	
	December AD 672	Battle against Dos Pilas	
	December AD 677	Defeated in battle at Dos Pilas	
	April AD 679	Defeated and possibly killed at Dos Pilas	
Hasaw Chan K'awil			26th
(Heavenly Standard Bearer)	AD 682	Accession as Kalomte of Tikal	
	March AD 692	M Group dedicated, Altar 14 and Stela 30	
	August AD 695	Victory against Calakmul (L. 3, Temple I)	
	August AD 695	Capture of Ah Bolon of Calakmul (5D-57)	
	September AD 695	Sat upon captured Palanquin from Calakmul followed by bloodletting ceremony and dedication possibly of Temple 5D-33-1st (L.3, Temple I)	
	November AD 695	Captive of Calakmul taken? (Incised bone)	
	May AD 703	Wife died (Lady Twelve Macaw?)	
	December AD 711	Stela 16 and Altar 5 dedicated in N Group commemorating end of Katun and deceased wife	
	AD 732–734	Death following construction of Temples I and II	

CHAPTER TEN

A FAMILY AFFAIR: HASAW'S DESCENDANTS

The love for his wife which Hasaw demonstrated through his public actions suggests that he was also was a good family man. Consciously or otherwise he had established a tradition through his descendants who demonstrated a reverence for the "great man" in many ways. Hasaw's new style of temple architecture was continued by the son and grandson who followed in his line of descent. With their guidance, Tikal achieved new heights of glory in its public architecture demonstrating the presence at the city of both great wealth and power, while all the time reverence for the pivotal ancestor was maintained by means of specific architectural planning.

Hasaw's immediate successor was his son Yik'in Chan K'awil, the 27th ruler in the succession. Yik'in's own parentage record states that his father was Hasaw Chan K'awil and his mother was the "Lady Twelve Macaw" (her other names not withstanding). Following Yik'in, the line of descent is briefly unclear, specifically because information is still lacking about one king, Ruler 28 in the succession. Also the succession is confused by the existence of many differing interpretations of the names of the remaining few rulers before the ultimate silence descended upon Tikal.

Yik'in's name has not been easy to translate. Epigrapher Steve Houston has offered the likely translation of "Darkness of the Night Sky." Given the traditional Maya habit of naming a child, especially a royal child, by the father stepping out of the birthing quarters and looking for a "sign" of a soul spirit or *nahual* for the new being, we can speculate how Yik'in got his name. Hasaw, the father, although innovative in character would not likely have settled for artificial means of naming his royal heir. While the sighting of a jaguar, a significant snake, a butterfly, or a crocodile would certainly have been convenient in terms of prestige, Hasaw had to settle for what he saw: the "darkness of the night sky." The honesty, as well as the beauty of the naming cannot be lost in modern times. Although there is no recognized birth date in the hieroglyphic record, the name suggests that Yik'in was born during the dark of the moon even though the night sky at Tikal would not normally be considered "dark." The brilliance of stars alone is enough to illuminate the landscape. Therefore, this birth must have been in the season when the night sky was obscured by cloud.

Enough is known about the reign of Hasaw's first successor to indicate that he built even more public works on a grand scale than did his father. Much of this he did in honor of his father. It is likely that the rule of Yik'in Chan K'awil represented the peak of the Late Classic achievement and wealth at Tikal.

*Night Sky
(Yik'in Chan K'awil)*

Yik'in Chan K'awil (Ruler B, and Yaxkin Kan Chak)

There are numerous known dates at Tikal associated with the reign of Yik'in. The following is a sequential reconstruction of what we know and can reasonably guess for the life of the ruler who oversaw the peak of Tikal's glory.

Yik'in acceded to power in the role of *chacte* of Tikal on 8 December AD 734,[1] the same year assumed to mark his father's death. This accession was recorded in two places, on Stela 21 and Stela 5. The former (*ill. 88*) is an extremely fine example of the delicacy of stone carving which marked this period, but unfortunately it is only partially preserved. The dates on a stela which was placed before a major structure usually include the date of dedication of the structure itself. In the case of Stela 21, the structure is Temple VI, the Temple of the Inscriptions, which associates Yik'in with this very important temple. In turn, the temple associates him with numerous later inscribed dates which deserve separate description below in their chronological sequence. However, the dedication date on Stela 21 is the next known event in his life. This date is 22 July AD 736[2] and by association it is also assumed to be the date of construction of the Temple, if not of the roof comb to be discussed later.

88 *The intricate carving on Stela 21 is well preserved, but only a part of the stela survives. The inscription records the accession date of Yik'in Chan K'awil in* AD 734.

The other text which mentions Yik'in's accession date is on Stela 5 and contains quite a lot of other information about him, including his parentage statement. This stela was located in front of Temple 5D-33-1st, built by his father, Hasaw, and it was set in place on 10 June AD 744,[3] ten years after Yik'in acceded to power. The date has other importance. It is the 13-katun anniversary of the event described on the adjacent stela (Stela 3). The significance of this lies in the fact that the earlier date, at 6 March AD 488,[4] was placed by the 13th ruler, a son of K'an Ak, and an illustrious ancestor of Yik'in. Thus Stela 5 links Yik'in to his past by both place and time. It serves as a monument to his father (who built Temple 33), his grandfather (buried under Temple 33) and the date marks an event in his more distant ancestry. The same stela records Yik'in's own immediate family history, but lamentably, not the date of his birth.

The lintel of Structure 5D-52-1st

An imposing tiered palace, often called the "five-storied palace," forms part of the southern boundary of the Central Acropolis (*ills. 89 and 90*). It was actually constructed as two separate buildings at different time periods. The only text associated with this architectural complex comes from the middle doorway of the first story of the smaller upper building. This is the earliest component of the five stories and the hieroglyphic date at 26 June AD 741[5] coincides with a date from the Temple IV lintels and therefore must be attributed to Yik'in. The palace lintel shows a dwarf in attendance to the figure of the king, a similar device to that depicted on Lintel 3 of Temple I, perhaps another example of Yik'in's imitation of (or homage to) his father (*ill. 91*). Also depicted are two long-necked water birds now recognized as cormorants, an iconographic motif that was quite popular in the Early Classic period at Tikal.

Structure 5D-52-1st contains two ranged rooms which were later divided into smaller chambers. Neither the original first story, nor any of the two later stories show evidence of family residence. The structure faced south only, out over the ravine which includes the Palace Reservoir. When built by Yik'in, the new structure blocked a fine view from the south side of 5D-57 which we now know was the house of Hasaw, Yik'in's father. This apparent ritual "killing" of a view must be considered with anthropological care, as it superficially seems to be a mark of disrespect, or disregard for his father's house on the part of Yik'in. The function of the new building must be the key and to this we can only guess. The attributes of the building suggest a temporary residence or retreat house – a house of meditation.[6] The upper zone decoration which surrounds the surviving ends and rear of the building consisted of simple panels containing a stylized eye of Kinich Ahau, the sun god, whose image is borne on the shield carried by Yik'in on the lintel within the new building. Therefore, when Yik'in completed this new building, the old house of Hasaw looked upon multiple images of the eye of the sun god lying to the south of a small courtyard (*ill. 92*).

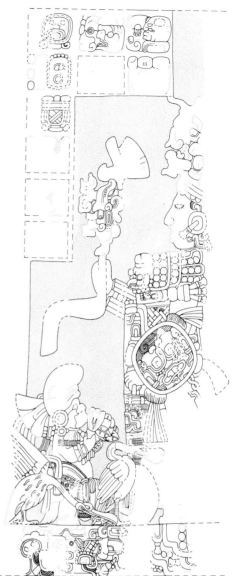

89 (*left above*) *The first story of Structure 5D-52 was one of Yik'in's building projects probably in* AD 741. *Two more stories were later added. In 1959 the structure was overgrown by forest.*

90 (*left below*) *The north side or rear of 5D-52 shows the good state of masonry preservation of the first story and the decorative panels in the upper zone.*

91 (*right*) *Drawing of the surviving part of Lintel 2, Structure 5D-52, first story depicts the lord Yik'in attended by a dwarf and in the presence of a cormorant, which may have been part of his personal livery.*

92 (*below*) *Detail of one of the decorative panels on the upper zone of Structure 5D-52. The squared corner design may be an abstraction of the eye of the god Kinich Ahau whose face also appears on the lord's shield on Lintel 2 of the same building.*

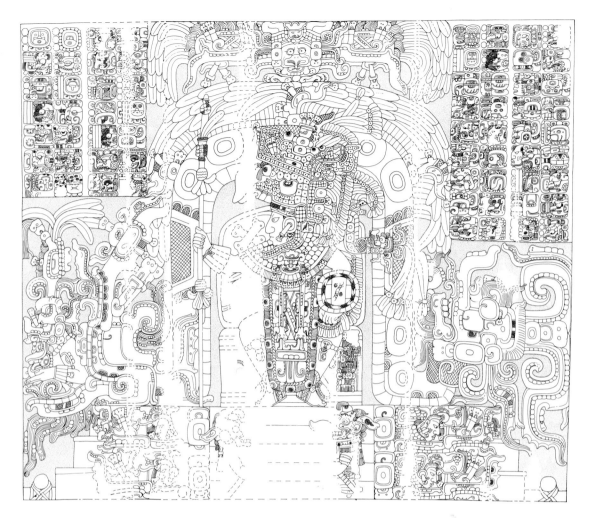

94 *Drawing of the carving on Lintel 3 of Temple IV, showing the lord seated on a captured palanquin in victorious glory. The scene reflects a similar one on Lintel 3 of Temple I portraying his father, Hasaw, in a similar situation.*

Yik'in's greatest project: Temple IV

The construction of Temple IV (*ill. 93*) is physically the largest construction project which is associated with Yik'in's life. The information provided by the Temple derives both from its physical placement in the sacred space of the city, and from the detailed texts on two carved wooden lintels which decorate the second and third doorways inside the temple itself. These lintels each depict a scene featuring images of Yik'in himself, showing the lord riding upon captured palanquins from two different cities and representing the successful results of two different "wars." The text on Lintel 3 (*ill. 94*) also includes the statement that the king is the son of Lord Hasaw and his wife, "Lady Twelve Macaw," verifying the parentage statement mentioned earlier on Stela 5. The stories told on these lintels provide a fascinating, albeit stylized, glimpse into the life of a royal leader at the peak of Maya glory in the lowlands. These texts

93 *(left) The largest construction project of Yik'in Chan K'awil was Temple IV, possibly built to commemorate his father. It remains the tallest pre-Columbian structure in the New World.*

are histories, possibly colored by propaganda, the tale of events as the king wanted them remembered, and therefore they are structured through a series of dates. This series is a great boon to the archaeology of the city, ranking in importance with the inscriptions on Stela 31 and Temple VI.[7] The progression of events is listed here in their chronological order which requires that the readings move back and forth between Lintels 2 and 3 of Temple IV.

The temple itself stands c. 64.6 m (212 ft) from the base of the great supporting platform to the surviving top of the roof comb, making it the tallest surviving New World structure. By comparison, the Tigre Complex at El Mirador is 55 m (181 ft) and the Pyramid of the Sun at Teotihuacan rises a little over 61 m (200 ft). In both cases the actual mass of construction was greater than Temple IV due to the size of ground dimensions, but Temple IV remains the tallest. The pyramid is formed by seven stacked terraces of diminishing size, with a central grand stair leading to the temple. The proportion of the temple building is somewhat longer and squatter than on Temples I and II, and 5D-33-1st, the prototype. There is however, the single doorway which was introduced as the signature of Hasaw for this style of temple architecture. The massive roof comb suffered loss of detail as a result of the early clearing done by Maudslay, but the heavily sculpted figure of the seated king can still be discerned, facing eastward over most of the city (see ill. 69).

The temple plan is the same in concept, if not in dimension, as Temples I and II, with stepped-up rooms from front to rear, with an exterior single side-inset which disguises the presence of a third room (see Chapter Twelve). The view from Temple IV encompasses all the other Great Temples, III in the near ground; II and I in the distance, Temple V off to the right or south, visible behind the massive South Acropolis (see ills. 3 and 19).

Reconstruction of the Lost World Pyramid has exposed this giant construction to view of Temple IV today. One realizes that from this vantage point, looking east, all of central Tikal was visible in ancient times when the foliage was under control, and not covering the plazas as it does today. Spaces that had been designed to be open are now hidden by the rainforest.

Inside the temple there were three doorways separating the three narrow rooms, each narrower than the one before from front to rear, in the fashion of the Great Temples of Tikal. The lintel over the front doorway, now gone, is assumed uncarved. Those over the second and third doorways now reside in Basel, Switzerland. A cast of Lintel 3 can be seen in the National Museum in Guatemala City. These great masterpieces of Maya art, including the lintels of Temples I and II, must now be viewed outside the realm of their creation. The lintels had been carved from the wood of the zapote tree, apparently outside the temple and installed after the artwork was rendered. Impressions in the plaster of the lintel beds high above the doorways tell us that the wooden beams were wrapped in reed mats for protection and tied with ropes for transportation. These reconstructed details of the intricate engineering that was required to raise this exquisite temple only reveal traces of the energy, thought, and design that resulted in such a magnificent architectural achievement. From the doorway, far beyond the temple realms of the city, one can see the Pine Ridge that borders the great Bajo de Santa Fe to the east of Tikal – the route that the early pioneers of the city followed on their way to settle this city, traveling from the east, the direction of the color red. Beyond that in the hazy distance are the Maya Mountains, today in the neighboring country of Belize – not a separate political entity when Tikal was first settled, just a physical landmark visible in the distant countryside – on the far side of Tikal's sometimes friendly neighbor, Naranjo.

A single plain stela and altar stood at the base of the stair of Temple IV just like the huge plain stela and its altar found at the base of Temple II, also an east-facing Great Temple.

The lintel dates and their events

The earliest lintel date for Temple IV is 28 July AD 743[8] and comes from Lintel 3. This records a "star war" event, waged against a city called Yax Ha La'in Wakah, thought to be either the site known today as El Peru or possibly another western site whose location was only discovered in February 1997.[9] The subject of the text accompanying this date is the seizure of the royal palanquin of the conquered city, an action performed by Yik'in, Lord of Tikal.[10] There exists a very interesting parallel here between both the subject matter and the scenes shown on the carved lintels of Temple I, the work of Yik'in's father Hasaw. In each case there is one lintel showing a jaguar protector deity and one showing a plumed serpent protector. Despite the fact that the two temples face each other, one facing to the west (Temple I) – the other facing to the east (Temple IV) – the relative positions of the jaguar and serpent iconography remain the same: serpent imagery on the east and jaguar imagery on the west. Additionally, there is a difference in the jaguar imagery. On Temple I the protector is a very large and clear figure of the animal. Even traces of the tail are visible. On Temple IV the imagery is of a very large human figure wearing jaguar identifiers – spots on the visible arm and leg. Another possible difference (or perhaps it is incomplete knowledge) is that both lintels on Temple IV appear to deal with the victories and capture of enemy palanquins. However, on Temple I, Lintel 3, we have evidence only for an identical event (capture of palanquin) at a different city (Calakmul). For lack of the complete text, the event celebrated on Lintel 2 of Temple I is not known, but the elements identifying a palanquin are certainly present with a great deal of plumed serpent imagery paralleling that on Temple IV, Lintel 3. While there is no reason to question the truth of the events recorded on Temple IV, the likelihood that they are recorded in imitation of those on Temple I cannot be ignored: like father, like son.

One day later[11] some kind of damage or destruction was performed against the captured palanquin from El Peru (or the new site). It may have been a desanctification ceremony designed to dissociate the holy object from its place of origin. The textual phrase ends with the arrival back home of the Lord of Tikal (Yik'in).

About six months later,[12] another ceremony was recorded 15 days after a near total solar eclipse at Tikal. The action seems to be the placing of an offering in a cache plate by Yik'in, but its timing is related to the conquest which is the main theme of the narrative on Lintel 3 of Temple IV.

One day later, on 4 February AD 744[13] a new "star war" event was recorded on Lintel 2. This time the place of attack was the city of Naranjo to the east of Tikal, and the object of attack the patron god of Naranjo. Again the action involved the royal palanquin of the attacked city. The capture of Yax May Kan Chac Sak Chuen, a known king of Naranjo, and his palanquin were recorded. The actor, once again, was the chacte of Tikal, Yik'in.

Three years after the capture of the palanquin of El Peru (or the alternate site),[14] yet another ceremony was performed by Yik'in in commemoration of what must have been the most significant achievement of his reign. This ceremony invoked a "renewal" of the god of the captured palanquin which is now identified as the "god of the chacte" of Tikal. The implications, both religious and political, are astounding. By right of capture, this inanimate object, viewed as a god of a foreign capital has, through ceremony, become a god of Tikal. The text describes how Yik'in was carried on the palanquin with its own name, and how he danced in the Great Plaza at Tikal. Probably these are anniversary celebrations of the capture of the palanquin and conquest of the distant city, accompanied by dedication of this holy object to use in its new home at Tikal.

The following year, on 7 March AD 747[15] we are told that Yik'in conducted a very similar event but this time celebrating the anniversary of the capture of the palanquin of Naranjo. This time the ceremony included a serpent vision experienced by the king, like the one depicted at Yaxchilan.[16]

We can only guess at the meaning of the parallels between the texts on the lintels of Temples IV and I. Like Temple I, Temple IV could be the mortuary structure for Yik'in, as is believed by many scholars. Nevertheless, he was clearly emulating his father in at least one regard, the recording of conquests in the most striking manner. Temple IV, the tallest structure to have ever been built in Tikal, was carefully placed in space, not only facing Temple I, residence of the god-ancestor Hasaw in such a way that no intervening structure (either before or after) obscured the view from doorway to doorway, but also in a way that fulfills truly remarkable geometric relationships to earlier important temples. The geometry of Tikal architecture is described in Chapter Twelve.

The dates recorded on the Temple IV lintels span a period of a little under four years. We do not know the date of construction of the building itself, although a suggested date based upon a variety of sources is in the year AD 741, coincident with the known date of construction of another building raised by Yik'in in the Central Acropolis, Structure 5D-52-1st, described earlier. However, the question always arises at Tikal concerning the relative dates of construction for a Great Temple as opposed to the dates recorded on its lintels. The reason for this problem is quite an interesting question about how the Maya built and completed a temple on these proportions. Like the pyramids of Egypt, the construction job was clearly a very big one, not accomplished in a few months. The same interpretative problem exists for both Temples I and IV concerning the dates recorded on the wooden lintels and the probable dates of the huge building's construction. In both cases there is a good argument that the dates of events on the lintels are a few years later than the probable dates of completion. This suggests that the lintels were installed several years after the construction. Conversely, what we know of the construction sequence argues against a later installation of the lintels. This would mean that Temple IV was not actually finished until some little time after March, AD 747, assuming that the lintels were carved before their installation.

Thus ends the hieroglyphic record from the largest monument raised by Yik'in, but by no means is it the last we hear of him.

95 Column Altar 1, found in the West Plaza in a secondary position was probably a ballcourt marker and depicts a minor victory of Yik'in Chan K'awil.

Column Altar 1 A small carved monument was excavated in the West Group Plaza in 1962 during my own excavations in that zone to the west of Temple II. This small but exquisite monument was found in a reset position, horizontally placed on a grand formal stair leading to the remains of a well-elevated palace, Structure 5D-15, which marked the north side of the West Plaza. The small altar was probably placed in such a prominent public position during the Post-classic activity at the site. Clearly it did not belong there and had been dragged from some other location in the post-collapse frenzy to observe badly under-stood ancient ritual. Most observers agree that this monument originated as a ballcourt marker, probably coming from the ballcourts in the East Plaza, where another similar monument was found. Nearly intact (*ill. 95*), the sculpture is finely detailed, showing a seated, bound prisoner. There are sculptural parallels with Altar 8, also showing a bound prisoner and dating to Yik'in's twin-pyramid group (Group 3D-2) of slightly later date. It is suggested that the same artist carved both monuments.

The inscribed date is 10 December AD 748[17] and the text records the capture of a noble by the name of Chac Toh Waybi Wuk Tzuk[18] (no translation), thought to be from Naranjo because his name also appears on more than one ceramic vessel from that site at the same time period.

Group 3D-2 The twin-pyramid group which marks the end of the 16th katun (AD 751) is known as "Complex P," or Group 3D-2. This group, including the carved Stela 20 and Altar 8, was discovered by Edwin Shook in 1937. The group is located on the west side of the North Zone also identified on the maps as Group H. This very important architectural feature of greater Tikal is located at the confluence of the Maler and Maudslay Causeways. These causeways may also have been built by Yik'in, but about this we have no information. The position of the twin-pyramid group on the west side of the large pyramid Temple Structure 3C-43 is significant. The big temple-pyramid we see today is surely late in date and the placement of the twin-pyramid group next to it suggests that an earlier temple already existed at this location. Excavations conducted in 1978 did demonstrate that there is a very important Early Classic component to Structure 3C-43. In terms of the cosmic layout of the city this spot is the northern apex, the ultimate location of "heaven," just as the north side in a twin-pyramid group is where the king resides in heaven, and just as the North Acropolis represents the heavenly resting place to the north of the central sacred space of the Great Plaza. For the site as a whole, Temple 3C-43 is the ultimate northern point.

Stela 20 shows the ruler in full profile, facing to his right, very like Stela 21, also raised in Yik'in's honor. Instead of the usual ceremonial bar, Yik'in holds in his right hand a vertical staff ending in a three-bladed weapon while his left arm supports a small shield. He stands before a throne bearing the face of a jaguar wearing a "tie" knotted under its chin. The ruler holds a bag in his left hand probably holding incense or tobacco. His large back-mask is topped with a bent human leg as on his earlier Stela 5. The iconography of this detached human leg must bear some meaning to his conquests.

Toward the north end of the Maler Causeway, which leads to the North Group, there is a very large rock sculpture, the only one of its kind known at Tikal, carved into the exposed and hardened bedrock. The scene depicts two figures, one a prisoner. The accompanying inscription, although eroded, suggests that the actor/victor is Yik'in.[19]

Temple VI: The Temple of the Inscriptions

The Temple of the Inscriptions was deemed to be a Great Temple at the time of discovery because of its imposing size and connection to the central zone by the

96 *Temple VI, known as the Temple of the Inscriptions, was dedicated by Yik'in and could well be his burial monument. The roof comb with the inscriptions is thought to have been added after Yik'in's death.*

Mendez Causeway. This was the last discovered of the large temples of Tikal, found during exploration in 1957 by Antonio Ortiz, foreman of the excavation project of Pennsylvania. Although measuring more than 25 m (80 ft) tall, this temple differs quite markedly from other Great Temples at Tikal. It has three doorways and is proportioned in the squat wide fashion characteristic of architecture before the reign of Hasaw (*ill. 96*). However, the remarkable roof comb measures 12.5 m (40 ft) in height and the central panel at the rear contains one of the longest inscriptions at the site. Since inscriptions are our main source of historical reconstruction of the city, this panel is very important. The two-room temple faces west into a large walled courtyard, devoid of other significant architecture. The Mendez Causeway leads from the southeast corner of the East Plaza down a long incline interrupted by the presence of G Group, a palace complex, and ending along the north side of the courtyard that fronts Temple VI (*ill. 97*).

In front of the Temple stairway and facing west are Stela 21 and Altar 9 (*see ill. 88*). Although half-missing, enough text remains to know that Stela 21 was

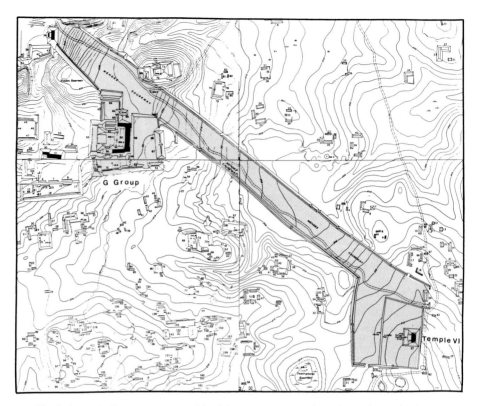

97 *Shaded area indicates a group of building projects attributed to Yik'in which are connected by the Mendez Causeway. They include Group G near the upper (left) end of the Causeway, and Temple VI at the bottom of the Causeway (right).*

one of Yik'in's monuments, and its location indicates dedication of the temple before which it stands. There is also reference to Yik'in in the great inscription of the roof comb. There is a possibility that the roof comb was added at a later date by a later king, but nevertheless construction of the monument is associated with Yik'in. Because of the architectural integration of the Mendez Causeway and the palace Group G, these features can also be associated with this ruler.

The mystery of the dates from Temple VI

The recorded dates included in the massive inscription extend over a period of 1905 years, reaching back into what must have been mythological time for the Maya who carved the text.[20] Further dates concern later historical events that remained in the oral tradition or were contemporary.

The chosen location for the temple may well relate to the earliest mythological dates. Christopher Jones[21] has argued that Tikal was first settled in this region and Patrick Culbert has demonstrated that one of the earliest ceramic deposits of trash came from the immediate region of Temple VI. In this inscription, were the Maya trying to reach back in time to recreate an entire story of the settlement of the site, skipping most of the middle parts but telling of early settlement and then relating this to contemporary events? The location itself may be an attempt to raise a monument at the point of first arrival.

The earliest date at 1139 BC[22] is a time when Tikal could have been one of those small villages described in Chapter Three, although it is earlier than any archaeological evidence for humans on the site. If this is the true date of the founding of Tikal, then its maintained memory until the 8th century is truly remarkable. The alternative is that the date is a mythological guess.

The next date is 457 BC,[23] which falls during the Tzec ceramic period of the Middle Preclassic, and Tikal definitely was occupied at this time. The third date of 156 BC[24] is during the Late Preclassic, by which time the North Acropolis was already an established and sacred entity.[25] These early dates are all followed by a Tikal emblem glyph, strongly suggesting that they represent a review of the early historical events in the settlement and growth of the site. Just what these events are remains a mystery.

The next five dates on the Temple VI roof comb are also found carved on various stelae set on the North Terrace of the Great Plaza and so were readily available to Yik'in. What these record are some tun-ending dates and other unknown events falling between AD 514 and 528.[26]

The remainder of the text is historical in nature and deals with the life of Yik'in, including his mother's name, the Lady Twelve Macaw (the romantic figure in Hasaw's life) as well as Yik'in's claim to be in the fourth katun of his life, meaning that he was over 60 years of age. In this series, the last two dates fall only three years before the succession date of Yik'in's son, known as Yax Ain II, or Ruler C. The last recorded date in this historical series is 15 February AD 766.[27] There is an exact interval of 30 years between the date on Yik'in's Stela 21 in front of the temple and the final date on the roof comb series. The roof comb itself could be an addition erected after Yik'in's death. The alternative possibility is that Yik'in made the addition himself very late in life, placing himself in the chronological flow of the entire history of Tikal. There remains little doubt that the temple itself and its accompanying stela and altar were one of Yik'in's projects.

Yik'in's monumental architectural projects were prodigious, exceeding even his father's work in sheer quantity. The construction of Temple VI on the east and Temple IV on the extreme west of the city created a new, expanded cosmos for the city. Temples VI and IV face each other in the manner of Temples I and II. There is a known geometric relationship between Temples IV and VI with Structure 3C-43 in the North Zone[28] as well as the formation of a new triad, paralleling the triad formed by Hasaw in the Great Plaza with Temples I, II, and 5D-33-1st. The role of geometry in city planning is discussed in greater detail in Chapter Twelve.

In summary, known works of Yik'in's architectural contributions to Tikal include Temple IV, Group 3D-2, palace Structure 5D-52-1st, Temple VI, and possibly the roof comb attached to it. Associated by inference, we must also include the Mendez Causeway, Group G palace complex, which may have been Yik'in's private palace quarters, and possibly the Maler Causeway, including as it does, the giant rock sculpture attributed to Yik'in, as well as the East Plaza "market place."

The burial place of Yik'in

The question of this great ruler's place of burial is complex and unresolved. Either of the Great Temples which he built, Temple IV and Temple VI, might have been raised for mortuary purposes. In the absence of excavation there are arguments against both. The only east-facing Great Temple that has been archaeologically tested is Temple II where no burial was discovered. On the basis of this single example it is risky to conclude that all three of Tikal's east-facing Great Temples (II, III, and IV) served only as commemorative cenotaphs to ancestors, and yet this possibility is real. While the inscriptions on Temple IV are a celebration of Yik'in's own exploits, the location and position of the monument were set in such a manner that homage to his deceased father (Hasaw) was integral to the building's existence. We still do not know if any tomb is covered by either Temple IV or Temple III.

The identity of the personage in Burial 196 is important because its contents clearly belonged to a member of the royal family. This burial was discovered by Nicholas Hellmuth beneath Structure 5D-73, a very curious structure in its own right . Located immediately south of Temple II, the structure is a pyramidal series of platforms with no building at the summit. Comparable in height to many temples in the North Acropolis, the mystery of why a pyramid containing a lavish royal tomb would be raised with no masonry building at the summit is unanswered. The contents of the tomb – ceramics and stylistic designs of non-ceramic objects – place the tomb as nearly contemporary or slightly later than that of Hasaw (Burial 116 under Temple I). This would place the tomb at about the right time for Yik'in's burial. The grave included one adult male laid centrally, face up, with his head to the west (*ill. 98*). The grave goods were superb and on a par with those of Burial 116. They included some truly remarkable polychrome vessels and a jade carving of a baby jaguar, in addition to one item of special interest. This is a lidded cylinder vessel of jade mosaic (*pl. XI*) which is an apparent companion piece to the one described earlier from Hasaw's tomb. The piece from Burial 116 has a male human head as a handle to the lid, and an incised inscription which identifies Hasaw's name. Conversely, the vase from Burial 196 has no inscription while the human head on the lid has features which match those of Maya women, especially the hair design. A protuberant device extending from the cylinder vessel's exterior wall has been interpreted by some as phallic, but its complexity of design suggests a more abstract concept. The two vessels (from Burials 116 and 196) look like a pair manufactured simultaneously of a male and female couple. The male

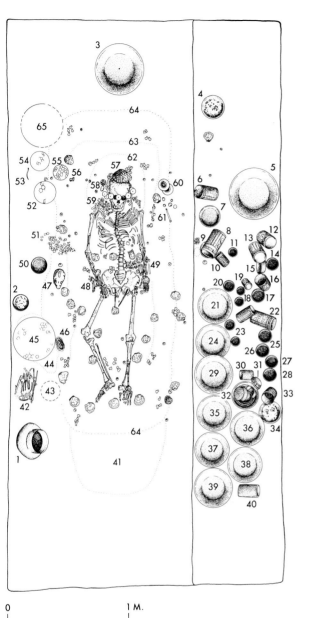

98 (left) Drawing of Burial 196 discovered under Structure 5D-73 just south of Temple II in the Great Plaza. Clearly a royal burial, the male personage is somehow related to both Hasaw and Yik'in.

99 (below) A closeup of the remains in Burial 196 shows the richness of jade jewelry worn by the lord.

version was placed in Hasaw's tomb (*ill. 87*). The second vessel with female head likely represents Hasaw's beloved wife, to whom considerable attention had been paid following her death, including the construction of Temple II. Yik'in may have placed the vessel bearing his father's image and name into his father's tomb but retained the representation of his mother for inclusion in another grave. The fact that this second tomb was buried beneath a structure adjacent to and facing Temple II, the mother's monument, is compelling. The question still remains of who is buried in Burial 196 (*ill. 99*). Could it be Yik'in himself, as some have suggested – or could it be another brother of Yik'in's, one who never ruled?[29] Finally, Burial 196 could be Ruler 28, who followed Yik'in in succession.

Related to the mystery of Yik'in's burial place is the question of the authorship of Structure 3C–43 in the North Group. The triadic relationship of this structure with Temples IV and VI is a strong indication that this northern building was part of Yik'in's greater architectural scheme. However, we know very little about the date of this large Classic period temple other than its geometric relationships to Temples IV, VI, and I and that an important Early Classic structure forms its base.

The second from last date on the roof comb of Temple VI is connected to an event which has a particularly relevant reading made by Schele and Grube.[30] The date is 12 February AD 766[31] and the reading says: "Smoke entered the *waybil* shrine taken by the 28th king in the succession." Two points are important: smoke entering a shrine describes a ritual found to be associated with death in other contexts, and Yik'in was the 27th ruler in the succession, not the 28th. The 28th ruler was his successor for a brief time and we do not know who he was, perhaps Yik'in's first son – and perhaps also, the personage in Burial 196 under Structure 5D-73 in the Great Plaza. The implication here is that the whole inscription on the roof comb was added by the 28th successor who recorded the life of Yik'in and only alluded to himself in this last phrase which deals with a death ritual connected to Yik'in's burial.

The very next available date in the history of Tikal is AD 768[32] two years later from Stela 22, and this is a retrospective date telling of the succession of Yik'in's son, Yax Ain II, to the throne of Tikal. The intervening time was presumably filled by the unknown 28th ruler, but the record is incomplete. The mystery of the location of Yik'in's burial remains, but beneath Temple VI is the most favored location. Like Temple I, Temple VI faces west, toward the direction of death and the underworld. Yik'in is known to have emulated his father in many respects, including the formation of a new and spatially expanded cosmos for the city. For these reasons, Temple VI is the better candidate for the location of his burial.

Table 5
Chronology of the middle Late Classic at Tikal
Time span AD 734–AD 766 (32 years)

Name	Date	Event	Ruler No
Yik'in Chan K'awil			27th
(Darkness of the Night Sky)	8 December AD 734	Accession to power as chacte of Tikal on Stela 21 and Stela 5	
	22 July AD 736	Stela 21, dedication date/also date of Temple VI(?)	
	26 June AD 741	On Lintel 1, 5D-52-1st: dedication of the building(?), and Lintels 2 and 3 of Temple IV	
	1 August AD 743	On Lintel 3, Temple IV: "star war" against El Peru	
	2 August AD 743	On Lintel 3, Temple IV: captured palanquin from El Peru	
	3 February AD 744	On Lintel 3, Temple IV: ceremony at Tikal, cache commemorating conquest of El Peru	
	4 February AD 744	On Lintel 2, Temple IV: another "star war" event against Naranjo	
	10 June AD 744	Placement of Stela 5 before 5D-33, on Stela 5	
	13 July AD 746	On Lintel 3, Temple IV: dedication of the palanquin from El Peru as a sacred object of Tikal	
	7 March AD 747	On Lintel 2, Temple IV: celebration of anniversary of capture of palanquin of Naranjo	
	10 December AD 748	Column Altar 1: capture of a noble from Naranjo(?)	
	5 May AD 751	Stela 20 dedication of 16th katun	
28th Ruler			28th
(Dark Sun?)	12 February AD 766	Smoke in shrine ceremony by 28th successor: anniversary of death of Yik'in(?) from roof comb of Temple VI	
	15 February AD 766	On Temple VI roof comb: 30-year anniversary of Stela 21 and dedication of Temple VI, and possibly the date of the addition of the roof comb	

CHAPTER ELEVEN

THE LAST THREE LORDS

The final throes of dynastic rule at Tikal were to last for slightly more than another century with only three more known rulers filling this time period. They are Yik'in's son, now known as Yax Ain II; the ruler who built Temple III, now known as Nu Bak Chak II (or Shield Skull II); and finally Hasaw Chan K'awil II, obviously named after the "great man" of Tikal. This chapter deals with the contributions of these last three rulers, even though little can be reconstructed. As the fortunes of Tikal begin to decline, information becomes scantier for each ruler. Less construction was done and fewer, if any, inscriptions exist to help in the reconstruction of the decline. This next-to-last epoch is the end of history as recorded by the Maya of Tikal. The final epoch has no history and is restored solely from the archaeology.

Yax Ain II (Ruler C; Chitam; Ak)

*Curl Nose
(Yax Ain II)*

Yik'in's son is known by many names. The patronymic glyph was recognized from the earliest investigation to be that of an animal, but identification of the animal has varied through time. Thought first to be a peccary, he received names in Maya for this beast, "Chitam" in Chol, "Ak" in Yucatec.[1] At the 1995 meeting of the Austin Group, the glyph was re-interpreted as a crocodile, re-introducing the name of "Curl Nose" from the Early Classic period. Thus one of the heroes of Tikal rulership was revived in name 357 years after the death of the original. The monuments of these early heroes were preserved in the Great Plaza telling not just of their names but of their exploits. The revival of such an early name could well reflect an attempt to bring back the golden age at a time when the fortunes of the great were slipping once again. The monumental public works of Yax Ain II still were a major contribution to the configuration of the city as we know it, but there are hints that the moment of greatest glory had passed with the life of his father.

Yax Ain II's public works are sharply divided between those that are certain by associated inscription and those that are inferred by stratigraphy and archaeology. The latter are the largest and more important, but they bear no unarguable signature.

The certain works include two separate, but adjacent twin-pyramid complexes each marking the end of katuns 17 and 18 and spaced 1 katun (20 years) apart. These monuments were Yax Ain II's declaration that he was ruler at the time of the ending of these katuns. Because they are physically adjacent, the

100 Reconstruction drawing of Complex Q by Norman Johnson, made in 1959. The stela enclosure is on the north side (top) with a nine-doorway palace on the south side. The configuration represents a world cosmos.

two complexes were called collectively "Group E" on the map and differentiated by the terms Complex Q and Complex R.[2] These two groups are distinguished by being the two physically largest twin-pyramid groups built at Tikal, and also, by location, the first architectural entities that are encountered by the modern visitor to the site.

As noted before, Yax Ain II's accession date is 25 December AD 768,[3] a date provided on Stela 22 in Group Q, the earlier of the two groups. There are only two fixed dates after this time, one from each dedicatory stela in each twin-pyramid group.

Group 4E-4 (Complex Q)

This architectural monument was constructed roughly half a kilometer northeast of Temple I. The location lies directly east of Group 4D-1 (Complex O) built by Hasaw, and may have been deemed auspicious for this reason. Complex Q is the largest twin-pyramid group ever constructed at Tikal (*ills. 100* and *103*). It is raised on a high platform covering 1.88 hectares, nearly three times larger than the group immediately before it at Complex P. The dedicatory monument for Complex Q is Stela 22 accompanied by Altar 10 (*ills. 101* and *102*) and the date of the katun-ending is 20 January AD 771.[4] The artistic

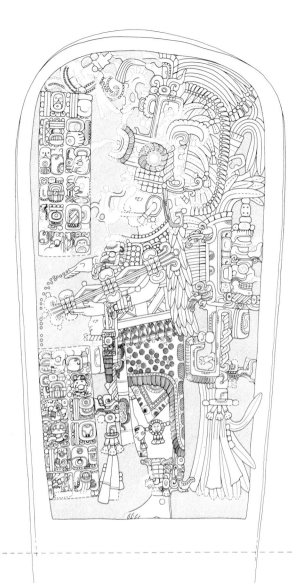

101 (left) Drawing of Stela 22 from the north enclosure of Complex Q. The date commemorates the beginning of the 17th katun and is celebrated by lord Yax Ain II in AD 771.

102 (above) Stela 22 and Altar 10 are still to be found in the enclosure of Complex Q, the first stop on a tour of Tikal.

103 The east pyramid of Complex Q, a twin-pyramid group, is the only restored example of this type of architectural group at Tikal. The flat summit was reached by each of four stairs.

style is a close imitation of Stela 21, erected by Yax Ain II's father in front of Temple VI some 35 years earlier. As with many stelae at Tikal, the profile figure faces to the left of the viewer, which is west. Yax Ain II is shown scattering drops from his right hand in a gesture variously interpreted as a bloodletting ceremony or the scattering of something solid. In this case, the occasion is observation of a successful completion of a 20-year katun ending. The visual message says in essence: "We give thanks that our existence has successfully completed another 20 years and did so under my guidance."

While Yax Ain II named Yik'in as his father, he did not name his mother in this text, nor had Yik'in ever named his wife as such, and so this important woman has passed unidentified.

Group 4E-3 (Complex R)

Twenty years later, Yax Ain II dedicated another twin-pyramid group immediately west of his most grandiose Group 4E-4. The new complex was not raised on a high platform and is somewhat smaller in scale. As a result, one steps down to what appears to be a much lesser monumental group. The eastern pyramid is built almost abutting the platform of the earlier and grander group, while the western pyramid abuts an interruption in the architecture of the Maler Causeway. The whole group seems squeezed between the Causeway and the earlier Complex Q (*ill. 104*).

The dedicatory inscription is recorded on Stela 19 accompanied by Altar 6. The inscription includes the date of the 18th katun ending which the whole group commemorates at 7 October AD 790.[5] The figure of Yax Ain II is yet another imitation of Stela 21 and now also of Stela 22 just before it. Although badly eroded, it shows that the similarities of design were strong.

The altar contains a new element. The usual bound prisoner shown on the surface is not identified while the side border displays four dignitaries who are clearly not prisoners. One is reminded of Altar Q at Copan which depicts the entire royal lineage of the city seated in progression from the founder to the

104 Complex R is another twin-pyramid group immediately adjacent to the open space of Complex Q. Its pristine state demonstrates the condition in which an unexcavated group was found. Note the fallen stelae.

105 (right) *The top of Temple V is visible over the roof of Maler's Palace in the foreground. Although built on opposite flanks of a ravine, the two structures are thought to be the work of the same lord, Yax Ain II.*

106 (below) *The view from the front of Temple I in the Great Plaza over the roof of Maler's Palace in the Central Acropolis, shows the alignment with Temple V, overgrown in the background.*

current ruler. On Altar 6, there are only four figures, and they are separated by large glyph panels which lamentably are illegible.

Yax Ain II named himself as the 29th ruler in the succession on Stela 22. The relative lack of dated monuments from his reign suggests some decline in his ability to command the wealth to build large public monuments. Only the two twin-pyramid groups contain concrete associated dates and trace definite authorship to him. However, there are other and larger works that can be

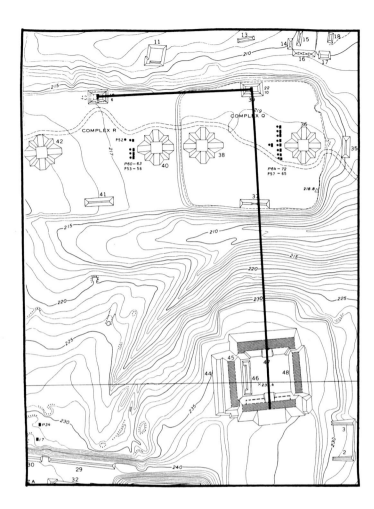

107 A detail from the map shows the right-angled relationship between the two carved stelae in Complexes Q and R, both the work of Yax Ain II, with the central axis of Group F, a palace complex, and likely the same lord's residence.

deduced to originate in his reign either by stratigraphy that connects them to works of his father, or by stylistic elements. These include the Great Temple V and the impressive palace in the Central Acropolis known as "Maler's Palace" (5D-65), named after the turn-of-the-century explorer who left his name engraved on the jamb of one of the palace's doorways (*ill. 105*). These two buildings are related by stylistic details of form and decoration, including the pattern of facing stones and masks in the upper zone of both structures, even though one is a palace, and the other a temple (*ill. 107*). Further, there is a very strong geometric relationship that binds the structures together, suggesting that they were constructed simultaneously.[6]

There is yet another link between Temple V and Maler's Palace. The raising of the palace involved much more construction labor than the mere building itself would suggest. Court 2 of the Central Acropolis was built up as a base for the palace, as well as to provide the ambient space for the courtyard. The quantity of fill required to complete the Courtyard measured 26 m (85 ft) in height on the ravine side (south) and approximately 7 m (23 ft) on the north side where previous constructions already existed. The raising of Maler's Palace was comparable in effort and volumetric fill to the building of a medium-sized temple – for example, Temple VI.

The justification for ascribing this massive effort to the reign of Yax Ain II is based upon the stratigraphy of the Central Acropolis. It is known that Structure 5D-52-1st, the basic element of the Five-Story Palace was built by Yik'in, and the evidence of construction demonstrates unequivocally that Maler's Palace is later in time than the former project, but not by many years. It is conceivable that Yik'in was responsible for both projects. It is far more tenable, however, that the joint construction of Temple V and Maler's Palace was the work of the next major ruler (Yax Ain II). Temple V is positioned in such a way that by geometry it pays homage to both Temples I and IV, both of which preceded it. The most convincing explanation is that Yax Ain II, as grandson, was honoring his father and his grandfather simultaneously by the construction of Temple V.

There is one other architectural project that can be attributed to Yax Ain II, calculated on the basis of geometric relationships. This is the palace group known as "Group F," a quadrangular compound located to the north of Group G, at the top of the Mendez Causeway. The Group F palaces lie south of Yax Ain's giant twin-pyramid group, Complex Q (Group 4E-4). A line connecting Stelae 19 and 22, both erected by Yax Ain II, forms a perfect right-angle with the north–south axis of Group F (*ill. 107*). The relationship cannot possibly be accidental. Rather, it suggests that Group F was constructed together with the later Complex R (Group 4E-3) maintaining the right-angle exactly at Stela 22.

Despite these quite fruitful inferential attributions of a number of architectural monuments at Tikal, there remain a significant number of features for which no attribution, however speculative, is possible at this time. For example, the Bat Palace (Structure 5C-13), the entire complex of the South Acropolis (5D-104 et al), the East Acropolis, the whole of the Seven Temples group (5D-96) including its major southern palace (5D-91), are all unattributed, to name a few. Hopefully, future research will be able to improve this situation.

If pushed to speculate, one might guess that the Bat Palace was a royal court built by the 30th Ruler (see below) for two reasons: proximity to Temple III, which was built by this ruler; and the similarity of the layout of the spacious east-facing forecourt which imitates the entrance of G Group, likely built as the royal court of Yik'in. The imitator had to come later. Further the stepped vault style of interior finish is a late feature at Tikal. These factors add up to a tentative attribution to the 30th ruler.

The South Acropolis, devoid of any benefit of excavation, remains an enigma with only alignments and geometric connections as a clue. These connections (*ill. 108*) show relationships to many far-flung structures built by many different rulers. The central temple serves as a fulcrum for relationships to at least seven other structures outside the South Acropolis.

It is a long reach by iconography, but one can note a similarity of decoration

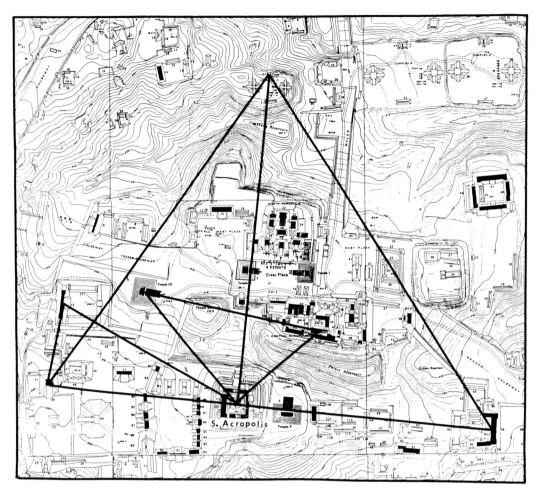

108 A series of interconnected integral right triangles reflect a series of relationships among numerous structures centered around the South Acropolis. The author of these projects is not known.

between the crossed bones on the rear of the central temple in the Seven Temples group and those that appear as decoration on the headgear of one of the figures of Altar 5. The "Lord of Calakmul" bears this same heraldic device on his headdress. Also, Hasaw's skirt on the associated Stela 16 bears multiple references to crossed bones. This thin association could indicate that the Seven Temples group was built in the time of Hasaw Chan K'awil I, but much better evidence is required for a positive association.

The final two rulers

Identification of rulers by name, and association with monuments, either stelae or buildings, can only come from inscriptions, and towards the end of

109 Only the restored temple and roof comb of Temple III are visible above the forest canopy as viewed east from Temple IV.

Tikal's glory these are very scant. The last cluster of such inscriptions centers on Great Temple III: one from the carved wooden Lintel 2 of the temple itself and the other from Stela 24, erected in front of Temple III; both relate to the 30th ruler of Tikal. A single inscription on Stela 11 in the Great Plaza relates to the last recorded ruler of Tikal, the 31st in succession.

Nu Bak Chak II (Shield Skull II)

Like most of the rulers of Tikal, the name of the 30th in succession has undergone a number of interpretations. The name "Dark Sun" appears on the stela in front of Temple III (Stela 24) as well as on Stela 20, one of Yik'in's stelae. This name has been attributed at different times to Rulers 28 through 30. Respectively, these are: the ruler mentioned on the roof comb of Temple VI, who we have suggested, was the eldest son of Yik'in and the personage in Burial 196; Yax Ain II (Ruler C); and the ruler mentioned on Stela 24 connected to Temple III, who is now called Nu Bak Chak II[7] (Shield Skull II). It is the same name as the father of Hasaw I, the "great man." The name "Dark Sun" may indeed be a variation on Yik'in's name, now translated as "Darkness of the Night Sky."

110 The carving on the side of Altar 7 at the foot of Temple III shows a deity head lying in a footed vessel. The royal mat symbol flanks the scene.

It is unfortunate that the second last ruler of the great city is represented only by a single Great Temple (*ill. 109*) with a carved lintel and the stela and altar that stand before it. However, it is more than we have for the final ruler. The date on Stela 24 is 24 June AD 810[8] which in fact is a katun-ending date, the end of the 19th katun in the Maya count. Such a date should have been included in a twin-pyramid complex but none was built for this katun. We infer that resources were badly down by this time and that the ruler had to choose among his options, and the construction of a Great Temple won out over a twin-pyramid group.

The accompanying altar is a notable work of art. The carving wrapping around the periphery of Altar 7 is divided into four sections with figures separated by eroded mat symbols as found earlier on Yax Ain II's Altars 6 and 10. One of the four figural designs is clear – a deity head resting in a tripod bowl (*ill. 110*).

Temple III stands roughly 60 m (180 ft) in height, faces east and has two interior tandem rooms instead of the three found in Temples I, II, and IV. Little detail of the sculpture on the roof comb has survived, but its height and verticality render the temple comparable to Temple I in proportion.

The specific reasons for the choice of location of Temple III would be speculative: for example, why does it face east? Does this mean that the Temple does not have a burial and serves only a commemorative function like Temple II? Why is it located between the earlier Temples II and IV and why does it not have a role that we recognize in expanding the cosmic plan of Tikal? However, there are a few things which we can recognize about the reasons for its location which fit well with the rest of the geometry of Tikal. The integral right triangle

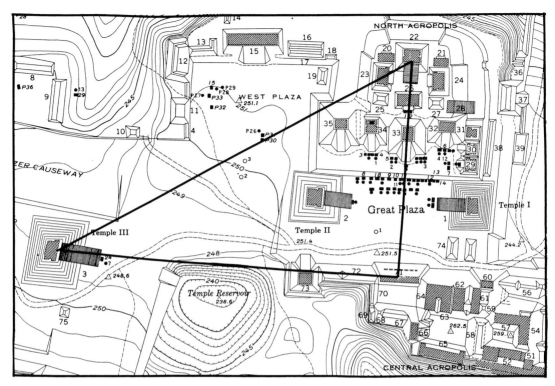

111 The location of Temple III was determined by an integral right triangle that used the sacred axis of the North Acropolis as its baseline.

centered on Temple III is connected to the sacred north–south base line of the North Acropolis. The right-angle occurs on the north doorway of 5D-71 of the Central Acropolis, connecting with Temple 22 in the North Acropolis and the doorway of Temple III. The 3-4-5 integral triangle is nearly perfect (*ill. 111* and see Chapter Twelve).

Lintel 2 (*ill. 112*), which separates the interior rooms is carved in a style that is consistent with the stela date.[9] The front doorway and its assumed uncarved lintel had collapsed. On Lintel 2 the central figure once again has a jaguar-related theme, being clothed in a jaguar suit that is closely fitted over the obese frame of this ruler. The lord is attended by two obeisant individuals, their status indicated by their clothing and postures. All three figures hold trident flint objects recalling a similar object in the hand of Hasaw Chan K'awil on Altar 5 in AD 711, 99 years earlier.

The argument that the central figure is a pregnant female has occurred several times. There is little to support this argument, however, as the figure has no indication of breasts, and the hands and feet are the same size as those of the obviously male attendants. Evidence from an abundance of painted ceramics demonstrates that male royal corpulence was a commonality during the Late Classic period.

112 Drawing of Lintel 2, Temple III. The portly lord in a tight-fitting jaguar costume has variously been identified as Shield Skull II and Dark Sun. The date is AD 810.

113 *A magnificent jade pendant was discovered in Burial 77 in the West Plaza. The burial is very late in the Tikal sequence but the identity of its occupant is unknown.*

According to the Austin Group (1995) this ruler's name is Nu Bak Chak II, which makes him "Shield Skull II", the name of the great Hasaw Chan K'awil's father, who was buried under Temple 5D-33-1st. The full reading of the text tells us a bit more about the changing times. The text says that this ruler "erected a stela near Temple III in the company of Yokom He of Twelve Servants, Holy Lord of Aguateca." The *yokom* title identifies this lord as a member of the Calakmul hegemony. His friendly presence suggests that a rapprochement has occurred by this time between Tikal and the Dos Pilas polity of which Aguateca was a part.

These scant data indicate that the 30th ruler oversaw a time of peace between Tikal and its traditional enemies. Of course, this could be historic propaganda.[10]

The final ruler: Hasaw Chan K'awil II

A single date on a single stela provides information on the final recorded lord of Tikal. The paired monuments of Stela 11 and Altar 11 stand on the North Terrace in front of Temple 33, close to the now ancient sacred axis of the North Acropolis. The stela date is, like on Stela 24, a katun-ending date. However, two full katuns of 20 years have been skipped. The ending is for the second katun of the tenth cycle at 10.2.0.0.0 in the Maya count. The date is 13 August AD 869 with a gap of 59 years since the previous date on Shield Skull II's Stela 24

178

in front of Temple III. The inscription on Stela 11 identifies this katun-ending ruler as Hasaw Chan K'awil II. If there were no intervening rulers, he would be the 31st in succession and the last recorded lord of Tikal.

The extremely important date for the change of baktun into the 10th cycle is missing from our record. Given the history of the past century, with each lord lasting more or less 32 years in reign, it is possible that these last two kings did indeed fill the gap between Yax Ain II (Ruler C) and the end of the record, a probable span of 69–70 years. They would have to have been years relatively free of war given such long ruling spans.

A burial found under Structure 5D-11 in the West Plaza contained a rather remarkable tomb of a young individual. The grave goods strongly indicate a member of the late royal family. A very fine jade pendant had been suspended around the neck of this unknown personage (*ill. 113*).

The last three rulers all reached back in time to reuse names of illustrious predecessors. The last two rulers repeated an earlier father–son relationship. The final recorded ruler of Tikal ended the known history with the same name as the man who fathered the zenith of the site – a fitting end to a remarkable city.

Table 6
Chronology of the end of the Late Classic at Tikal
Time span: AD 768 – 869 (101 years)

Name	Date	Event	Ruler No
Yax Ain II			29th
(Curl Nose; First Crocodile II)	25 December AD 768	Accession on Stela 22	
	20 January AD 771	Dedication Group Q, Stela 22	
	7 October AD 790	Dedication Group, Stela 19	
Nu Bak Chak II			30th
(Shield Skull II)	24 June AD 810	Ruling, conclusion of 19th katun on Stela 24 Probably depicted on Lintel 2, Temple III	
Hasaw Chan K'awil II			31st
(Heavenly Standard Bearer)	13 August AD 869	Conclusion of 2nd katun of 10th cycle, on Stela 24	

CHAPTER TWELVE

LATE CLASSIC ARCHITECTURE, CITY PLANNING, AND THE GROWTH OF TIKAL

The history of a great city like Tikal is the story of its rulers and their works. A great portion of the archaeological field research performed at Tikal has yet to be published, but this drawback is compensated for by the speed with which epigraphers have dealt with old as well as new texts. In following the course of the city's history, I have dealt with topics of city growth, buildings raised by certain rulers, when this information was available, along with the succession of rulers and Tikal's vacillating fortunes. However, there are sufficient gaps in the knowledge that coverage of the architectural style and growth is necessarily uneven. This chapter will continue where Chapter Seven left off with discussion of style and growth during the Late Classic period. Because of its central importance to city growth in the Late Classic, mention has already been made in Chapters Nine, Ten, and Eleven of the use of geometry and alignment as a device for planned growth. This important feature of Tikal architecture will be further explained in this chapter.

In general, the city did not have any progressional pattern of development, such as from the center outwards. We saw that the earliest settlement was in a series of villages scattered near the edges of the Bajo de Santa Fe. Settlement then spread westwards to a series of locations which included the site of the North Acropolis as well as the Lost World Pyramid. These scattered settlements were likely unified into a definable small city by the time that Dynastic rule began, probably around AD 200. The architecture of Tikal took on its own distinctive qualities during the Early Classic, partially reflecting an influence from Teotihuacan. By the completion of the Early Classic, Tikal was already a dominant force engaged in warfare and alliance with its neighbors in the Peten. By AD 600 Tikal was a substantial city with a population that could have been anywhere between 25,000–50,000 inhabitants, or more.

The Great Temples of Tikal, the city's signature style of architecture, all date to the Late Classic period, beginning with 5D-33-1st (AD 672–682) and concluding with Temple III (AD 810), spanning a period of approximately 135 years and six lords of Tikal. Stylistically, this period was not without architectural variation. Only three of the six named Great Temples have the basic interior three rooms. Temple VI reverted to an earlier style of proportion with three frontal doorways. During this period many other Late Classic temples of smaller scale were built without reference to the magnificent "Great Temple" style, but rather conforming to the ancient three-doorway, low/broad proportion established in the Preclassic including for example, 5E-38 in the East Plaza (*ill. 114*), 3D-43 in the North Group, as well as dozens of smaller temples scattered throughout the site and of unidentified authorship.

Palaces, twin-pyramid groups and ballcourts form the other most significant clusters of architectural style. Of these, palaces demonstrate the greatest variety in form while twin-pyramid groups are the most rigidly stylized with little variation in form. Such broad generalizations are subject to challenge on a micro-academic level since two identical buildings of the same type are rare.

Twin-pyramid groups

Twin-pyramid groups are a Tikal type of architectural assemblage that has been found in few locations outside this city. The group functioned as a sacred marker of the change of a time period (the 20-year katun) and served the ruling lord as a means of public declaration of his success in seeing the end of the katun, whether he was in power at its beginning or not. His power as a ruler dominating a conquered victim is the usual theme of the north-placed stela and altar pair. The group was an architectural cosmogram of the cardinal directions always placing the king in the north, the heavens, while the southern "palace" structure displayed the nine doorways of the nine lords of the underworld.

114 Temple 5E-38 stands at the top of the Mendez Causeway on the east side of the East Plaza. Its role in Tikal's history remains unknown.

115 Reconstruction drawing of the small ballcourt between Temple I and the Central Acropolis. Note the viewing shelter on the highest architectural element. This shelter is on the axis of the ballcourt.

An analogy to this theme is found in the Great Plaza itself, where Temples I and II form the pyramidal functions marking the movement of the sun; the North Acropolis served in the role of the northern heavens (and in this case, burial place of kings); while a pair of multi-doored palaces of differing date mark the southern boundary. Structure 5D-71 was an Early Classic building whose central axis marked the sacred north–south axis of the North Acropolis. Still of Early Classic date, an adjacent nine-doorway palace (Structure 5D-120) was later raised to the immediate east, but off the sacred axis.

Altogether nine twin-pyramid groups are known from the site, but it is not known if they are consecutive. The earliest groups are in incomplete condition and have no associated inscriptions. However, the beginnings of the practice are clearly in the Early Classic period, while the Late Classic versions are better preserved, dated and larger in scale.[1]

Ballcourts

The few ballcourts known from Tikal vary more in scale than in form. One large example is located in the East Plaza[2] and is of Late Classic date but not associated as yet with any particular ruler.

The most obvious ballcourt today is the small group in the Great Plaza just south of Temple I. Numbered 5D-74, the axis of this court aligns with a building high above in the Central Acropolis, and the northern room of this structure likely served as a royal viewing stand (*ill. 115* and *see ill. 73*).

The other most prominent examples are found in the Plaza of the Seven Temples where three playing courts spread across the entire north side of the plaza. The structure numbers are 5D-78-81. From the north side, the Plaza of the Seven Temples could be entered only by passing through one of the playing fields of the three parallel ballcourts. All known examples at Tikal of ballcourts are tentatively assigned to a Late Classic date, but their authorship by ruler is not available.

The playing courts are all oriented north–south. Sloping side benches were used in the game to bounce the ball back into the playing field (*see ill. 115*). Adjacent at a higher level were platforms accessible by stairs where viewers could watch the game. The court in the East Plaza showed evidence that these viewing platforms were covered. Our only evidence for the specific type of game played is in the form of displaced carved monuments that could easily have served as ballcourt markers. Column Altar 1 was described in Chapter Ten as one of the works of Yik'in. A very similar monument was found re-set in the East Plaza, just as Column Altar 1 had been in the West Plaza. The two markers may have originated from the East Plaza court, which would imply that it was built by Yik'in. A much smaller fragment of another similar monument was retrieved from the Postclassic debris in the Central Acropolis, telling us that these small monuments were dragged from the ballcourts and often destroyed during the collapse of the city.

Palaces

The category of palace architecture is perhaps the most complex in ancient Maya society because the functions of the widely varied group are so poorly understood. Only two functions are clear: family residence and administration. How these two functions combine to form a royal court in the European sense is not clear in its details but very strongly indicated from a number of lines of evidence (*pl. XII*).

Other functions of buildings we call palaces most certainly occurred: royal retreat houses for men or women; judiciary courts (in the legal sense); schools for the training of children of the royal families in the arts, sciences and religion; perhaps even storage houses for major paraphernalia. We have to remember that the texts from both Temples I and IV speak of the capture and singular importance of the royal palanquins of enemy cities. Such large and elaborate items had to be stored somewhere appropriate, and Tikal would have had its own similar paraphernalia, presumably in greater quantity than those that were captured.

The Central Acropolis is the only palace group that was extensively excavated as a surviving above-ground group. Excavations elsewhere at the site show that earlier palace groups were buried in their entirety, either as the result of conquest or by deliberate retirement, for example Group 6C-XVI. This remarkable group, excavated by Juan Pedro Laporte, appears to have consisted of an entire palace complex from the Early Classic period which was partially razed and fully buried, as if the entire group had been ritually killed.[3] Similar remains found beneath the East Acropolis in the East Plaza suggest a comparable event.[4]

The Central Acropolis is unique at Tikal because of its location on the south side of both the Great Plaza and East Plaza at the sacred core of the city; and also by its known length of developmental growth, ranging from the Preclassic through to the very collapse of the city, a period of roughly 1200 years. This important group will be discussed at some length, but first it is useful to look at other types of palace structures and groupings that are different from those found in the Central Acropolis.

Limited courtyard palace groups

There are a number of palace complexes at Tikal which have grouped the main buildings around a single or double courtyard. These complexes stand out markedly as different from the long-term growth and multi-courtyard configuration of the Central Acropolis. The few examples that exist in the central core of the site have the appearance of the Inca royal court as found in Highland Peru. In the latter tradition each king built his own royal court and it was maintained after his death as his personal property. These constructs (called *panaqas*) were quadrangular in formation and contained residential as well as religious functions. Also they date to half a millennium after the downfall of Tikal, so there is no connection other than analogy. At Tikal there are four such groupings arranged almost (but not quite) in a cardinal distribution about the site center. They are: Group G, associated with the Mendez Causeway and Temple VI possibly built by Yik'in (Ruler B); Group F associated by geometry only with the works of Yik'in's son Yax Ain II; a group called the Bat Palace to the immediate west of Temple III; and a group to the south of Temple V, including Structures 6D-42 through 65 in two courtyards, facing east. Three of these examples face east (all but Group F), the direction that a residence should face towards the rising sun and the direction of life and rebirth. The east-facing groups are fronted by large spacious platforms. Both the Bat Palace grouping and Group G have broad stairways that connect their spacious eastern approaches to the surrounding terrain. In the case of Group F the orientation is south, as the map clearly shows that the open ambient space "fronting" the enclosed group lies to the south. The southern group (6D-42-65) is made more complex by the presence of a greater number of small buildings and is without the large approach space on the eastern side, although the courtyards do open to the east. This group is very important in the configuration of the Late Classic geometry of the city in that it ties together the locations of Temple VI, Temple IV and the temple called 3D-43 in the north group, known as Group H.

116 A view of the interior courtyard of Group G, the palace complex which integrates into the Mendez Causeway and is thought to be the work of the 27th lord of Tikal, Yik'in.

Only Group G has been partially excavated, and none of the open eastern spaces have been investigated. However, standing architecture allows some knowledge of the room arrangements in Groups F, G, and the Bat Palace (*ill. 116*). In each of these groups, the known room arrangements are complex. There are transverse rooms and rooms in tandem, sometimes interconnected, sometimes not. In all observable cases there is evidence that the room arrangements were changed over time: big rooms were divided into smaller ones, and routes of access altered, common features of palaces.

These limited courtyard groupings are all raised on elevated platforms, with some buildings raised even higher. The decision to designate certain groups as an "acropolis" or not is to date entirely subjective and without analytic justification. It is relatively easy to ascribe Group G to Yik'in and Group F to his son Yax Ain II, but the other two groups are still shrouded in mystery, though they are visibly Late Classic in date, excepting the 6D group about which nothing is known other than what can be seen on the map.

Freestanding major palaces

This category is quite diverse and somewhat artificial, serving as a means of handling a number of important structures. There are at least two types: (1) highly elevated and large-scale structures with tandem rooms that face only in one direction, and (2) elevated single, or multi-room structures that face equally in two directions.

The functions of these two types are clearly different, but no doubt both are ceremonial, as opposed to residential. Type 1 includes structures in a variety of locations around the center of the site. The nine-doorway structure, 5D-15, is unique in that it faces south, while all other nine-doorway structures known at Tikal face north. Other examples are 5D-77, facing south in the Lost World Pyramid group; 5D-105, facing east, on the east side of Temple V; and 5E-51, probably facing north, to the west of Group G.

Type 2 is a passage structure, serving the function of passage from a public space into a ceremonial space. The most prominent example is 5D-91 (*ill. 117*) on the south side of the Plaza of the Seven Temples. A formal ceremonial stair is visible on the south side of this major palace. All other counterparts are found in the context of groups, specifically the Central Acropolis. Structure 5D-71 is already known to have vast importance because its axial line lies on the sacred axis of the North Acropolis. The structure offers highly limited access from the Great Plaza into Court 1 of the Central Acropolis.

Similarly, the palace known as 5D-44 apparently served a combination of ceremonial functions. Seven doorways face northward into the East Plaza. However, access was available when the building was first built (date uncertain), through the north gallery into the south gallery, and hence into Court 6 of the Central Acropolis. With time this access was closed in keeping with a general closure of access into the Acropolis during the later part of the Late Classic period.

117 Detail of a painting by Diana Nobbs of the Seven Temples Group. Structure 5D-91 in the background is typical of a "passage" type of palace.

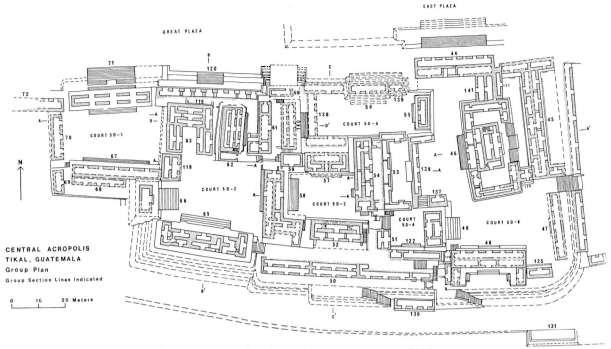

118 The Central Acropolis is a complex of multi-level courtyards surrounded by palaces of differing function and constructed over five centuries.

The Central Acropolis

The most extensive investigation of a palace complex (*ill. 118*) was made in this group, and the results have provided the greatest amount of information for interpretation of structure functions as well as the techniques used at Tikal for architectural planning and surveying. The architectural arrangements in the Central Acropolis have revealed how the Maya of Tikal dealt with organization of space – how they planned for new major construction. A simple method of architectural surveying is involved that allows a precise method for laying out the floor plan of a proposed building using reference points from earlier, pre-existing buildings. The principles are simple once recognized and multiple examples are available from the Central Acropolis courtyards.

The survey technique

(1) Each building has a single critical point in its plan that determines the location for the new building. This point is the juncture of the two lines that will be formed by the front wall of the building and the central axis through the central doorway. These lines intersect at right-angles. Their point of intersection is the location point of the building (*ill. 119*).

(2) Alignment of location points was apparently important to the Maya of Tikal, so that placement of a third building in alignment with the placement points of two earlier buildings demonstrated respect or honor of these earlier buildings.

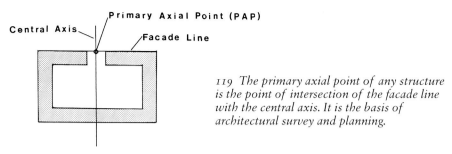

119 The primary axial point of any structure is the point of intersection of the facade line with the central axis. It is the basis of architectural survey and planning.

(3) The placement of the location point is established by reference to the location points of two earlier buildings which have importance to the new building. The most common reason for importance is ancestry, that is, structures raised by ancestors who will be honored by this new building. The three points, two pre-existing and one new, are connected in an integral right triangle (*ill. 120*).

(4) The new building may now find its floor plan, with the location point already fixed, by a direct-sight survey from one of the two pre-existing reference points on the triangle (*ill. 121*). The surveyor stands over his reference point, and, holding an instrument, sights the turning right angles from all the visible corners or other architecturally important points on existing buildings that are in view. Two clear examples of this technique are available in Court 2 of the Central Acropolis. The result is that sufficient new points can be laid out on the flat surface of the proposed building, and with the application of symmetry, the entire floor plan can be achieved.

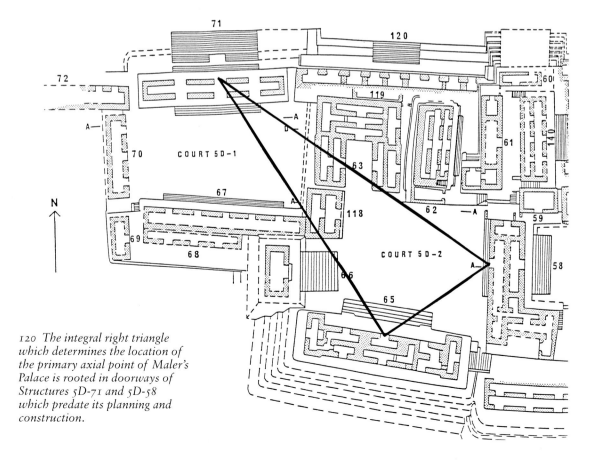

120 The integral right triangle which determines the location of the primary axial point of Maler's Palace is rooted in doorways of Structures 5D-71 and 5D-58 which predate its planning and construction.

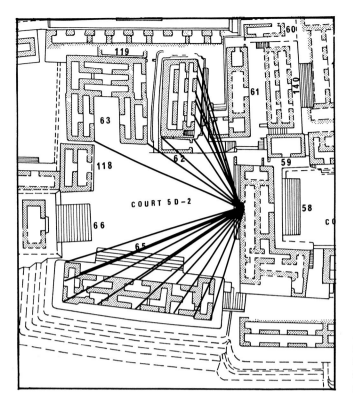

121 *Key points on the ground plan of Maler's Palace were surveyed by turning multiple right-angles from visible points on earlier buildings as viewed from the doorway in 5D-58.*

The survey instrument

The instrument for sighting right-angle turns is a flat celt-shaped object, which could be made of wood, but only examples in jade are known. Three perforations in the surface form the right-angle. Pegs placed in these perforations become the sighting rods. Such objects are frequently depicted hanging around the necks of kings, and are usually identified as "pectorals." The object shown in *ill. 122* is from a royal tomb in Caracol. None has been retrieved as yet from Tikal. Numerous examples have been found in Costa Rica, and while these are recognized as traded Maya pieces, we do not know their places of origin.

While the Central Acropolis has proved the best laboratory for revealing this system of urban planning, it extends over the rest of Tikal.

122 *An Early Classic jade pectoral found in a tomb in Caracol may be a prototype survey instrument for turning right-angles.*

Tikal's planned growth

The date of origin for application of the triangulation and right-angle system is not known. There are examples of such usage in the Early Classic period, but much more investigation and study of the available data are required to confidently say anything more definitive on the matter. However, a number of quite significant progressions mark the Late Classic, particularly during the period of the three apex kings: Hasaw Chan K'awil, Yik'in Chan K'awil and Yax Ain II. Hasaw's planning of the Great Plaza at *c.* AD 730–732 is the earliest highly dramatic example, a configuration already described in Chapter Nine. His triangle honored his late wife and an unknown ancestor buried beneath the pyramid temple of 3D-43. An even more dramatic example is the triangular connection that unites Temples I, IV, and V.[5] As the latest structure in this group is Temple V, the builder of this Great Temple was the creator of the formation (*ill. 123*). I have argued that this was Yax Ain II (Ruler C). Temple I was the creation of Hasaw; Temple IV is the work of his son Yik'in; and so the grandson, Yax Ain II honored his father and grandfather with the creation of Temple V. The right-angle sits at Temple I, the earliest in the group, and the triangle is a perfect 3-4-5 configuration in the Pythagorean series.

A third example already noted is the relationships that unite Temple IV and Temple VI with the northern 3C-43 and an obscure (but notable) structure in the south (6D-61).

A final example is the alignment from an Early Classic temple in the Lost World group to the palace complex of Group G, passing through the main temple of the South Acropolis. This latter serves as a fulcrum for a number of relationships, in which a right-angle to Stela 20 in twin-pyramid Complex O, way in the north, serves as the basis of two integral right triangles, dividing central Tikal into two spatial entities. Several other relationships spin off of these in a progression of triangulations (*see ill. 108*). It would be inappropriate to attempt to detail every such example in this volume. Suffice it to say that the city's growth was anything but haphazard. It was a carefully planned progression in which each new monumental building served as an honorific to two earlier structures of similar importance.

This system of architectural planning is not unique to Tikal.[6] Incidents of its use are observed at Palenque, Copan and a number of other large Maya cities. In fact, every lowland site for which a detailed map exists shows some evidence of this system of building triangulation.

Observation of this remarkable feature of Tikal architecture raises more questions that it solves. Where did the knowledge come from? How, in practicality, was it executed over large distances on the surface and quite formidable ones in the vertical dimension. Some answers may be derived from outside sources. The ancient Egyptians used the exact same system as a means of land measure to re-survey their fields after every annual flooding of the Nile. Later, the system found its way into the design of their art and architecture. While

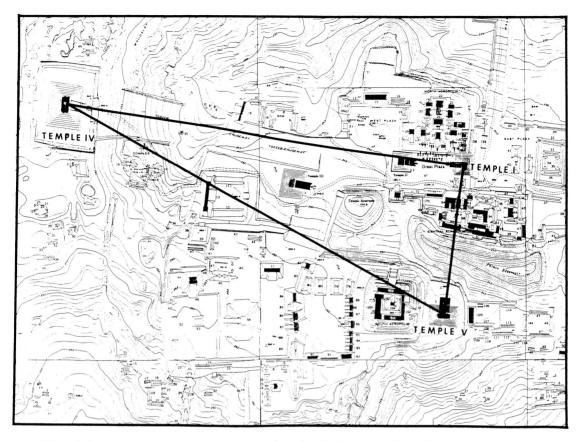

123 Map of the integral right triangle which served to plan the location of Temple V relating it to the earlier Temples I and IV.

there is no connection between the two societies, a similar process of development undoubtedly was in operation. As an agricultural society dependent upon a shifting field system, the use of land measure is logical. The transmission of this measuring technique to art and architecture follows, and this is what we see in the Central Acropolis and throughout Tikal.

The greenstone survey instrument found by Arlen and Diane Chase in Caracol was an instrument belonging to a member of the elite. Knowledge of the movement of stars and of the calendar represented power to the elite class of the Maya because it related to essential food production. Knowledge and control of the manipulation of space likely was understood by every farmer who used it to lay out his milpa. At the elite level, it was used for the veneration of ancestors expressed by city planning. In light of these observations, the layout of the city of Tikal is a massive expression of ancestral veneration over more than one-and-a-half millennia.

CHAPTER THIRTEEN

DECLINE AND FALL:
THE LAST DAYS

The decline of Tikal had already begun before the last recorded inscription at 13 August AD 869 (10.2.0.0.0). The absence of a record for the important katun-endings which preceded this last one testify to the fact that the city was in trouble.

There is a small ceremonial center called Jimbal that lies 12.5 km to the north of the Great Plaza inside the settlement range of the greater city. This center erected a carved stela at the Maya date of 22 June AD 879 (10.2.10.0.0), ten years after the last date at Tikal. The inscription contains some non-Maya, probably Mexican, glyphs and makes no mention of Tikal. It is probable that this small center at this time considered itself independent, lying outside the original Tikal settlement boundaries.

Inscriptions continue to occur at a few other sites in the Peten, such as Ixlu and Seibal, but generally the peak of civilization in this part of the lowlands is over by AD 870.

Archaeological evidence for the last years of occupation give us a confused and mixed picture, as one might expect during a period of cultural disintegration. However, the evidence does not provide any clues to the cause of the decline. Whatever the causes were, they did not pertain to Tikal alone, but to the Peten landscape in general. The subject continues to be debated by scholars on a broad geographical scale.

The Terminal Classic

The period which is characterized as the "collapse" at Tikal is referred to as the "Terminal Classic," associated in turn with the Eznab ceramic complex. The dates ascribed to this complex are AD 850–950. That the collapse lasted for a century is based on a "guesstimate" of how long it would take for stone architecture to deteriorate from natural causes. The pattern of architectural disintegration found at Tikal depends largely upon the loss of the wooden lintels which support doorways. When these lintels are removed, by whatever agency, the vault stones above fall, creating an unnatural arch above the doorway. Eventually, the whole roof will fall inward. In cases of multiple-storied buildings, the upper story is particularly subject to this form of natural deterioration, while the lower stories are protected somewhat. The pattern is quite clear.

Where a second story wall coincided directly over a lower story wall, the lower story remained preserved intact. However, where the second story covered only part of a building below, the part of the lower floor that was exposed on its roof was subject to collapse.

David Freidel has argued with reference to the northern lowlands that this condition of semi-collapsed structures is the result of "ritual termination" of the building, and he offers evidence of terminal conflict. In this interpretation Freidel found that the debris and artifacts over the floor of a collapsed building had been ritually placed there with "white earth" deliberately spread over these objects.[1] Such a case was found at the site of Cerros in Belize. However, the patterns of protected versus unprotected structure and their coincidence with physical collapse at Tikal indicate that there is no intentional termination involved at this site. At Tikal we interpret the objects found on a structure floor as evidence of the very last occupants of that structure, and we date the objects to the Eznab phase.

The largest body of evidence for this phase was found in the Central Acropolis during my excavations of that architectural complex. Bill Haviland also discovered extensive deposits of Eznab material similarly distributed in a palace located in a more remote part of the city. The evidence described here will be that from the Central Acropolis.

The physical material used for evidence can be examined in several differing categories. These are midden deposits inside rooms; midden deposits in exterior locations; and burials. Within these categories there are further interesting divisions of types of material, the most intriguing of which are food remains and musical instruments. Because the Maya were so meticulous about cleaning up, probably in cyclical occasions related to the calendar, midden deposits from periods of earlier occupation are very rare. Ancient garbage is most often found as part of construction fill in large buildings except where middens are found in association with rural houses. The Maya were apparently very good about re-cycling. Therefore, the deposits from the terminal occupation of the city that never were cleaned up offer us a glimpse of daily life at this time in a manner that is not available from the peak of the Classic itself.

The three major sources of these deposits in the Central Acropolis are from Courts 5D-2, 5D-4, and 5D-6, the latter two being the more extensive and productive. For discussion purposes, the important middens will be identified by their operation and sub-operation designations from the excavations.

Court 5D-2, Operation 80C

The midden called Operation 80C was located in an alley between structures 5D-62 and 5D-63, a U-shaped structure. This deposit contained ceramics of Eznab date and also human bones. The bones represent one of several cases of real burials in middens found in the Central Acropolis for this time period. The location suggests occupation of the east rooms of 5D-63 and probably also the rooms of 5D-62 (*see ill. 118*). These buildings are of types that had ceremonial, possibly specialized, but not domestic residence, during their peak in the 8th and 9th centuries. The domestic refuse found for the terminal period is not consistent with the original functions of these buildings. Although we do not have middens for the earlier Classic period to verify the functions for that period, the domestic nature of the Eznab midden in Operation 80C is definitely at variance with the ceremonial nature of the original building. During the terminal phase original functions of the structures have been abandoned, and any stone building in good condition was occupied by surviving residents of Tikal as shelter. Elsewhere, the midden contents provide evidence that these people were using objects that belonged to the elite ruling class, but they were living in conditions that are very different from those of the Classic period. The very fact that the middens were not removed is indicative of this difference.

Court 5D-4 and Operation 96
Although much of this courtyard contained midden material, the most concentrated and important parts were located both inside and outside Structure 5D-51 and along the front (north side) of Structure 5D-122 – in other words, on the west and south sides of the courtyard. Probably related to the occupation of this area was another midden at a lower level in a cul-de-sac south of Structure

124 A view into the open space of Court 4 in the Central Acropolis. The court is surrounded by small Late Classic palaces that were occupied during the collapse of the site and the location of many trash middens of this date.

5D-124 (*ill. 124*). This refuse was no doubt thrown from the living area in the courtyard above.

The stratigraphy of the midden inside 5D-51 is of greatest interest. Immediately over the floor the refuse of occupation included the remains of an atlatl (spearthrower) with carved bone handles. This is the type of object that was introduced from Highland Mexico back in the times of Jaguar Claw I in the 4th century. This example, indicative of purposeful food collection by hunting (or warfare), was associated with ceremonial paraphernalia such as fragments of polychrome ceramic vessels and ceramic figurine whistles. Above this, were collapsed stones from the vault of the front room. A thin layer of *guano* (bat dung) on top of the stones indicated a period of abandonment. Above the *guano* was another occupation layer with most interesting contents. A fire pit had been excavated into the layers below and this was surrounded by organic food remains including not just corn, beans and squash but also a wide variety of seeds from fruits and nuts. Associated ceramics were a mix of broken domestic vessels and ceremonial polychrome vessels, some identical to those of the earlier Late Classic Imix phase. It is possible that these latter originated in a Late Classic tomb which had been looted, but such a thesis is unprovable. Even more interesting was the presence of a human coprolite (feces). The combination of ceremonial and prestige ceramics with the evidence of cooking and absence of hygienic measures provides a very strange and uncharacteristic view of Maya habits. It has been suggested by a member of the Austin Group that this room may have served as a prison, an intriguing suggestion supported by the presence in the doorjambs of the entrance of secondary holes that indicate uncharacteristic closure of the doorway.

Midden 97A, Court 5D-6

Nearby, just to the north of Court 5D-4 was a long, linear midden designated 97A. The inventory of the contents of this midden best exemplifies the curious blend of material from domestic, daily life with ceremonialism and indications of wealth.

The mundane pursuits of daily life were represented by: 19 flint cores; 33 fragments of chert or obsidian bifaces (axes or knives); 24 *mano* fragments (used for grinding grain or nuts); 32 *metate* fragments (grinding plates); 10 hammer or rubbing stones; 1 fragment of a chert dagger; 1 fragment of a ceramic colander; 1 stone spindle whorl; 6 perforated sherds, probably used as spindle whorls; and 248 fragments of animal bone. Not counted were detritus of chert and obsidian, human bone fragments, charcoal, and many kilograms of domestic ceramic fragments.

On the other hand, items reflecting wealth and high status included the following: 14 ceramic pellets (from rattle feet on ceramic vessels); 242 figurine fragments; 45 fragments of modeled-carved vessels; 34 censer fragments (for burning incense); 3 identifiable whistle fragments; 1 ceramic box (almost complete); 6 effigy vessel fragments; 1 ceramic flute fragment; 1 ceramic ear-flare

125 In the foreground is Structure 5D-128 in the Central Acropolis with Court 4 in the background, both locations of collapse period middens. The tall structure in the rear is 5D-52, the "Five-Story Palace."

fragment; 2 polychrome sherds (one with painted hieroglyphic text); 23 stucco fragments (architectural adornment); 1 bone tube (probably a fan handle); 1 each of shell: finger ring, fan handle, pendant, and 4 shell tinklers. This list is typical of the contents of a Terminal Classic midden in the Central Acropolis and demonstrates a curious blend of domestic daily refuse and costly ceremonial paraphernalia (*ill. 125*).

The middens of 5D-46

Once again, the clan lineage house built by Jaguar Claw I in the mid-4th century figures in the story of Tikal, even at the very end. Whether the last members of the lineage were indeed the last occupants of this house, or whether it had been taken over by interlopers is not known. The longevity of this structure as an important building is rare in Maya archaeology.

There were five important middens associated with this structure, two in the outer courtyards of the building and three inside rooms. Two of these will be summarized here because of their special importance for the reading of the last days of Tikal.

Midden A (Operation 98A) was located in the north patio of 5D-46, a space that had been added sometime quite late in the Late Classic. The exterior midden was heaped against the north wall of the Early Classic building and extended halfway across the patio (*ill. 126*). There was a fire pit excavated into the original patio floor and associated with food remains, animal bones and charred seeds. The remarkable feature here was the presence of human bone that had been partly charred and exhibited tooth marks. These human bones included a large skull fragment with burning on the interior surface. The suggestion of cannibalism is strong. However, the fact that human remains are found frequently in midden deposits during this period has led some to interpret this evidence as just another burial that was attacked by rodents. As excavator, my own interpretation is that these particular human remains were mixed with other food refuse together with direct evidence of cooking and they represent part of the kitchen midden. Such mixture with kitchen material was not the case with the true midden burials.

Midden C (Operation 98K) was an interior midden in the central room on the western side of the building . The midden was banded by alternating soil

126 Reconstruction of Court 6 in the Central Acropolis with 5D-46 on the left, the house of Jaguar Claw I. Palaces visible in this group span 500 years of building and were the scene of final occupation during the collapse.

colors and piled up against the rear (east) wall of the room, sloping down through the doorway and out onto the exterior platform. The layers of debris were dense with typical Eznab midden artifacts, and the banding indicated periods of cyclical deposit. Hopes for some stratigraphic divisions of the Eznab phase were dashed when parts of the same polychrome vessel were retrieved in both upper and lower levels of the deposit. The time period for accumulation of this midden, 1.8 m (5.9 ft) in depth, must have been relatively short. The method of accumulation can only be explained by the presence of a hole in the ceiling of the now absent roof. Remnants of rooms on the second story showed that individuals could have been living on the upper level, dumping their trash into the room below. The wide physical separation of two parts of the same vessel further suggests that wide intervals occurred between bouts of cleaning. This, again, is not typical behavior with any parallel in the modern ethnography of the Maya.

Nearly all exterior doorways in the heavily occupied parts of the Acropolis showed evidence that attempts at blocking them with something more substantial than the usual curtains were employed in the Classic period. Whether these door blocks were designed to keep things out or to keep people in is a matter of conjecture. They do suggest a time of small population and high stress. This stress is evident in many signs: the charred and chewed human bones, the presence of kitchen items mixed with ritual and rare items of wealth, the blocking of doorways. A number of ceramic specimens are of a type known to come from Belize in this same Terminal Classic period. The idea that a trade network was still in operation under these conditions of declining social order seems strange, but the evidence is that this was the case.

Musical instruments

One of the more interesting features to emerge in the artifactual assemblage for the Terminal Classic is the number of musical instruments that found their way into the midden deposits. Those found included ceramic drums, a ceramic "flute" with an anthropomorphic figure, a set of ceramic pan pipes, a bone rasp and numerous whistles scattered throughout the acropolis. This orchestra of instruments may well be representative of types that were present throughout the Classic period and only happen to be preserved for our edification because the refuse of the final occupation was not cleaned up (*ill. 127*).

Causes of the collapse

This topic has already produced a multiplicity of academic papers with dozens of explanations. The volume titled *The Classic Maya Collapse* edited by T. Patrick Culbert has most extensively explored the variety of offered causes. Very briefly, the major causes favored by scholars include social unrest and revolution, disease, drought, change in water-level, land mismanagement in food production, and warfare. Over the years scholars have agreed upon one thing:

127 (left) A flute-like ceramic wind instrument that was recovered in the Central Acropolis provides a hint of pre-Columbian music.

no single factor is sufficiently supported in the evidence to stand out as a sole cause of the collapse. Many factors were involved in a process that was enormously complex, took many years to occur, and varied geographically over the spread of the Maya lowlands.

Recently, the work of Arthur Demarest, Stephen Houston, and Takeshi Inomata in the Petexbatun (Dos Pilas) region has demonstrated convincingly that warfare was a primary factor in that region. Certainly, the history of Tikal, as now interpreted from the inscriptions, shows a deep involvement in conflict with its near and far neighbors. This factor must have exerted considerable influence on the eventual downfall of the site. Equally certainly, other factors were involved. Change in the water-levels in the Peten is now strongly argued to be evident during the latter part of the Late Classic period. Such lowering of the water-levels in the wetlands that surrounded Tikal would have had a powerful influence upon the ability to exercise intensive agriculture in those environments. Stress introduced by any of the above factors would be expected to be accompanied by social unrest and probably disease. Years of warfare, and the added stress of a lowered water supply, and hence less food, could have brought about the disruption of the socially stratified society at Tikal, which we call the "collapse."[2]

The painting produced in 1915 by Santa Fe artist, Carlos Vierra, probably shows Tikal most accurately as it looked in the Terminal and Postclassic (*pl. XIII*). Made without ever having visited the site, Vierra captured the image of a magnificent city falling into decay and succumbing to the creeping inroads of the rainforest.

The Postclassic

Little is known of the Postclassic at Tikal because the occupation was so slight. The ceramics are distinguished by the complex name Caban, and examples have been retrieved from scattered portions of the site. These ceramic types relate to other sites that preserved a strong occupation during this late period, especially small sites close to or on Lake Peten Itza some 60 km to the southwest. Sites like Motul de San Jose, Ixlu, Punta Nima and Tayasal surrounded the lake and continued to be occupied into the Postclassic period. The dates for evidence of this occupation at Tikal are set rather arbitrarily at AD 950–1200. The small number of artifacts found suggest that visitors from the lake sites passed through or stayed briefly at Tikal, perhaps on pilgrimage, and left behind some evidence of their visit. As described in Chapter One, the site of Tayasal continued to be occupied until the late 17th century when it was finally conquered by the Spanish. By this time, it seems that there was no memory of Tikal, as the Spanish neither heard of it nor did they leave a record of visiting the abandoned ruins.

Finally, there was a small settlement at Tikal in the 19th century for which remnants have been recovered – late Colonial forms of pottery and even metal instruments. The name "Tikal" was attributed to these people as described in Chapter One. One tradition says that the late settlement was eventually driven from residence by a plague of rabid bats. After this occupation, the ruins lay abandoned once again until the arrival of the various early visitors and the University of Pennsylvania project in 1955. Since this date, the site has enjoyed permanent occupation and hopefully will continue to do so, since abandonment equals destruction.

Retrospect

Even though the first occupation of Tikal was somewhat late in the framework of the entire lowlands, it nevertheless was occupied for at least 1,670 years. The early stages of development reflected those of the lowland Maya as a whole, seeing the evolution from scattered farming villages into a cohesive community with an agricultural economy and a strong ritual framework.

By AD 200 the concept of family dynasty was introduced, a concept that gripped the city until its last ruler carved and set his last monument in AD 869. Almost certainly the family line did not stay intact, but was broken and usurped by interlopers from outside more than once. The longest break was the Hiatus, lasting 133 years when Tikal was under outside domination, likely from the southeastern city of Caracol. The Early Classic period ended in darkness and silence in the inscribed records.

With the emergence of the Late Classic, Tikal struggled in a difficult renaissance which finally burst into flower by AD 680 with the appearance of its greatest ruler Hasaw Chan K'awil I. Wealth and power grew under this man and reached a peak in the rule of his son Yik'in Chan K'awil. Despite continued wealth, there then began a decline with the 29th ruler Yax Ain II, Hasaw I's grandson, who died around AD 800. The decline accelerated with the final record, after long gaps, in AD 869.

Investigations of the history and archaeology of the site have been extensive, perhaps greater than at any other New World site. The results of these investigations are only partially available to date, and when fully available will still represent knowledge of only a small percentage of the vast city. Certainly Tikal still holds secrets and surprises yet to be revealed. The history of a single city like Tikal casts light on the Maya civilization as a whole. Study of Tikal has illuminated many facets of Maya culture: how the Maya engaged in politics and warfare; the function of royal courts; the manner of architectural surveying and city planning; the role of outside influence, particularly from Mexico; and not least, attributes of a city's style in art and architecture.

As visitors to the site still experience at Tikal, the presence is overwhelming. The horizontal and vertical scales are vast – the expenditure of human effort hard to comprehend. The beauty and dangers of the setting are humbling. This volume has only been able to scrape the surface of many complex topics. We all wait with bated breath for the next chapter in Tikal studies.

Visiting Tikal

The cycle of rainy and dry seasons has made the best time to visit Tikal from February to May, the traditional dry season. However, there is no way to accurately predict just when the cycle of rains will occur, especially in recent years when the influence of El Niño has displaced the normal cycles. In the dry season, there are fewer flying insects, less humidity, and even fewer tourists, making a visit ideal.

The political situation for the country of Guatemala must always be checked in advance, but in the past this has had very little effect on the safety of tourism.

There are two entrance fees to pay if entering the park in your own vehicle. The first is for the vehicle and is payable at the gated park entrance several miles south of the archaeological zone on the paved road. The second is a day fee paid at another gate located a short distance west of the hotel and museum zone. A ticket is good for each day allowing multiple entries and costs 10 US dollars, subject to raises.

At Tikal there are several hotels and a camp ground operated mainly for the youth group who choose to travel on a very low budget. The hotel favored by most visitors at the site is the *Posada de la Selva* (or Jungle Lodge) which offers semi-detached bungalows with overhead fans, but no air conditioning. There now is a welcome swimming pool on site (don't drink the water), a moderately good dining room and bar. For those who wish more luxurious accommodation there are resort hotels in the areas of Flores and Santa Helena, where the airport is located. The choices are many in this area and one needs to consult a travel agent for current information. Popular with the tour groups are the Villas Maya located on a small lake a few miles east of the airport at Santa Helena. Another, even grander hotel, at the east end of Lake Peten Itza and closer to the Tikal park is the Westin Hotel, Camino Real. Bus communication to the park is not provided by hotels unless one is part of an official tour group, which is recommended. At present, in the 1990s, it is still possible to enlist on a tour group that is led by one of the original University of Pennsylvania archaeologists. Such a group is highly recommended because it has a time limit and these archaeologists can recount intriguing anecdotes of the "good old days" in a way that no other tour guide can communicate.

At the site, there are a number of facilities available. These include two museums of major importance, neither of which should be missed. Both are located near the entrance to the site as approached from the road from Santa Helena (the airport). One is the government-supported Stela Museum, connected to the official Visitor Center and restaurant, just west of the entrance to the site. The Visitor Center includes an extensive sales market with an astounding range of goods, including books, local and imported native crafts, reproductions of famous pieces from the tombs of Tikal, and much, much more. Take an extra suitcase for purchases.

The other important institution at the site is the Sylvanus Morley Museum, across the way at the entrance (north of the old airport), a facility which was opened during the heyday of the Pennsylvania Project and which contains many of the best pieces from the major tombs. This Museum has an entrance fee which maintains the building and staff. All facilities, including museums, hotels, restaurants and bars are located close to the entrance of the park where the road connects with the old and now defunct airport at the site.

While it is perfectly possible to visit the ruins on one's own and without a guide, it is not really recommended. The site is spread over a very large terrain and the possibility of missing something very important is high, not to mention the latent dangers of the rainforest of the Peten of which the visitor must be aware. The wildlife of the rainforest is still there, and the unwary need to be accompanied by an experienced guide. For the visitor who stays at the site overnight there is a special feature available. The park staff will issue special permits for a fee to enter the archaeological zone outside of the regular park hours, which vary by season. The fee pays for the time of a park ranger who must always accompany visitors in these off-hours. The attraction is to reach the Great Plaza, or Temple IV, in time to view the sunrise and hear the sounds of the rainforest as it comes to life each day. Conversely, a visit at night, especially during a full moon, is a powerful experience, allowing the visitor to view the rising of the moon behind Temple I from the top of Temple II. Most visitors find this experience worth the extra price.

Visiting Tikal is a major experience. No one has failed to be impressed by the magnitude of the achievement of the Maya at this major city, nor by the ambience of the environment. The best advice is to be both careful and wary and to take more film than you think you might need, especially film of high speed, since the forest casts a dappled shadow at all times.

Notes to the text

Chapter 1

1 *Prehispanic Maya Agriculture*, edited P.D. Harrison and B.L. Turner II, 414 pp., University of New Mexico Press, 1978. *Pulltrouser Swamp, Ancient Habitat, Agriculture, and Settlement in Northern Belize*, edited by B.L. Turner II and Peter D. Harrison, 294 pp., University of Texas Press, 1983.

2 "Warfare, Demography, and Tropical Ecology: Speculations on the Parameters of the Maya Collapse," by Arthur A. Demarest. Paper presented at the 89th Annual Meeting of the American Anthropological Association, New Orleans, 1990. "The Petexbatune Regional Archaeological Project: Peace, War and Collapse of an Ancient American Civilization," by Arthur A. Demarest. In *Five Hundred Years After Columbus: Proceedings of the 47th International Congress of Americanists*, edited by E.W. Andrews V and E.O. Mozzillo, pp. 98–102, Tulane University, New Orleans, 1994. *Hieroglyphs and History at Dos Pilas: Dynastic Politics of the Classic Maya*, University of Texas Press, Austin, 1993. *Politics and Hierarchy Amongst Classic Maya States*, by Simon Martin and Nikolai Grube, in Archaeology Magazine, 1994.

3 *The Santa Marta Rock Shelter, Ocozocoantla, Chiapas, Mexico*, R.S. MacNeish, and F.A. Peterson, NWAF Paper 14, 1962.

4 *Cuello, An Early Maya Community in Belize*, edited by Norman Hammond, 260 pp., Cambridge University Press, 1991.

5 "The Revolution in Ancient Maya Subsistence," Peter D. Harrison, pp. 99–113 in *Vision and Revision in Maya Studies*, edited by Flora S. Clancy and Peter D. Harrison, University of New Mexico Press, 1990.

6 "Eighth Century Physical Geography, Environment and Natural Resources in the Maya Lowlands," pp. 11–63 in *Lowland Maya Civilization in the Eighth Century AD*, edited J.A. Sabloff and J.S. Henderson, Dumbarton Oaks, Washington D.C., 1993.

7 "Tikal as a Trading Center," Christopher Jones, mss. Paper presented at the XLIII International Congress of Americanists, Vancouver, Canada, 1979.

8 "Aspects of Water Management in the Southern Maya Lowlands," pp. 71–119, in *Economic Aspects of Water Management in the Prehispanic World*, Research in Economic Anthropology, Supplement 7, edited by Vernon L. Scarborough and Barry L. Isaac, JAI Press, 1993.

9 "Preliminary Investigations of Agronomic Potentials in 'Bajos' Adjacent to Tikal, Peten, Guatemala," by Bruce H. Dahlin, pp. 305–312, in *Actes du XLIIe*

Congres International des Americanistes, Vol. 8, Paris, 1979. "Bajos Revisited: Visual Evidence for One System of Agriculture," pp. 247–254, by Peter D. Harrison, in *Pre-Hispanic Maya Agriculture*, ed. by Peter D. Harrison and B.L. Turner II, University of New Mexico Press, 1978.

10 *The Vegetation of the Peten*, Carnegie Institution of Washington Publication No. 478, Washington D.C., 1937.

11 *The Ceramics of Tikal: Vessels from the Burials, Caches, and Problematical Deposits*, Tikal Report No. 25, Part A, by T. Patrick Culbert, The University of Pennsylvania Museum, 1993.

12 "New Perspectives on Old Problems: Dynastic References for the Early Classic at Tikal," by Juan Pedro Laporte and Vilma Fialko C., pp. 33–66, in *Vision and Revision in Maya Studies*, edited by Flora S. Clancy and Peter D. Harrison, University of New Mexico Press, 1990.

13 For example, *The Maya*, 6th edition, by Michael D. Coe, Thames and Hudson, 1999; or *The Ancient Maya*, 5th edition, by Robert J. Sharer, Stanford University Press, 1994.

Chapter 2

1 Maler, 1911, Peabody.

2 C Coggins, 1986 (Guatemala); Jones, 1988.

3 Stuart, D., nd mss unpublished.

4 A. P. Maudslay, *Biologia Centrali-Americana*, Archaeology, Vols. I–IV, 1889–1902. This publication made available the maps and incredible photographs taken throughout the Maya area, including Tikal.

5 Teobert Maler, *Explorations in the Department of the Peten, Guatemala*, Vol. V, No.1, Tikal, Cambridge, 1911.

6 A. M. Tozzer, *A Preliminary Study of the Prehistoric Ruins of Tikal, Guatemala* Vol. V, No. 2 of Memoirs of the Peabody Museum, Harvard University, Cambridge, 1911.

7 Sylvanus G. Morley, *The Inscriptions of the Peten*, CIW Pub. 437, 1937.

8 R. B. Woodbury and A.S. Trik, *The Ruins of Zaculeu*, United Fruit Company, 1953.

9 *Secret of the Rain Forest*, Life Magazine, Vol. 45, No. 15, October 13, 1958, pp. 84–96. *Rich Find of Maya Bones*, Life Magazine, Vol. 47, No. 17, October 26, 1959, pp. 93–96.

10 My own Project number was 22, marking me as an early entry into the research group.

11 J. P. Laporte and Vilma Fialko C., "New Perspectives on Old Problems: Dynastic References for the Early Classic at Tikal," in *Vision and Revision in Maya Studies*, ed. F. S. Clancy and P. D. Harrison, UNM Press, Albuquerque,

1990, pp.33–66.

Chapter 3

1 P. D. Harrison, "Aspects of Water Management in the Southern Maya Lowlands", in *Economic Aspects of Water Management in the Prehispanic World*, ed. V. Scarborough and B. L. Isaac, JAI Press Inc., 1993, pp. 71–119.

2 D. S. Rice, *Eighth Century Physical Geography, Environment, and Natural Resources in the Maya Lowlands*, 1993.

3 Chert is the American variety of flint, having a slightly different chemical composition from the European sources, but being very similar in attributes, especially in its suitability for knapping and thus shaping into useful cutting, scraping and digging tools.

Chapter 4

1 J. P. Laporte, ibid.

2 W. R. Coe, TR 14, 1990.

3 ibid.

4 R. J. Sharer, *The Ancient Maya*, 5th edition, p.145.

Chapter 5

1 In Maya notation 8.12.14.8.15.

2 The reading of this name most commonly published in the past has been "Yax Moch Xoc."

3 Other interpretations of the word "xok" include "the counter" and "the reader," connoting a scholarly man – fitting concepts for the founder of a dynasty.

4 C. Jones, paper presented at the Maya Weekend, University Museum, Philadelphia, 1996.

5 This situation changes almost daily, and definitely with every new meeting of the epigraphers who are constantly at work on the topic. Thus it is inevitable that some of the names used in this volume will have been modified by the time it is in print.

6 In Maya notation 9.0.10.0.0

7 Maya Early Classic Monuments and Inscriptions, in *A Consideration of the Early Classic Period in the Maya Lowlands*, ed. by G. Willey and P. Mathews, Albany, NY, 1985.

8 In Maya notation 8.12.14.8.15.

9 As with all rulers in the early part of the Early Classic Period there is controversy over the interpretation of the name phrase. Here there is no reading yet made in Maya and the word "moon" sometimes precedes the "zero" in the various scholars' readings.

10 In her re-analysis of *The Rulers of Tikal*, Genevieve Michel has now rejected Zero Moon Bird as a ruler of Tikal.

11 The identification of this ruler's name is another that remains controver-

sial. The name translation alone has changed in recent time. Originally known as "Jaguar Paw" and published in this form in many places, the orthography has come to be recognized as emphasizing the claw rather than the soft paw. Whether one or two rulers are represented within the same texts remains unresolved as of February, 1998. A single ruler by the name of Jaguar Claw I with a long reign is assumed in this presentation.

12 Schele and Freidel, *A Forest of Kings*, William Morrow, 1990.

13 "The Arrival of Strangers": Teotihuacan and Tollan in Classic Maya History, by David Stuart, prepared for the Symposium "The Classic Heritage: From Teotihuacan to the Templo Mayor," Princeton University, revised February 1998.

14 P. D. Harrison, *The Central Acropolis, Tikal, Guatemala: a Preliminary Study of the Functions of Its Structural Components During the Late Classic Period*, Ann Arbor, 1970.

15 Excavations at the site of Dos Pilas southwest of Tikal, made by Demarest, Houston and Inomata have demonstrated the power of warfare in Maya history. See also Martin and Grube, 1996.

16 Harrison, 1970, as in Note 13.

17 As noted by Simon Martin, the word *chacte* has been read in error. The newer reading is *kalomte*, a word of unknown meaning. See Copan Note (Austin, Texas) No. 58, Stuart, Grube and Schele. I have sometimes chosen to retain the term "chacte" in this text as it is still broadly understood in the meaning of highest ruler.

18 Peter Mathews and John Justeson did most of the groundwork leading to recognition of this title.

19 Laporte and Fialko, 1990, in Vision and Revision in Maya Studies.

Chapter 6

1 Clemency C. Coggins, *Painting and Drawing Styles at Tikal*, Doctoral Dissertation, Harvard University, 1975.

2 The other is the text on the roof comb of Temple VI. Stela 40, recently recovered at Tikal has also provided new material for the Early Classic history of the city.

3 Clemency C. Coggins, 1975, ibid.

4 Excavation of Nu Yax Ain's tomb was conducted under the supervision of Dr. Edwin M. Shook, Director of the Tikal Project at the time. Archaeologist Stuart Scott was in charge of North Acropolis operations during the summer of 1959, and I had the privilege of joining him briefly in the excavation of the grave goods in Burial 10.

5 The term *chan k'awil* turns up frequently enough in ruler's names to indicate a kind of title. Unlike *ahau* and *kalomte* it is more a reverential title that

was not part of *all* ruler's names. The loose translation is "great, heavenly one." Its use was more popular in later times during the Late Classic. The phrase is integrated into the name glyph in such a way that it cannot be separated from the individual's personal name, such as, in this case, "Siyah", one translation of which is "gift."

The phonetic translation, both of this ruler and most other rulers of Tikal is taken from the work of a group of epigraphers called herein "the Austin Group" who meet annually in Austin, Texas to discuss and update the on-going work of translating the corpus of Maya hieroglyphs. The principal leaders of this group are Linda Schele of Austin, Texas; Nikolai Grube of Bonn, Germany; and Simon Martin of London, England.

6 In Maya notation 8.18.15.11.0.

7 In Maya notation 8.19.10.0.0.

8 In Maya notation, these two dates are: 9.1.0.8.15 and 9.1.2.17.17 respectively.

9 In Peter Mathews' detailed discussion *Maya Early Classic Monuments and Inscriptions* (1985) a forty year period of activity is described spanning the adult life-span of Stormy Sky.

10 Coggins, 1975.

11 The Maya reading is tentative.

12 In their chronological sequence these 16 stela are numbered 40, 9, 13, 3, 7, 15, 27, 8, 6, 23, 25, 14, 12, 10, 26 and 17.

13 This reading is a speculative one provided by the present author and is explained later in the text.

14 The translation of this ruler's name could be debated for pages. We now know that the animal whose head is carved in the glyph is indeed that of the peccary, identified by the trefoil element in its eye. "K'an" can mean either "precious" or "yellow." In this case the latter seems appropriate although we could well be missing the point entirely. The peccary is a specific symbol in the heavens representing rebirth, and the reference in this glyphic phrase could well be to the heavenly constellation. See *Maya Cosmos*, by Freidel, Schele and Parker, 1993. Previously in the literature this ruler has been called "K'an Boar."

15 *Estela 40 de Tikal: Hallazgo y lectura*, by Juan Antonio Valdes, Federico Fahsen and Gaspar Munoz Cosme, published by the Instituto de Antropologia e Historia de Guatemala, August, 1997, 48 pp.

16 The Maya notations for these 2 dates are respectively and in chronological order: 9.1.3.0.12 and 9.1.13.0.0.

17 In Maya notation 9.2.0.0.0.

18 In Maya notation 9.2.13.0.0.

19 *The Rulers of Tikal*, revision in press, Publicaciones Vista, Guatemala.

20 Because the name glyph of this ruler includes a skeletal lower jaw, he was previously called "Jaguar Paw Skull I." This is now known to be a glyph variant for the basic name Jaguar Paw which has

been reinterpreted as "Jaguar Claw."

21 In Maya notation 9.3.0.0.0.

22 In Maya notation 9.3.2.0.0.

23 Schele and Grube, Texas Note 67, 1994, Austin, Texas.

24 In Maya notation 9.4.0.0.0.

25 Recent studies of both the texts on Stela 23 and related glyphs on Stela 26 have suggested that the woman's glyph may refer to an event rather than a person, the event being the founding of the dynasty. In this case, the main figure on Stela 23, being so badly defaced *could* turn out to be that of a male member of the lineage. If so, we do not know who this person may be.

26 In Maya notation 9.3.9.13.3.

27 Coggins, 1975.

28 The term *kalomte* is the revision made by Martin and Grube to the title *chacte* used in this text. Martin and Grube say that the meaning of "kalomte" is not yet known.

29 Previously published as "Jaguar Paw Skull II" by both Jones and Michel.

30 In Maya notation 9.5.3.9.15.

31 In Maya notation 9.6.3.9.15.

32 In Maya notation 9.6.8.4.2.

33 See Schele and Freidel in *Forest of Kings*, and subsequent papers by Grube and Martin.

34 Previously published as Animal Skull II (Michel and Jones).

Chapter 7

1 Harrison, 1970, dissertation; and Harrison, Ancient Maya Architecture, in *Maya, Treasures of an Ancient Civilization*, ed by C. Gallenkamp and R. Johnson, Abrams, 1995, pp. 84–96.

Chapter 8

1 Schele and Freidel *A Forest of Kings*, 1990; Hassig, *War and Society in Ancient Mesoamerica*, 1992; Martin, Simon and Nikolai Grube, Maya Superstates, in *Archaeology* , Vol. 48, No 6,1995, pp. 42–46; Martin and Grube, Evidence for Macro-Political Organization among Classic Maya Lowlands States, unpublished mss.

2 The same name glyph is read Spearthrower Shield and is shown both as an owl and a shield in different versions of text.

3 From Temple I, Lintel 3. In Maya notation 9.12.9.17.16.

4 Martin, Simon and Grube, Nikolai, *Politics and Hierarchy Amongst Classic Maya States,* Archaeology Magazine, 1994. Also, Grube, N., Schele, L., and Fahsen F., *Epigraphic Research at Caracol, Belize*, 1993, ms.

5 In Maya notation 9.5.12.0.4.

6 In Maya notation 9.6.2.1.11.

7 Schele and Grube, 1994, p. 101.

8 In Maya notation 9.6.8.4.2.

9 In Maya notation 9.6.18.12.0.

10 In Maya notation 9.7.14.10.0.

11 In Maya notation between 9.8.0.0.0 and 9.12.0.0.0.

12 The specific date in Maya notation is 9.12.0.8.3, a little later than the period of silence noted above.

13 Identification of the war event and relationship with Tikal was made by Stephen Houston and David Stuart. See also Arthur Demarest in National Geographic, 1993.

14 In Maya notation 9.9.12.0.0.

15 A tentative Maya translation provided by Schele in the Austin Symposium of 1994.

16 Also known in the literature as "Animal Skull", and unofficially translated into Maya as "E te II."

17 Translation by Simon Martin, personal communication, 1997.

18 Also called "Bird Head" in some references, cf. Hales.

Chapter 9

1 In Maya notation 9.13.0.0.0.

2 Linda Schele and Nikolai Grube, *Some Revisions to Tikal's Dynasty of Kings*, Texas Note 67, March 1994, Texas Notes on Pre-Columbian Art, Writing and Culture, Austin, Texas.

3 The name has a variety of readings from different occurrences in texts. It has been read as Nu U Bak Chak, and once at Dos Pilas, as Nun Bak Chak.

4 In Maya notation 9.11.6.16.11.

5 In Maya notation 9.11.6.16.17.

6 In Maya notation 9.12.0.8.3.

7 In Maya notation, respectively 9.12.5.10.1 and 9.12.6.16.17.

8 This translation remains uncertain, like most royal names at Tikal.

9 In Maya notation 9.12.9.17.16.

10 In Maya notation 9.12.11.5.18.

11 In Maya notation 9.12.13.17.7.

12 In Maya notation 9.13.0.0.0.

13 This is a subjective observation. In this author's opinion Hasaw Chan K'awil had the greatest effect on the greatness of the city than any of its other mighty lords.

14 In Maya notation 9.13.3.7.18.

15 While Schele and Grube utilized the "Jaguar Claw" translation, Martin prefers "Jaguar Paw Smoke" as the name of this ruler of Calakmul (Martin, personal communication, 1997).

16 In Maya notation 9.13.3.8.11.

17 A variation on the Tikal usage of Chak Toh Ich'ak (Jaguar Claw).

18 In Maya notation 9.13.3.9.18.

19 The giving of proper names to sacred inanimate objects has been revealed in certain readings of texts, not just from Tikal, but from several royal capitals. As in the case here, the glyphs representing this name can be read in Maya, but not accurately translated into meaningful English.

20 Bloodletting ceremonies were conducted to solemnize events of great importance, such as the accession of a ruler into power, or the death of a ruler. The performance of such a ceremony at this time indicates the great importance

to the people of Tikal of this conquest event.

21 In Maya notation 9.13.3.13.15.

22 As knowledge of the hieroglyphic writing of the Maya progresses, and it is progressing rapidly, all readings from texts of this kind may be subject to revision.

23 Chris Jones, personal communication, 1995.

24 In Maya notation 9.14.0.0.0.

25 The geometry and use of alignment that is involved in the placement of Altar 5 will be discussed in a later chapter dealing with this extraordinary feature of the layout of the city.

26 Interpretation of the reading of the glyphs on Altar V, as well as the meaning of the figures depicted on it follow the work of Grube and Schele as described in Texas Note 66, *Tikal Altar V*, 1994, Texas Notes on Pre-Columbian Art, Writing, and Culture, Austin, Texas.

27 The identification of the *wayas* glyph and its association with Calakmul was first made by Simon Martin, who also is responsible for recognition of the link between the two men in the picture by a common denominator of relationship to the same woman. Earlier contributors to study of this title were Steven Houston and David Stuart.

28 In Maya notation 9.13.11.6.7.

29 Epigraphic research leading to recognition of the verb for "exhumation" was done by David Stuart.

30 Flora Clancy, Seventh Palenque Round Table, Vol. XI, pp 237–242, 1989.

31 Jones, 1982.

32 In Maya notation 9.14.15.1.19.

33 In Maya notation 9.14.15.6.13.

34 In Maya notation 9.15.0.0.0.

35 In Maya notation 9.15.3.6.8.

36 Clemency Coggins, *Painting and Drawing Styles at Tikal*, Doctoral Dissertation, Harvard University, 1975.

37 Aubrey S. Trik, "The Splendid Tomb of Temple I, at Tikal, Guatemala," *Expedition*, Vol. 6, No. 1, 1963, pp. 3–18.

Chapter 10

1 In Maya notation 9.15.3.6.8.

2 In Maya notation 9.15.5.0.0.

3 In Maya notation 9.15.13.0.0.

4 In Maya notation 9.2.13.0.0.

5 In Maya notation 9.15.10.0.0.

6 The analysis was described in *The Central Acropolis, Tikal, Guatemala: A Preliminary Study of the Functions of Its Structural Components During the Late Classic Period*, Harrison, Doctoral Dissertation, University of Pennsylvania, 1970.

7 The readings that are included in this text are abstracted from the work of the Austin Group, specifically including the work of Schele, Grube, Martin and Stuart in April, 1994. See also Simon Martin, *New Epigraphic data on Maya Warfare*, paper presented at Primera Mesa Redonda, Nueva Epoca, Septem-

ber 28–30, 1995, Palenque, Chiapas; Martin, *Tikal's "star war" against Naranjo*, in Eighth Palenque Round Table, June 1993, ed. M. Macri and J. McHargue, Pre-Columbian Art Institute, San Francisco.

8 In Maya notation 9.15.12.2.2.

9 Both of these sites lie to the west of Tikal and both are located on or near the Rio San Pedro Martir, the water route to the west. El Peru is the closer site, but recent discovery of a new site, locally called *Lo Veremos*, places it even further west on the Rio Chocop, a northern tributary of the San Pedro. The further site could not have been attacked by Tikal without the cooperation of El Peru. The politics of the situation become intricate. The newly discovered city is closest to Piedras Negras, a known ally of Calakmul. Hopefully, new inscriptions will help to resolve this puzzle from the mid-8th century Maya heartland.

10 See reference to Simon Martin in Note 7.

11 August 2, AD 743 (9.15.12.2.3), a date recorded also on Lintel 3 of Temple IV.

12 February 3, AD 744 (9.15.12.11.12), Lintel 3, Temple IV.

13 In Maya notation 9.15.12.11.13, on Lintel 2, Temple IV.

14 July 13, AD 746 (9.15.15.2.3), on Lintel 3, Temple IV.

15 In Maya notation 9.15.15.14.0, on Lintel 2, Temple IV.

16 The comparable artwork is from Lintel 25, Yaxchilan, in which Lady Xok, while doing sacrifice, received a serpent vision. This work dates from AD 725 and thus was earlier than the event recorded on Lintel 2 of Temple IV.

17 In Maya notation 9.15.17.10.4.

18 Simon Martin, 1995.

19 This identification has been made by Simon Martin who adds that the identification is not conclusive.

20 The primary reference for translations and dating of the Temple VI roof comb text is from Christopher Jones, "Inaugural Dates of Three Late Classic Rulers of Tikal, Guatemala," in *American Antiquity*, Vol. 42, No. 1, 1977, pp.28–60.

21 Christopher Jones, *Commerce and Trade Routes of the Maya*, in Historia de Guatemala, Vol. I, nd (written in 1992).

22 In Maya notation 5.0.0.0.0.

23 In Maya notation 6.14.16.9.16.

24 In Maya notation 7.10.0.0.0.

25 In order for these dates to conform to the Schele correlation which has otherwise been used in this volume, the three dates of 1139 BC, 457 BC and 156 BC should read 1143 BC, 456 BC and 157 BC respectively.

26 In Maya notation respectively: 9.4.0.0.0 to 9.4.13.7.7.

27 Called Date I in the series of Temple VI dates, the Maya notation is 9.16.15.0.0

28 Two integral right triangles share a

baseline that runs between 3C-43 and 6D-61 in the south. The western triangle has its right angle at Temple IV, while the eastern triangle has its right angle at 6D-61. The significance of the latter structure is not known, but its location is close to due west of Temple VI, and it could have been the burial place of a member of Yik'in's family (wife, sister?).

29 The location of Burial 196 to the south of Temple II and in the immediate proximity of the Great Plaza shows great reverence for the individual in the tomb. However, during these times, its location does not conform to the need to be buried in a location of cosmic significance – a consideration that was escalating in importance in Tikal at this time. This fact suggests a lesser member of the royal family is involved, rather than a king. This line of reasoning favors a brother of Yik'in of unknown name.

30 Texas Note 67, March, 1994, *Some Revisions to Tikal's Dynasty of Kings,* Schele and Grube.

31 In Maya notation 9.16.14.17.17.

32 From Stela 19, December 25, AD 768. In Maya notation 9.16.17.16.4.

Chapter 11

1 The first identification of this personage was made by Chris Jones who simply called him Ruler C. Next G. Michel used the Chol Maya word for peccary (Chitam, 1989), which Coggins revised for the Yucatec version (Ak).

2 In the formal designation of the Pennsylvania excavations these complexes became Group 4E-4 (Q), and Group 4E-3 (R).

3 In Maya notation 9.16.17.16.4.

4 In Maya notation 9.17.0.0.0.

5 In Maya notation 9.18.0.0.0.

6 This very important geometric relationship is described in Chapter 12.

7 This translation is from Schele and Grube, Maya Hieroglyphic Workshop, March 9–18, 1995, Austin, Texas.

8 In Maya notation 9.19.0.0.0.

9 Coggins, 1988.

10 Joyce Marcus has suggested in *Mesoamerican Writing Systems* (1992, Princeton Press), that all texts had a propaganda function, recording history in only the way that the rulers wanted it to be remembered.

Chapter 12

1 C. Jones, *The Twin-Pyramid Group Pattern: A Classic Maya Architectural Assemblage at Tikal, Guatemala.* Doctoral Dissertation, University Microfilms, 1969. C. Jones is also preparing the final report on twin pyramid groups at Tikal as Tikal Report 18.

2 Recorded on the map as three structures numbering 5D-31, 5D-41 and 5D-42.

3 Laporte, 1990 in *Vision and Revision in Maya Studies.*

4 Culbert, personal communication, 1997.

5 The right angle at Temple I was recognized by Aveni and Hartung originally, but not the significance of the triangle itself.

6 Harrison, "Spatial Geometry and Logic in the Ancient Maya Mind, Part 2: Architecture," in *Seventh Palenque Round Table,* 1989, pp 243–252, San Francisco.

Chapter 13

1 David Freidel, Archaeology of Cerros, 1995.

2 See Harrison, "The Rise of the Bajos and the Fall of the Maya," in *Social Processes in Maya prehistory: Studies in Memory of Sir Eric Thompson,* ed. N. Hammond, pp 470–508, Academic Press, NY, 1977.

Bibliography

COE, MICHAEL D. *Breaking the Maya Code,* Thames and Hudson, London, 304 pp., 1992.

COE, W. R. II Tikal Report No. 14, *Excavations in the Great Plaza, North Terrace and North Acropolis of Tikal,* 6 volumes, Monograph of The University of Pennsylvania Museum, 1990.

—*Tikal, A Handbook of the Ancient Maya Ruins,* The University of Pennsylvania Museum, 127 pp., 2nd edition, 1988.

COGGINS, CLEMENCY C. *Painting and Drawing Styles at Tikal, An Historical and Iconographic Reconstruction,* Dissertation, 2 volumes, Harvard University, 1975.

CULBERT, T. PATRICK Tikal Report No 25, Part A, *The Ceramics of Tikal: Vessels from the Burials, Caches and Problematical Deposits,* Monograph of The University of Pennsylvania Museum, Philadelphia, 1993.

— *Maya Civilization,* Smithsonian Institution, Exploring the Ancient World Series, edited by Jeremy A. Sabloff, St. Remy Press, 160 pp, 1993.

HARRISON, PETER D. *The Central Acropolis, Tikal Guatemala: A Preliminary Study of the Functions of its Structural Components during the Late Classic Period,* Dissertation, University of Pennsylvania, Ann Arbor, 327 pp., 1970.

— Edited by Harrison and B. L. Turner II *Pre-Hispanic Maya Agriculture,* University of New Mexico Press, Albuquerque, 414pp. 1978.

HAVILAND, WILLIAM A. Tikal Report No. 19, *Excavations in Small Residential Groups of Tikal: Groups 4F-1 and 4F-2,* Monograph of The University of Pennsylvania Museum, Philadelphia.

HOUSTON, STEPHEN D. *Hieroglyphs and History at Dos Pilas, Dynastic Politics of the Classic Maya,* University of Texas Press, Austin, 181 pp., 1993.

JONES, CHRISTOPHER Tikal Report No. 16, *Excavations in the East Plaza of Tikal,* 2 volumes, Monograph of The University of Pennsylvania Museum, Philadelphia, 98 pp, 1996.

— and LINTON SATTERTHWAITE Tikal Report No. 33, Part A, *The Monuments And Inscriptions of Tikal: The Carved Monuments,* Monograph of The University of Pennsylvania Museum, Philadelphia, 128 pp., 1982.

MALER, TEOBERT *Explorations in the Department of Peten, Guatemala: Tikal,* Memoirs of the Peabody Museum of American Archaeology and Ethnology, Harvard University, Vol V, No. 1, Cambridge, 91 pp., 1911.

SCHELE, LINDA and DAVID FREIDEL *A Forest of Kings, The Untold Story of the Ancient Maya,* William Morrow and Co, Inc. New York, 542 pp., 1990.

— and PETER MATHEWS *The Code of Kings,* Scribner, New York, 431 pp, 1998.

SHARER, ROBERT J. *The Ancient Maya,* 5th edition, Stanford University Press, Stanford, 892 pp., 1994.

TOZZER, ALFRED M. *A Preliminary Study of the Ruins of Tikal, Guatemala,* Memoirs of the Peabody Museum of American Archaeology and Ethnology, Harvard University, Vol. V, No. 2, Cambridge, pp. 93–135, 1911.

Acknowledgments and illustration credits

AMF = Albuquerque Museum Foundation; JPL = Juan Pedro Laporte; UPM = University of Pennsylvania Musem, Philadelphia

Scholarship on the city of Tikal has been extensive, involving more than 100 individuals. These are divided between archaeologists who worked at the site in the field, and epigraphers as well as other specialists who have studied the materials recovered from the site. Inadvertently, one benefits from the efforts of all of these scholars, but a number of them have been of special assistance in the preparation of this volume. Tikal is an ancient city of such singular importance to the world of Maya studies that it is under constant examination and this is particularly so in the field of epigraphy. Changes occur in the understanding of the city on a daily basis. In preparing this synthesis I have relied heavily on the work of many others in addition to my own excavations at the site. Of particular help with the editing and correction have been Teddy Dewalt of the Art Museum of Denver, Christopher Jones of the American Division, University of Pennsylvania Museum, Mary Miller of the Department of Art at Yale University, Simon Martin of London University, William A. Haviland of the Department of Anthropology, University of Vermont, and Genevieve Michel of Seattle, Washington, all of whom generously shared their knowledge and spared me some embarrassment. Of course, errors will still exist, and these are solely my responsibility. At another level of editorial guidance I owe a great debt to Colin Ridler of Thames and Hudson who has ensured a consistency of presentation, and to Jeremy A. Sabloff, American Editor of the series, Director of the University of Pennsylvania Museum, and friend as well as colleague. Special thanks are owed to many who generously made available some rare illustrations, especially Justin Kerr, Nicholas Hellmuth, Edward E. Crocker, Terry Rutledge and Charles Gallenkamp. Also, I am greatly indebted to many soldiers-at-arms with whom I worked at Tikal and came under its lasting spell: William R. Coe II, Christopher Jones, William Haviland, Patrick Culbert, Hattula Moholy-Nagy, and Virginia Greene, to mention a few. Finally, my wife, Alexandra M. Harrison not only worked at Tikal, but has given freely of her encouragement in completing this project.

Illustrations are by the author, except for the following, which are by courtesy of:
I photo Nicholas Hellmuth; **IV** photo Stuart Rome, courtesy AMF; **V** Diana Nobbs; **VI** Diego Molina; **VII** Diego Molina; **X** painting Terry Rutledge; **XI** photo © Justin Kerr, File # 4887; **XII** photo © Justin Kerr, File # 2697; **XIII** painting Carlos Vierra, courtesy Museum of Man, Balboa Park, San Diego; frontispiece and **81** drawing Terry Rutledge; **5** map Philip Winton, after UPM, Neg # Tikal 61-5-5; **6** map Philip Winton; **8** after a photo courtesy Hans Rudi-Hug; **9** Diego Molina; **12, 13** Trustees of the British Museum; **16** after Tikal Report 11, University Museum, Temple IV and Great Plaza Sheets, 1959; **19** painting Diana Nobbs; **22** JPL; **24** JPL; **25** UPM, Neg. # Tikal 67-5-113; **26** photo Stuart Rome, courtesy AMF; **28** after general map of Tikal ruins, TR 11, University Museum, 1959; **30** UPM, Neg. # Tikal 69-5-21; **32** UPM, Neg. # Tikal 69-5-22; **35** UPM, Neg. # Tikal 69-5-177; **36** UPM, Neg. # Tikal 98-5-2; **39** UPM, Neg. # Tikal 65-4-1139; **40** UPM, Neg. # Tikal 66-5-5; **42** JPL; **46** UPM, Neg. # Tikal 69-5-51; **49** UPM, Neg. # Tikal 64-5-29; **51** UPM, Neg. # Tikal 69-5-175; **52** UPM, Neg. # Tikal 68-5-74; **53, 54** drawings Federico Fahsen, courtesy Juan Antonio Valdez and IDEAH of Guatemala; **55** photo Edward E. Crocker; **56** photo Stuart Rome, courtesy AMF; **57** UPM, Neg. # Tikal 69-5-9A; **58** UPM, Neg. # Tikal 69-5-18B; **59** UPM, Neg. # Tikal 68-5-75; **61** drawing H. Stanley Loten, UPM, Neg. # Tikal 98-5-1; **68** UPM, Neg. # 73-5-936; **74** Simon Martin and Nikolai Grube; **77** UPM, Neg. # Tikal 69-5-96; **79** UPM, Neg. # Tikal 69-5-55; **80** UPM, Neg. # Tikal 69-5-75; **82** UPM, Neg. # Tikal 63-5-87; **83** UPM, Neg. # Tikal 69-5-97; **85** UPM, Neg. # Tikal 73-5-X3; **86** UPM, Neg. # Tikal 62-3a-48; **87** photo Stuart Rome, courtesy AMF; **91** UPM, Neg. # Tikal 69-5-100; **94** UPM, Neg. # 69-5-99; **97** after general map of Tikal ruins, TR 11, Philadelphia, 1959; **98** UPM, Neg. # Tikal 73-5-993; **99** photo Nicholas Hellmuth; **100** drawing Norman Johnson; **101** UPM, Neg. # Tikal 69-5-59; **107** after general map of Tikal ruins, TR 11, Philadelphia, 1959; **108** after Great Plaza Quadrangle, TR 11, Philadelphia, 1959; **111** after Great Plaza Quadrangle, TR 11, Philadelphia, 1959; **112** UPM, Neg. # Tikal 69-5-195; **113** UPM, Neg. # Tikal 62-4-812; **115** drawing Terry Rutledge after Peter Spier; **117** detail of painting by Diana Nobbs, courtesy the artist; **122** photo Diane and Arlen Chase; **123** after a compilation of several quadrangles, TR 11, Philadelphia, 1959; **126** after a drawing by Wilbur Pearson; **127** photo H. Stanley Loten.

Index

Numerals in *italics* refer to illustration numbers